the Geese Theatre Handbook

DRAMA WITH OFFENDERS AND PEOPLE AT RISK

Edited by

Clark Baim, Sally Brookes and **Alun Mountford**

WATERSIDE PRESS

the Geese Theatre Handbook

Drama with Offenders and People at Risk

Edited by Clark Baim, Sally Brookes and Alun Mountford

Published 2002 by

WATERSIDE PRESS
Sherfield Gables, Sherfield-on-Loddon
Hook, Hampshire RG27 0JG
United Kingdom
Tel 0845 2300 733 / +44 (0)1256 882250
Fax + 44 (0)1256 882250
Email enquiries@watersidepress.co.uk
Web www.WatersidePress.co.uk

ISBN 978 1 914603 06 8

Key words Theatre—Offenders—Young people at risk/ Youth at risk—Criminal Justice—Rehabilitation—Group Leadership Skills—Criminology—Drama

1. Offender rehabilitation—handbooks, manuals, etc. 2. Theatre and youth—handbooks, manuals, etc. 3. Drama in education—handbooks, manuals, etc. 4. Theatre therapy, dramatherapy, psychodrama—handbooks, manuals, etc.

Cataloguing in Publication Data A catalogue record for this book can be obtained from the British Library

Printing and binding: MPG Biddles Ltd, Kings Lynn

Cover design: Waterside Press in association with John Good Holbrook, Coventry. Front cover photograph Sally Brookes. Back cover photograph Richard Tomlinson.

Reprinted: 2003, 2006, 2009

the Geese Theatre Handbook

DRAMA WITH OFFENDERS AND PEOPLE AT RISK

Edited by

Clark Baim, Sally Brookes and Alun Mountford

Contributors

Clark Baim
Sally Brookes
Irene Brown
Vivienne Cole
Hilary Dawson
Mark Farrall
Camilla Gibbs
Louise Heywood
Wendy Meakes
Stephen Morris
Alun Mountford
Juliet Raynsford
Mark Robinson
Jeremy Thomas
Andrew Watson

WATERSIDE PRESS

Quick Reference to Essential Concepts

Three Key Concepts (*Chapter 1*)

- **Mask** A metaphor for the 'front' we present to others, with our private thoughts and feelings underneath. Leading to the well-known Geese Theatre phrase, 'lifting the mask,' used to describe attempts at deeper personal disclosure and communication.
- **Expanding the Role Repertoire** Broadening our range of life roles, skills and strategies.
- **The Challenge Comes Through the Role** Participants are encouraged to challenge their own attitudes and beliefs when they play roles representing other points of view (e.g. a victim; a witness to a crime; a relative of a victim; the police; one's self at a different point in time). Rather than the challenge coming from facilitators or other group members, the best challenges often come through the first-person portrayal of another role.

Guidelines for Structuring Drama-based Work (*Chapter 3*)

- **Degree of Distance**
  - **One step removed** Scenarios and discussion based on fictional or actual events not directly involving anyone present (e.g. events in the news).
  - **Personal level** Scenarios and discussion focused directly on the personal life experiences of someone present.

- **Levels of Focus** At a given time, the degree of focus placed on any member of the group: Low, medium, high or passing.
- **Readiness Levels** The readiness of an individual, the group, the facilitator, co-workers and the agency as a whole to engage in a particular piece of work.
- **The Four Areas of Involvement in Applied Drama**
  - **Games and Exercises** (*Chapter 5*) Structured activities with a pre-determined focus, used to build group cohesiveness, improve disclosure and safety, encourage problem solving and co-operation skills, or focus on offending behaviour themes, among other uses.
  - **Interactive Observer** (*Chapter 6*) Scenes or characters presented to prompt debate among the audience and interaction with the characters. Includes pre-designed scenes directed by facilitator with participants in role (e.g. *Narrated Scenes*) and scenes presented by the facilitator(s) (*Worker in Role*).
  - **Frozen Pictures** (*Chapter 7*) Static scenes presented by the participants. Also called: Sculpts/ Tableaux/ Still Images.
  - **Role Play** (*Chapter 8*) Scenarios enacted by the participants or modelled by the workers, for the purposes of learning, expanding awareness, demonstrating problems, trying out alternatives, getting feedback, developing empathy, general personal development/ creativity, practising skills and other uses.

Quick Reference to Essential Concepts (continued)

Processing Techniques (*Chapter 4*)

Processing means drawing out the responses of the participants, enabling them to deepen their thinking and helping to make the work more relevant. The main techniques used to process dramatic work are:

- **Opening Up Discussion ('What do you think is going on?')** Gathering initial impressions of a scene.
- **Inner Voice from the Audience** Members of the audience speak the inner thoughts and feelings of onstage characters.
- **Inner Voice from the Characters** The characters speak their inner thoughts and feelings directly to audience.
- **Lifting the Mask** The characters are encouraged to speak more honestly and reveal what is beneath their mask, or 'front.'
- **Interview in Role** Worker and audience interview a group member in a given role. Group member responds in role.
- **Role Rotation and Role Reversal** In role rotation, onstage roles are re-distributed among the group members. In role reversal, two key figures in a scene exchange roles.
- **Re-working the Scene** Advancing, rewinding, exchanging roles, adding or subtracting characters, adding plot twists, or any of a wide range of other directorial moves made in order to increase the relevance and usefulness of a given scene.

Building New Skills (*Chapter 8*)

The sequence of steps which form the basis of social learning and skills building:

- **Assessment/ Self-assessment** of skills needs, using role play or other means.
- **Instruction** The new skill is explained step-by-step.
- **Modelling** The new skill is modelled by the leader or a more able group member, with each step labelled.
- **Practice** The participant practises the new skill in increments of increasing difficulty.
- **Testing** Where appropriate, participants take part in spontaneous role tests and receive feedback.
- **Real-world practice** The participant uses the skill in real life and undertakes further practice where needed.

How to Use this Book

The Geese Theatre Handbook is primarily intended as a practical manual. For those who want an insight into the interactive performance style of the company, we include a chapter on our performance approach. While the book is not meant to convey the last word on our approach, it does represent a snapshot of our current work and the thinking behind it. The work itself will always remain fluid and evolving—a work in progress.

THERE ARE TWO WAYS YOU CAN READ THIS BOOK

1. **For issue-oriented or offence-focused work**
   If you want to use this handbook to help plan and run offending behaviour sessions or any other type of issue-oriented work with any client group, we recommend that you to read *Part 1* (*Chapters 1* to *4*). These chapters cover theory, safe practice and basic techniques for making the most of the exercises and structuring sessions. You can then use the rest of the book (*Part 2: Chapters 5-9*) as an ongoing source for ideas. *Appendix A* contains forms that can help with assessment and evaluation of issue-based work, and *Appendix B* outlines a suggested structure for programmes using drama. *Appendix C* offers a range of sample session plans for various types of offending behaviour groups.

2. **For creative theatre and drama**
   If, on the other hand, you plan to run purely creative sessions, with no focus on specific issues, you may want to give the introductory chapters a cursory reading and use the rest of the book (*Part 2: Chapters 5-9*) as a source of ideas.

The book has been designed with both uses in mind. Indexes at the back will help you quickly locate exercises. We hope that, in practising these methods, you become inspired to adapt, expand and transform the material in new and creative ways.

A NOTE ABOUT TERMINOLOGY

Some of the terms we use in this book are defined differently by other authors. Although we have tried to point out these differences, some readers may still find gaps or unacknowledged links to similar exercises and techniques. This is due to the very wide spread of drama-based methods. If you are able to, please let us know about any such oversights, and we will make the correction in future editions.

WORDS IN ITALICS

In otherwise plain text, names of exercises and other terms written in italics are described in this book and are included in the indexes.

GENDER

In this handbook, participants are referred to alternately as ‘he’ or ‘she’. This style is used in order to reflect our work with both males and females.

Foreword and Acknowledgements

This handbook is Geese Theatre Company's contribution to the growing knowledge about effective and humane interventions with offenders and people at risk of offending. We work from the premise that most people—offenders and non-offenders alike—are capable of personal change when motivated, given the chance to express themselves differently and the opportunity to try out new ways of relating to other people. We believe that the dramatic process, with its focus on alternatives and the development of new skills and roles, can provide practical assistance in helping participants who want to work towards a more positive future for themselves and their community. We hope this handbook will encourage the further development of active, dramatic methods and inform future interventions in the criminal justice system and youth justice system.

Acknowledgements
We are very grateful to those people who have helped in the preparation of this handbook. Many thanks to Paul Forty, Susie Taylor, Ted Eames, Jim Farebrother, Andy Marshall, Alyson Coupe and Jane Green for their assistance, advice and editorial support. We are also enormously grateful to Bryan Gibson of Waterside Press for his enthusiasm, boundless patience and commitment to seeing the project through five years of drafts.

There are also many people we must thank for their support and hard work over the years, whose contributions have kept the company alive and developing. First and foremost, thanks to Geese Theatre's administrative team, Administrative Director Vivienne Cole and Administrator Irene Brown, and the members of the Board of Governors, present and past. In particular, we would like to acknowledge long-serving Chairman of the Board Norman Rush and also past Chairman Clive Barker for their commitment. Thanks also to past company members Mark Ball, Matthew Britton, Joe Butler, Simon Casson, Helen Cave-Smith, Sharon Coggins, Hilary Dawson, Sue Deedigan, Alex Dower, Katy Emck, Jackie Evans, Mark Farrall, Gavin Ferris, Yvonne Gregory, Mario Guarnieri, Kenneth Guy, Sandra Hall, Saul Hewish, Victoria Lee, Una Morton, Jon Nicholas, Nena Nwankwo, Simon Ruding, Karen Sweeney, Patrick Tidmarsh, Ken Walker, Paul Wallis and Lizzie Watt, all of whom added enormously to the work over the years.

While mentioning the contribution of past company members, we also acknowledge, with greatest thanks, the extraordinary dedication and creativity of long-serving company members Louise Heywood, Mark Robinson, Stephen Morris, Juliet Raynsford, Andrew Watson and Wendy Meakes.

Our thanks also go to John Bergman, MA, RDT, for his inspiration and creative vision in starting Geese Theatre USA in 1980 and for his ensuing work with the UK company. In thanking John, we also thank the dozens of ensemble members of Geese Theatre USA, who from 1980 to 1989 forged the basis of much of what was to follow. Thanks to Mike Bael, Dan Brown, Shaun Landry, Ian Mackinnon, Jill Reinier, Scott Stevens, Ellen Stoneking, Tom Swift, Keith Whipple and the many other former members of Geese Theatre USA.

We would be remiss if we did not also thank the partners and families of members of the Geese Theatre, who over the years have endured our absences and unsociable hours with great tolerance and understanding.

For any charity, fundraising is important to survival. We have been fortunate to receive support from a wide variety of sources over the years, and thanks are due to those charitable funders, ranging from the Arts Council and regional arts boards, to the National Lottery, to charitable trusts and foundations and individuals, who have supported us through the years.

Our appreciation also goes to all of those criminal justice professionals who took the risk and invited us in, who have enjoyed the work, participated, supported us and had us back again. We also thank those probation services, prisons and other organizations—including many hundreds of inspiring, committed professionals—with whom we have formed lasting working relationships. Our successes owe a great deal to your support, and we have developed many of the exercises in this handbook in cooperation with you.

Geese Theatre is not alone in the field of theatre work with offenders. We thank and acknowledge the individuals and organizations who have come before us, and those who continue to do inspirational work in this small but developing field. In particular, organizations such as the TIPP centre, Clean Break and the Unit for the Arts and Offenders (and its member organizations) all deserve special thanks and recognition for advancing the field.

Most of all, we thank the scores of thousands of people who have attended the performances and joined in the workshops, who have shown a willingness to experiment with new roles and new possibilities. We gain enormous inspiration from you.

Clark Baim, Sally Brookes and Alun Mountford
Birmingham, January 2002

About Geese Theatre

Geese Theatre UK is one of the country's leading theatre companies specialising in work within the criminal justice sphere. The company of actors and group workers devise and perform issue-based plays and conduct workshops, staff training and consultations in or for prisons, young offender institutions, probation centres, youth offending teams and in related settings. Since its formation in 1987, the company has worked in almost every prison and probation area throughout the United Kingdom and in Ireland. Geese Theatre UK is a registered charity, formed originally as a sister organization to Geese Theatre USA which was founded by John Bergman MA, RDT in 1980.

Contact address

Geese Theatre UK For information about the company, training courses, performances workshops and other work please contact:

Address: Geese Theatre Company, Woodbridge House, 9 Woodbridge Road, Birmingham, B13 8EH, England
Tel: 0121 4496222
Fax: 0121 4491333
e-mail: mailbox@geese.co.uk
Website: www.geese.co.uk
Registered charity number: 327563 (Registered name: Albatross Arts Project)

About the Editors

Clark Baim established Geese Theatre UK in 1987 after touring in the mid-1980s with Geese Theatre USA. He was the UK company's first Director and is now an independent psychodrama psychotherapist, supervisor and theatre director/teacher. He continues to specialise in work with offenders and among his other responsibilities he is a trainer on accredited programmes for the National Probation Service.

Sally Brookes is the Artistic Programme Director of Geese Theatre Company UK. Since joining the company in 1993 she has undertaken a wide range of work within the criminal justice system as a trainer, performer, and groupwork facilitator. She also designs and makes the Geese Theatre masks.

Alun Mountford is a group worker, actor and trainer for Geese Theatre Company UK. Since 1989 he has worked extensively on Geese Theatre partnerships with probation areas. He has co-facilitated a wide range of programmes, including drug treatment programmes, and has co-designed programmes for men who have committed violent offences. In addition to his work with Geese Theatre, he also directs psychodrama groups at HM Prison Grendon.

the Geese Theatre Handbook

CONTENTS

From the Reviews

'The book's chapter on role playing is perhaps the most definitive exploration of the variety of applications and settings for the method .... This makes the *Geese Theatre Handbook* perhaps the best single compendium of experiential activities, warm-ups and such presently available .... In summary, I think this is an outstanding book about theatre therapy in working with offenders. Highly recommended.'

Adam Blatner, MD, TEP

'Five years in the making, the book is an invaluable resource .... this is a key accompaniment for exponents and would-be exponents of applied drama in prisons.'

Prison Service News

'It is almost impossible to accurately convey the depth and scope of this excellent publication .... if you're involved with offenders or other at risk groups—buy it.'

Howard Fay JP, *The Magistrate*

'This is a generous book. Not only does it explain the thinking behind the Company's work, it also provides a treasure-chest of games and exercises for any group setting. I defy any trainer or group facilitator across the social and communication skills spectrum not to find some stunning new off-the-peg idea to lift a jaded session on a wet Thursday.'

Julia Braggins, *Criminal Justice Matters*

'It is described by the editors as a practical manual, which it is—an absolute treasure trove for people who work with groups—in mental health, schools, training, social work—wherever.'

Kate Kirk, *Mental Health Today*

'The power of drama to involve and engage our deepest feelings and emotions is clearly seen in this impressive and generous publication. Impressive, because the professionalism of the approach and the complexity of the work shine through in the detailed scenarios and methods described. Generous, because the editors have provided for us all the hard-worked-for experience of years made readily accessible and available for consideration within our professional practice and for our personal learning and insight.'

Tim Newell, *Prison Governors Newsletter*

Introduction

To know my deed
'Twere best not know my selfe.

Macbeth 2. 2. 78-79

A SERIES OF SNAPSHOTS FROM GEESE THEATRE SESSIONS[1]

- Participants in a group for convicted car thieves create an image of a typical offence: Three young men approach a car in order to steal it and go joyriding. One of the three is clearly reluctant. He is subject to a suspended sentence and knows he will go to prison if he is caught. How will he deal with this situation?

- A group of prisoners take part in an active trust exercise where, in pairs, one partner leads the other safely around the room. The partner being led has his eyes closed. After each partner has had a chance to lead and be led, the group members discuss the experience and how the themes of trust, responsibility and vulnerability relate to their personal lives.

- In a group for convicted burglars, the participants play all of the roles in a fictional role play looking at the consequences of burglary and its effect on victims: A family of four, parents and two children, returns home to find their house has been ransacked. Many items, including the children's toys, are stolen. They talk with the police, a victim support worker, the locksmith and the loss adjuster. The burglars are brought into the room. What will the family say to the burglars?

- In a group of young women who have been convicted of violent offences, the participants create a short fictional scene where two women face each other in an argument and come to the brink of fighting. The participants rewind the scene and dissect the thoughts and feelings of the main character, exploring how she may have contributed to the build up to the offence and how she might have made different choices.

- In a group for men convicted for using violence against their partners, the participants interact with a group worker who is in role as a man arrested for attacking his wife. They ask the character questions, challenge his excuses and justifications, and later make links to their own thoughts about their offending.

- A participant in an offending behaviour group lists a number of the people who have been affected by his crime and then takes on the role of each person in succession, speaking in the first person about how the crime has affected them.

---

[1] These examples are based on actual sessions. The exercises and techniques described are, in order: *Frozen Pictures; Trust Walking; Whole Group Role Play; The Two-Person Exercise; Worker in Role: Hot Seating*; and *Victim Ripple Effect*.

INTRODUCTION: CREATIVE AND ISSUE-FOCUSED USES OF DRAMA

Theatre and drama take place in many prisons, young offender institutions and other criminal justice settings. This includes performances by inmates or visiting companies, drama workshops, playwriting and production classes, video production and related work. When used in prisons, these activities have been shown to counteract prisoners' sense of isolation and the stress of institutional life (Matarosso, 1997; Peaker and Pratt, 1990 and 1996). Live performances in prisons also help generate a positive atmosphere throughout the institution; they are often a unifying and inspirational community event.

There is also a wealth of evidence showing that involvement in theatre and drama—indeed, involvement in any co-operative art, such as music, dance or mural painting—often has lasting effects on the social development of a wide spectrum of participants ranging far beyond the criminal justice system (Phillips, 1997; Matarosso, 1997). This involvement can improve participants' sense of self-worth, their respect for and co-operation with others, and their self-determination.

Drama can also be used in a pragmatic way to focus on offending issues. The drama-based methods covered in this book have clear and demonstrated value as tools for intervening in offending behaviour and encouraging positive change. Moreover, research evidence tells us that not only is it possible to address offending behaviour work through experiential means, but in fact this approach is the very lifeblood of the most effective offending behaviour programmes. Effective programmes involve the whole person, in heart, mind and action.

So, is drama useful for encouraging general social development, or for directly addressing offending behaviour? It can be both. We enjoy the challenge of working in both ways, and have designed this book to incorporate both aims.[2]

THE ADVANTAGES OF A DRAMA-BASED APPROACH

Drama-based methods harness the power of 'learning by doing' in a uniquely powerful way. Because of this, these methods have significant advantages over discussion-based or instructional approaches. The memory of a discussion can easily be lost. The experience of *doing* is harder to forget, especially if the *doing* is closely related to one's own life experience. Some of the other advantages of drama-based methods are:

- **More personal** Drama can make learning more immediate and personally meaningful. In structured drama activities where we can take on roles representing other points of view and where we can also challenge characters who mirror back to us our own thoughts and beliefs, we in effect challenge our own thinking and beliefs in a first hand, living encounter. Because the discoveries are our own, we may be more willing to act upon our insights. Drama provides a test-bed for us to explore our best and worst impulses in a safe, laboratory context, in order to strike a better balance in the 'real world.'

- **Not reliant on literacy and verbal expression** Drama does not rely on literacy, nor does it necessarily require verbal fluency. When non-verbal methods are used, drama helps those who are less confident to express themselves. Drama can also help people to become more articulate.

- **Active and spontaneous** Drama is a highly suitable approach for action-oriented individuals. In games and exercises, for example, participants actively practise the essential social skills of co-operation, trust, tolerance, self-control and problem-solving, among other essential skills. These are not merely discussed as abstract concepts, but are instead made tangible and immediate.

- **Addresses thinking, feeling and behaviour** Drama addresses the person as a whole and takes into account thoughts, feelings and behaviour in equal measure. Programmes that take into account mainly the thoughts and behaviour of the offender, giving feelings only peripheral consideration, can miss out what for many offenders is the most important influence on their destructive behaviour: their misunderstood, misdirected or uncontrolled feelings. Acknowledging feelings, talking about them, enacting them, and experiencing them in a safe and contained way can bring enormous benefit to participants, enhancing their ability to appropriately express these feelings. The positive feeling engendered by a successful experience within the group can also provide a strong motivating force for change.

- **Practical and immediate** Drama is also a highly practical and efficient tool for exploring destructive behaviour and practising alternatives. Because drama evokes feelings, memories and internal connections in a powerful and immediate way, the participant is better able to access the thoughts and feelings associated with an event. Because the memory

[2] An independent, peer-reviewed study has looked specifically at the effectiveness of Geese Theatre's *Violent Illusion* five day residency for violent offenders. The study found evidence of positive effects on anger management and self-control among a group of mentally disordered violent offenders (Reiss et al, 1998). See Bergman and Hewish (1996) and Mountford and Farrall (1998) for detailed discussion of Geese Theatre's approach to work with violent offenders.

is more immediate, the practice of alternative solutions has more immediate importance.

- **Enables practice** Drama can be used to help the participant practise and test new skills and new roles, while at the same time practising self-reflection.

- **An instinctive approach** Finally, the use of drama-based methods taps into several basic human drives. Given the opportunity and the right setting, most of us welcome the chance to tell the story of our own lives, and to expand the range of our skills, our roles and our ability to cope with the challenges of life. Drama also harnesses the fundamental human ability to create and respond to stories. These can be stories addressing any aspect of human thought or conduct. They can reach profound levels and address universal themes such as the need in us all to feel worthwhile and to have a purpose in life.

FREQUENTLY ASKED QUESTIONS

WHO THE WORK IS FOR:

- **Do these exercises apply to people who have committed all types of offence?**
  In general, yes. Geese Theatre has used the exercises and methods contained in this book with all types of offenders, including people who have committed property offences, interpersonal offences (e.g. violence and sexual aggression), robbery, offences of dishonesty and all other types of crime. This includes work with males and females, both adults and young people.
  While there are many programmes designed for specific types of offender, the material in this book is designed to apply across the spectrum. You should be able to adapt the exercises and methods in this book to any group, as long as you have knowledge and experience in working with their particular needs.

- **Can these exercises be adapted for use with other, non-offender, groups?**
  Yes they can. The majority of the exercises and dramatic structures outlined in this book share much in common with work done in fields as wide ranging as community theatre, special needs education, adventure therapy, mental health, work with refugees, human relations training and corporate team development. Although we explain the methods in this book with reference to offenders and people at risk of offending, they apply equally well with almost any group of people, provided that you are familiar with the needs and interests of your group and can make the appropriate modifications.

- **Can these exercises be applied to one-to-one work or large groups?**
  Yes they can, although in describing the exercises we are referring to work in groups of between four to twenty people, as this is usually the type of work we do. At the top of each exercise description in this book, we provide a range of at-a-glance information, including the suggested group size. We also indicate recommended material for one-to-one work and large groups in the alphabetical index of exercises (p.221).

- **Can this material be used in work with young people?**
  In general, yes. We have applied most of the material in this book to work with people as young as 14. However, special conditions apply: if you are working with people below age 18, it is important to understand the particular needs and vulnerabilities of this age group, which will mean making constant adjustments to the level of intensity and focus of the work. (This applies whether or not the young people are considered to be 'at risk.') For example, we suggest that you be particularly careful about applying these methods on the *personal level* as opposed to the level of *one step removed.* See *Chapter 3* for more on this distinction and guidance about regulating the intensity of drama-based work.

- **How does this type of work take into account cultural differences and social and economic constraints?**
  Through the use of drama-based methods, we can be far more responsive to the learning styles of participants from different cultural and ethnic backgrounds. Because drama and story-telling are such universal methods, they cut across cultural boundaries and offer a non-Eurocentric approach to groupwork. Many cultures use story-telling, drama and metaphor as intrinsic parts of their cultural and moral education.
  Workers must also bear in mind the social and economic constraints that are widely acknowledged to influence offending, and balance these without encouraging a sense of hopelessness or that an individual's choices are only 'society's fault.' We must bear in mind the context of offending and never discount the importance of the wide range of factors and pressures confronting the participants. It means treating all participants individually, but within their social/ historical context, and constantly balancing individual responsibility with external influences.

- **Can I use these methods with people with physical conditions or impairments?**
  Certainly. There is no reason that someone with a physical condition or impairment need be excluded from drama-based activities. This includes workers as well as group members.

A few tips: Remember that there are both 'visible' (e.g. restricted movement, serious visual impairment, speech difficulty) and 'invisible' (e.g. epilepsy, heart condition, diabetes) types of condition, and it is important to lead sessions in such a way that no one feels excluded because of their impairment or compelled to explain why they do not wish to join in an exercise. Plan your sessions so that they do not discriminate against those with physical conditions, and when running exercises, lead in such a way that the participants feel able to vary and adapt the way in which they perform to suit their own creativity and capability. Plan a variety of different types of exercises, so that if someone feels the need to opt out of one, he is not therefore left out of a major part of a session. Very simple adaptations, such as slowing down the activity, using mime rather than spoken action, or directing role plays so that the actors stay seated throughout, can make all the difference between an off-putting exercise and one where everyone feels able to participate.

In structured groupwork programmes, it is worth including questions about physical and mental health and use of medications in the assessment process. For one-off sessions or in situations where there is no opportunity to assess participants individually, you may wish to include in your general introduction a statement about everyone working within their own safety limits and with sensitivity to the limits of others. Where appropriate, you may ask individuals to advise you directly, or, if they wish to, the entire group, about any conditions or impairments which will affect their participation.

- **Can these methods be used with learning disabled people or people with mental health problems?**
Although we are not specialists in these areas, we have used and adapted the methods discussed in this book with a range of offending behaviour groups provided for offenders with learning disabilities and for those in psychiatric settings (e.g. in special hospitals). As long as you have a solid grounding in the work with your particular client group, you should be able to adapt and structure the material in this book appropriately. It is worth pointing out that drama is often uniquely advantageous with learning disabilities groups, because it is based on social interaction, live situations and concrete examples. There are some excellent books about drama-based work with learning disabilities groups and in psychiatric settings, and we would recommend in particular Chesner (1995 and 1998), Jennings (1978 and 1987) or Cattanach (1996).

DRAMA, THEATRE AND THERAPY

- **Do I need acting skills in order to do this work?**
There are only two techniques in the handbook requiring a worker to take on an acted role (see *Worker in Role: The Enacted Scene,* and *Worker in Role: Hot Seating*). In all other cases, as worker you will be in the position of facilitator, not the performer, unless of course you decide to take on a character role more often because it is one of your skills.

- **What is the distinction between drama and theatre?**
The two terms are often used interchangeably. In this handbook we will make the distinction that *theatre* happens when one group of people—clearly identified as the audience—are observing a live performance presented by other people. *Drama*, on the other hand, occurs when everyone present is involved in the action. Obviously, there are overlaps between the two forms. For example, Geese Theatre's improvisational shows are a hybrid of the two forms, as they rely on a steady stream of dialogue back and forth between the audience and the characters, and audience members at times come onto the stage and enter the action. Similarly, Augusto Boal (1979) has developed the widely used method known as *Forum Theatre*, where members of the audience can come onto the stage and try to change the action by offering alternative solutions.

- **What is 'applied theatre and drama', and what is Geese Theatre's theoretical approach?**
While it is understandable that people should want to categorise our work, we are not certain it has a category other than the very broad category of *applied theatre and drama*—that is, theatre and drama applied to specific audiences and settings with particular outcomes in mind.

Our work also takes into account such fields as education, criminology, experiential therapy and cognitive-behavioural therapy, an approach used in many offending behaviour programmes. We add to this the wide-ranging innovations in the application of drama made in such fields as improvisational theatre, theatre-in-education, drama-in-education, theatre of the oppressed, dramatherapy and psychodrama. The result is a highly eclectic and holistic approach, blended by our collective experience of what works with offenders and people at risk of offending. The participants themselves have also taught us what works in the most practical way possible: by joining in.

Inevitably, we have found, as so often happens, that we 're-invented the wheel' by developing some methods only to find later that others have made similar discoveries before us. We have gained enormously, if mainly in retrospect, from innovators such as Dorothy

Heathcote, Viola Spolin, Augusto Boal, J L Moreno, Sue Jennings and others.

- **Is it therapy?**
Drama and psychological therapy have been professionally linked since as long ago as 1797, when the Abbé de Coulmier used theatre productions as a method of therapy for patients at his asylum at Charenton, near Paris (Jones, 1996). Nevertheless, it is important to stress that therapy is separate and distinct from drama, and its boundaries should be respected.

In the broadest sense of the word, however, drama can be therapeutic, just as all art, education and social interaction have the potential to be psychologically challenging and life enhancing. Nevertheless, when we apply drama intending to challenge participants' ideas and encourage positive change, and we do not have specific therapy training, we should know what constitutes the boundary between work that is broadly social/educational as opposed to that which is directly psychotherapeutic. This means having some insight into where the path might lead, so that we are aware when we are moving from the relatively safe ground of social experience—concentrating mainly on the social functioning of the participant—into the realm of therapy, which is purposely aimed at surfacing deeply personal material, tracing behavioural and emotional patterns back to their origins, and, where appropriate, working through earlier life experiences.

Chapter 3 provides practical guidance about how to structure your sessions in keeping with the boundaries between therapy and drama.

ABOUT GEESE THEATRE COMPANY

- **What is Geese Theatre Company and how did it start?**
Geese Theatre (UK) is a group of professional actors and group facilitators working in prisons, young offender institutions, probation centres, youth programmes and related settings throughout the UK and Ireland. We are an independent registered charity (officially registered as Albatross Arts Project) devoted to using theatre and drama to help participants learn and practise new solutions and more constructive options out of offending.

We do a wide range of work. In addition to performing issue-based plays, we facilitate workshops, conduct staff training events and make presentations at conferences for criminal justice workers and those in related fields such as social work and youth work. We also provide consultation on the development of a wide range of rehabilitative and prevention oriented programmes for offenders and youth at risk. And we provide training for magistrates, judges, prison officers, police, health service professionals, probation officers, social workers and other professionals.

Geese Theatre was established in the UK by Clark Baim in 1987, when he arrived from the United States after touring with the original Geese Theatre USA. The U.S. company, formed in 1980 by John Bergman, MA, RDT, has toured to hundreds of prisons across America and to a range countries, winning a wide variety of criminal justice awards and receiving national press coverage along the way.[3] Geese Theatre USA has paved the way for a great deal of innovative arts-based work in prisons across America. While Geese Theatre USA has not had a performance company since 1989, John Bergman continues to work independently as Director of Geese Theatre USA, conducting residencies and workshops in North America and elsewhere. Until 1997, he also directed our new productions. Although the two companies – Geese UK and Geese USA—are separate organizations, we still tour several of the productions developed by John Bergman and Geese Theatre USA. The foundation of our interactive performance approach and also our groupwork model in general offending behaviour programmes—known as *Lifting the Weight*—originated in the work of John Bergman and Geese Theatre USA. John Bergman was also the creator and director of *The Plague Game* and *Violent Illusion Part One*, and the co-creator with us of *Violent Illusion Parts Two* and *Three*, and *Stay* (see *Chapter 9*).

Equally important to the foundation provided by Geese Theatre USA have been the developments made within the UK Company itself under the directorships of Sally Brookes, Simon Ruding, Saul Hewish and Clark Baim. Sally Brookes has, in addition to her role as Artistic Programme Director, designed and made the masks which form the basis not only of our performance approach but also make up our most important groupwork tool. Early in the company's history, Patrick Tidmarsh made important strides in adapting our performance approach to groupwork. And in his role as trainer for the company for many years, Alun Mountford has helped us incorporate a wide range of experiential and humanistic approaches into our work. Other trainers and directors have helped us broaden our approach. Added to all of this has been the contribution of more than 40 past and present ensemble members, each of whom has added to our approach.

---

3 See Cleveland (2000) for an interview with John Bergman about Geese Theatre USA. See also *Time*, Nov. 9, 1987 and *The Wall Street Journal*, October 17, 1986, p. 1. The latter article mentions in particular the important role of Vera Cunningham—then Leisure Time Activities Co-ordinator at Stateville Prison in Illinois and director of the inmate theatre group The Con Artistes—who invited John Bergman and the original USA Geese in to do their first prison performances and workshops in 1980.

The Starting Place (Voices of the Participants):

I need a sense of hope. I don't know what hope is, or what it is to have a life. What it is to trust people or have a friend.

I want to find out what's going on inside my head, so I don't have to keep making the same mistakes.

I need a place to get my head sorted and find out the proper way to do things like have a relationship and have a proper life.

Victims are alright when they keep quiet.

I want to stop being so bitter and twisted, hating everybody.

I want to understand why I never take any responsibility for my actions.

Some people are sheep, some people are goats, and some are lions. I'm a lion.

I've done 20 years inside, and every time I go out I stay the same. I don't move on, because nothing has gone on while I'm inside. Time stops.

I have the sort of face people like to hit.

I don't give a shit.

PART I

Background and Essential Techniques

Photo: iD.8 Photography

CHAPTER 1

Theory and Key Concepts

I want to be **good** *Boyo, but nobody'll let me.*

Nogood Boyo in Dylan Thomas' *Under Milkwood*

This chapter covers:

- **Summary of the Research and Key Theories**
- **Three Key Concepts used by Geese Theatre Company**

SUMMARY OF THE RESEARCH AND KEY THEORIES

In stark contrast to the long prevailing belief that offenders are best dealt with through exclusion, containment and punishment, research over the past several decades has demonstrated the effectiveness of a far more constructive approach based on developing the social consciousness, self-control, self-esteem and sense of responsibility of offenders. Notably, this research demonstrates that experiential methods are at the heart of effective practice with offenders and people at risk of offending. Among the guiding principles highlighted in the research is that learning should be active, concrete and based on the use of role play to model and practise new skills (Antonowicz and Ross, 1994; Chapman and Hough, 1998; Goldstein, 1999; McGuire and Priestley, 1987; Melnick, 1984). To take just one example, in their widely-cited meta-analysis of outcome studies, Antonowicz and Ross (1994) identify drama-based methods such as *Role Play, Role Modelling* and *Skills Practice* as being present in most successful offending behaviour programmes.

Three underlying theories The most widely cited current evidence suggests that effective programmes for offenders and people at risk of offending are those based on *Social Learning Theory* and *Cognitive-behavioural Theory* - and their attendant methods - in combination with traditional discussion-based approaches (Vennard *et al.*, 1997). We would also include the field of *Role Theory*, which has the advantage of describing a theory of behaviour that uses terms related to drama, such as *roles* and *scripts*.

- **Social Learning Theory** (Bandura, 1977) explains the principles by which learning occurs in a social context. It describes how new skills are best taught through an interactive process involving the following standard sequence:

  —**Assessment/ self-assessment** of skills needs.
  —**Instruction** in the recommended steps or procedures for practising this skill, including the micro-skills that make up the overall skill.
  —**Modelling** of the behaviour or skill, by the group workers or other group members, with each micro-skill labelled. This can include 'anti-modelling' to demonstrate 'how NOT to do it.'
  —**Multiple Practice** of the new skill by the participant. The skill should be practised in a step by step fashion, with increasing levels of difficulty and realism, in order to encourage incremental reinforcement of the skill.
  —**Testing** of the new skill, where appropriate, to ensure it has been assimilated. This includes feedback and positive reinforcement.
  —**Real-world Practice** This includes opportunities for positive 'real world' experience of the new skill within a relatively short time.

  This sequence offers an important conceptual framework for helping participants to develop new skills in a conscious and structured way. We explain this further in the description of *Modelling Role Play* and *Skills Practice Role Play* (pp.173-179).

- **Cognitive-behavioural Theory** is widely cited as being among the most effective approaches in offending behaviour programmes (McGuire, 2000; Vennard et al, 1997). Cognitive-behavioural theory provides a framework for understanding the ways in which our fundamental beliefs and attitudes affect our thinking, our feeling and, ultimately, our behaviour (Beck, 1976; Ellis and Grieger, 1986;Beck & Freeman, 1990). Changes in these core beliefs are likely to produce a profound effect on behaviour, and much of the focus of cognitive-behavioural therapy- as it applies to offenders - is on addressing and modifying beliefs and habitual thinking and feeling cycles which prove self-defeating and which can lead to offending behaviour.

  One of the main aims of drama-based work used in a cognitive-behavioural context is to help create a gap between the participant's beliefs and his behaviour. Playing the role of a victim of crime, for example, will often challenge the participant's belief that nobody got hurt as a consequence of his offending and that it was 'just a laugh.' In a similar way, he may develop some personal insight and stop seeing himself as a victim who only gives other people 'what they deserve.' After a time, if the participant is motivated, he can use role play to help develop the thinking skills, the interpersonal skills and the confidence to make the changes he wants to make.

- **Role Theory** offers a common-sense framework for becoming more consciously in control of our own roles and our behaviour toward others. Much of human interaction can be understood by considering the roles and scripts we perform as we go about our daily lives. One of the central observations of role theory (Moreno, 1993 and Blatner, 1997) is that we are all role players; in the course of our lives we carry out scores, if not hundreds, of roles. These are roles such as parent, son, daughter, sibling, worker, friend, cook, customer, teacher, law-breaker, cleaner, pedestrian, counsellor and innumerable others, each role designating a cluster of behaviours generally associated with that role in a given cultural context. When we know how to perform a role, it can be said to be in our 'role repertoire.' In general, the greater the number of roles in our repertoire, the better able we are to meet our needs and function successfully, as long as we are able to utilise the roles effectively. Having more roles means we have more potentially successful strategies to choose from.

  Where we have no experience of a role that we require, role theory offers a means of identifying what skills and roles we would benefit from developing. For example, many young people have never experienced the role of employee. Moreover, they may not have seen the role modelled for them, for example by a parent or other responsible adult. As a consequence, they may avoid work entirely because it is so far out of their repertoire of roles, or they may try unsuccessfully to get a job or stay in a job. If motivated, they may benefit from practising roles such as *interviewee, worker, co-worker/ co-operator, commuter,* and any other roles associated with getting and keeping a job.

  A person's roles should not be seen as fixed, but rather as dynamic and evolving functions of a central self that can consciously choose what role to play and how to play it. It is the conscious choice that makes all the difference. Having conscious choice leads to the creative possibility that we can conduct ourselves differently than we have done in the past. We can create new roles, or new ways of performing old roles. We may want to play the role of son or daughter in a new way, for example, or play the role of parent, partner or worker in a way that we never considered before.

THREE KEY CONCEPTS USED BY GEESE THEATRE COMPANY

By combining social learning theory, cognitive-behavioural theory and role theory, three key concepts emerge which are of particular importance in Geese Theatre's approach: the concept of *the mask*, the concept of *expanding the role repertoire*, and the concept that the *challenge comes through the role.*

The mask The mask is among the oldest theatrical conventions, and we use the metaphor of the mask as one of the central tools in our approach. The concept of the mask provides a practical tool for looking both at the social roles we play and the inner processes that support those roles.

In simple terms, a 'mask' is the front we portray to the outside world. We all have many different masks - masks for when we are at work, masks for when we are in public, masks for meeting people at a social function, etc. All of these masks are facets of the same character - us. Participants often enjoy discussing and even portraying the various 'masks' they use in varying circumstances, for example 'me with my mates' versus 'me standing in court.' It is a highly accessible metaphor.

Once we have introduced the concept of the mask, we use two basic strategies to look at the meaning and function of masks:

- First, we can 'lift the mask' (i.e. 'go inside the head') in order to encounter the hidden thoughts, feelings, attitudes and beliefs of a character. This might be a fictional character or it may be the participant himself in a scene presenting an actual event or close-to-life situation. This gives us a highly practical way to demonstrate the connection between a character's inner process and how that process relates to his behaviour. By staying 'behind the mask,' we can then consider what thoughts, attitudes and beliefs need to change in order for the character's behaviour to change. Looking behind the mask encourages us to look beyond the automatic assumptions we make and beyond that which is obvious about ourselves and others. See the sections on 'lifting the mask' on pp.43, 183.

- The second strategy we use is to consider the nature of the mask itself and the purpose it serves. For example, it may be that a participant identifies a particular type of mask he feels he needs to wear in order to feel safe (for example an angry mask or a 'stone wall' mask). This can lead to discussions and role plays which examine where the masks can be useful and where they may be destructive or self-defeating. Other masks can be considered and adopted. Participants are often intrigued to consider when, if ever, they do not 'wear a mask' at all. Geese Theatre uses a variety of masks - called *Fragment Masks* - to represent various coping/ behaviour strategies. These are discussed more fully in *Chapter 9*, which explains our performance approach and the ways that we use mask in performance.

Expanding the role repertoire means that participants consciously take on new roles and practise their constituent skills. For example, a participant who has recently provoked heated arguments with staff at his hostel regarding what he considers to be unfair rules can be offered the chance to practise the role of a peaceable resident who is able to make a complaint without being abusive. Within this role, he can practise interpersonal skills such as listening, making an assertive but polite request, offering assistance to others, finding a compromise, and dealing with frustration or anger in a non-abusive way.

By seeing his own decision making and behaviour as being within his control, the participant may come to see that although he has indeed written his own 'life script,' he may have done so with a restricted range of strategies. This new consciousness can motivate him to move beyond the roles he has played in the past (Blatner, 1997).

The challenge comes through the role Because attitudes and beliefs play a vital role influencing our decision making and behaviour, offending behaviour programmes are most effective when they help participants to challenge their own (and each others') attitudes in a powerful and memorable way. The most powerful and lasting challenge often comes from the participant's personal identification with and empathy toward other points of view through the living experience of other roles. Again, this is a strategy common to social learning theory, cognitive-behavioural theory and role theory. In social learning theory and cognitive-behavioural theory, this concept is called perspective-taking and is used to encourage moral reasoning, among other aims. In role theory, the concept is known variously as identifying with the role, role taking or role insight.

As an example, an offender who is entrenched in the role of 'con artist,' 'hard man' or 'victim of society' may find useful challenge in taking on the role of a victim of a crime similar to his own and speaking as that victim. Likewise, he may benefit from taking on the role of a family member of the victim, his own partner or child, a witness to the crime, his arresting officer or indeed any role which will provide a fresh perspective. The aim is to strategically involve him in multiple roles that will help shift him from his narrow point of view within which he justifies and minimises the impact of his offending. In this way, the challenge comes through playing the role rather than primarily from the facilitator or other group members, as it would in more traditional, discussion-based groupwork.

Based on this concept, one of our most useful functions as facilitators of drama-based work is to orchestrate sessions that help participants to experience first hand the greatest possible number of different roles. We can ask ourselves at any point in a session, 'What *role* can best be used to challenge that point of view?'

It is also important to remember that, in many cases, participants will find it very challenging simply to portray their own role in a real-life event. For example, a participant who has committed a street robbery is asked to portray himself in a *Frozen Picture* (using another group member as his victim) based on the moment of his offence. This can often be a powerful moment as he sees, frozen in time, the reality that he has tried to minimise or avoid: that he is responsible for creating the victim in front of him. He may furthermore be challenged when the group member in role as the victim offers his feelings and reactions in relation to the robbery. Other group members may also offer suggestions of how the victim may be thinking or feeling. These are all equally useful examples of the concept that the challenge comes through the role.

Lifting the Mask

Photo: iD.8 Photography

CHAPTER 2

General Guidance

People are generally better persuaded by the reasons which they have themselves discovered than by those which have come into the mind of others.

Pascal, *Pensées*

This chapter covers:

- **Making Sessions Memorable**
- **Suggested Skills and Qualities of the Group Leader**
- **Working With Resistance and Promoting Group Participation**
- **Encouraging Deeper Communication**
- **Competition**
- **Non-Violence and Physical Touch**
- **Use of Materials**

MAKING SESSIONS MEMORABLE

If we could pass on only one piece of advice to the readers of this book, it would be to approach your work with the impulse to make learning active and memorable.

What makes a session memorable? Put simply, the most memorable work involves the *whole* person, physically, mentally and emotionally.

To illustrate this, consider the difference between starting a discussion on victim awareness in a group of male burglars on probation by asking the question 'what would you feel like if someone stole something of yours?' versus the following:

Ask the group to form a circle, then ask each group member to take out his wallet and place it on the floor at his feet. Ask the group members to move several places to the left so that they are now in front of someone else's wallet and someone else is in front of their own. *Now* ask them to consider the importance of these material possessions and how they would feel if you asked each of them to pick up the wallet in front of them (we recommend that you *do not actually ask them to do this*). There will be a reaction!

This approach is far more memorable. It is experiential in the truest sense of the word, because the participants are learning through live and emotionally engaging experience.

SUGGESTED SKILLS AND QUALITIES OF THE GROUP LEADER

Recently, we were asked by a social work manager to draw up a list of desirable qualities for a group leader using drama with offenders and people at risk of offending. We arrived at the following list, based on our own experience and mistakes made along the way. We offer the list only as a guide, and not as a test or screening tool. Most of these qualities develop with practice, so if you are just starting out and you feel you don't have all these qualities yet, remember that for even the most experienced workers these are working goals.

A good group worker using drama in work with offenders and people at risk of offending:

- is confident and willing to lead by example;
- has a genuine belief that participants can change and improve their lives, and also a firm belief in the participants' responsibility for their own decisions;
- is capable of building rapport with participants, but does not collude with offending behaviour or attitudes;
- can show appropriate empathy with the participant, but still maintain a facilitative distance;
- when listening to participants, avoids the twin pitfalls of over-cynicism and gullibility;
- has the ability to inspire infectious enthusiasm;
- has a good sense of humour;
- can contain his own anxiety in order to minimise the anxiety of the participants;
- is willing to trust the group, and does not dominate it or force insight or change;
- engages in reflective and honest self-critique;

- can assess the group's response and make appropriate adjustments while the session is in progress;
- understands that even the most experienced workers will have times when they feel they have fallen far short of best practice, and does not self-destruct when this happens, but stays focused on ways to retain and develop best practice.

WORKING WITH RESISTANCE AND PROMOTING GROUP PARTICIPATION

Resistance from participants, especially open or hostile resistance, is something we all dread as workers. Resistance can be particularly marked in offending behaviour programmes where participants attend involuntarily as part of their sentence. Yet, as fearful as resistance can be for workers, paradoxically it can also be used to great advantage (Harris and Watkins, 1987).

It is first of all crucial to acknowledge that the group member's agenda may be quite different from our own. If you are working in the context of an offending behaviour programme, for example, he may initially have little interest in being on the programme, and little or no motivation to change. He may have felt pressured to attend out of obligation to the courts, and see the programme as part of his punishment. This inevitably creates a power imbalance which can make him feel all the more vulnerable when asked to become involved in active, drama-based work. He may resent having to actively participate, and fear being 'brainwashed' or somehow forced to give up his core values. We must start by acknowledging this ambivalence and helping him to identify the reasons he *does* want to be here (e.g. 'I'm here because I don't want to go to prison,' or, 'I'm here because I want to stop getting arrested.') as opposed to focusing on the reasons he *doesn't*.

One way to understand resistance and harness its creative potential is to equate it with fear. Participants most often become resistant in direct proportion to their level of fear. So in order to address resistance, we need to ask, 'what is causing this person, or this group, to feel afraid?' Resistance now becomes something we as facilitators can address by modifying our approach. The problem with simply labelling it 'resistance' is that this implies the problem is located solely in the participant; it is more useful to see resistance as a product of the context in which we are working and the interaction between us and the participants. Of course there will also be occasions when all our best efforts will not engage an individual because the context is inappropriate; it is simply the wrong place and time.

Why should participants be afraid? Often this is because they have previously had a bad experience in other group contexts. Or they may have had a bad experience of drama or role play, and fear repeating the experience. They may fear being judged by other group members, or being made to 'look a fool.' They may also fear being physically harmed by one or more of the other group members. Similarly, they may fear that you will trick them or force them to become vulnerable. These are genuine fears and must be respected, especially because as group workers we are usually in a position of authority.

Some general observations about working with and minimising resistance are given below.

Making drama a natural process Initially, participants often dread the idea of doing 'silly games and acting,' as they have preconceptions about what drama-based work entails: 'You're going to make me be a tree.' A good way to overcome this reluctance is to use and explain the drama methods in a highly practical way. We can explain to the group members that drama is a very direct and practical tool they can use to look at their own lives and to try doing things differently. They need not consider what they are doing to be 'acting' at all. In group sessions, we normally avoid dramatic jargon, preferring to move into drama by using phrases such as 'show us how that is for you,' 'let's bring that to life,' 'let's look at that in real time' or other similar phrases. Often, calling what we are doing 'exercises,' 'challenges,' 'experiments' or 'examples' will help get past the initial resistance. Later on, once the group is accustomed to this way of working, we can call the activities games, sketches, role plays or what we will. More often than not, the group will soon join in the spirit and won't mind what we call it. If what they are working on is relevant and interesting, the participants often won't even realise they're doing something special called 'drama.' They will just think of it as a good session.

Seamless transitions To minimise resistance and make the work flow naturally, we can start from the simplest point and make a series of seamless transitions into drama.

For example, if we are seated in a circle with the group and we want to open up an active exploration of high risk situations, we might simply indicate an imaginary line across the floor, asking the group to imagine that the line is a tightrope. We can now ask:

Group worker: *If being on the tightrope represents staying out of trouble, what keeps you on the tightrope? How do you keep your balance? Does anyone else help you? What does falling off the tightrope mean for you? What could cause you to fall? What situations typically mean you're likely to fall off? What have been the consequences in the past?*

After discussion, the group members may be ready to create scenes based on the high risk situations they have described. This transition can be made seamless in the following way: point to an area of the room that can serve as the stage, and say something like:

Group worker: *What's over there?*
Participants: *It's a room in a house.*
Group worker *What room of the house is it?*
Participants: *A kitchen ... a front room ... the bedroom ...*
Group worker *If it's the kitchen, what's in it? Show us where things go.*

(Using chairs and other 'props' in the room, the participants and the group worker put in place the table, chairs, fridge, cooker and door.)

Group worker: *Who's in the room?*
Participants: *A woman and man ... their child ... a pet dog.*
Group worker: *What's just happened?*
Participants: *The woman just found out he's spent the last of the money drinking with his mates, there's no food in the house, and the dog needs to go to the vet.*
Group worker: *What's the man saying?*
Participants: *'Shut up, woman!'*
Group worker: *And what's he thinking to himself?*
Participants: *'She's doing it again. She's doing this to wind me up...'*
Group worker: *What are the feelings that go with that thought?*
Participants: *He's vexed. ... He's angry at her ... He feels guilty that he spent all the money ... He wants to hit out, he's losing it, he's really angry ...*
Group worker: *Sounds like he's about to fall off the tightrope. Let's see the scene. We'll change the roles around, so it doesn't matter who takes which part first. So let's have someone up as the man who's just come home, and someone up as the woman.* (as the participants take their places, the group worker continues:) *We may bring the child in at some point, but let's start with the man and woman ...*

Depending on the stage of the group and the variables discussed in *Chapter 3*, the group worker now facilitates the scene as an *Interactive Observer* scene, a *Frozen Picture* or a *Role Play.* Any and all of the *processing techniques,* covered in *Chapter 4,* may be used to explore the scene.

Simple is best As the above example demonstrates, drama can start from the simplest question, and often involves very simple scene setting and character background. It is very easy to over-complicate matters by putting unnecessary emphasis on rules, props, scene-setting, character details, or by having too many people in a scene. This can lead to confusion and resistance among participants. So keep it simple.

Making resistance part of the process It is often useful to bring the resistance out into the open and raise it for discussion. Resistance thereby becomes useful material for the group. It is all 'grist to the mill.' When the group members see that you are willing to respect their reservations and that their resistance does not make you anxious, they will generally feel less fearful and reluctant.

Rolling with the resistance can also be a useful strategy. At times, out of fear or anxiety, a participant might say something like, 'This is stupid. I can't be doing with this.' In response, rather than becoming defensive or trying to justify the exercise, we might 'roll' with this statement by briefly commenting about one possible aim of the exercise and clarifying that the intention was not to get the participant angry or to make him feel stupid.

Resistance can be an opportunity. The participant may be resisting or 'sabotaging' the group by using the same script he uses in any difficult situation. If we respond with criticism, the story ends in the same way it always has: he dismisses the group and shuts down, or he finds a way to get excluded from the group. The participant may actually *want* you to respond in a certain way that he is used to; at least he can predict what to say in that event. Rolling with resistance allows new energy and spontaneity to enter the exchange. It also demonstrates that interpersonal tension can lead to creative solutions rather than just conflict and power struggles.

Encouraging the motivation to change To increase motivation and participation, and thereby decrease resistance, it is useful to focus at the start of the group on the shared predicament of the group members as a basis for moving forward and helping each other. What are the drawbacks and consequences of their offending? What changes will lessen the likelihood of future offending? We might use the *Cycle of Change* exercise to facilitate this discussion.

Positive feedback Encourage each group member to negotiate achievable stages of change, and reinforce each positive shift, no matter how small. By the general standards of society a member of the group may still present an aggressive and anti-social 'front,' yet by his standards he may actually have made positive changes by being involved far less frequently in fights.

Engaging the best instincts of the participant We are all better than our worst deeds, yet it is surprising how often offending behaviour work focuses almost entirely on the worst deeds and the 'worst self' of the participants, paying only peripheral attention to their best instincts, their strengths and their abilities. Most offenders, for example, have a strong sense of justice arising from their own experiences of oppression (e.g. growing up in an abusive home, in poverty, or in a violent or racist community). With a proper balance, we can acknowledge and respect their experiences of oppression while at the same time encouraging the participants to expand their sense of justice to take into account the people they have hurt.

When we engage with the best instincts of participants, and work on the assumption that they do not want to re-offend and continue hurting themselves and others, we are less likely to face resistance because the participants will feel respected. Even with those participants who voice pro-offending attitudes in the session, we should still work in such a way that engages their alternative, 'anti-offending' thoughts. This might be called a 'pro-social approach', as opposed to an 'anti-offending' approach. It is a matter of emphasis.

At various points in this book, we use the concept of 'New Me' versus 'Old Me' thinking, feeling and behaviour (see, for example, *Thinking Reports*). This concept is a very useful way to help the participant develop his best instincts and neutralise his destructive or self-defeating instincts.

Confidence As workers, part of our job is to contain the group's anxiety, and this takes confidence on our part. By being confident, we convey to the participants that they can contribute honestly to the process without running the risk of destabilising us and then suffering the consequences. Even when we have moments of internal nervousness, it is important to project confidence. This means paying attention to how we are coming across to the participants, how we are using our voice, our gestures and our body language as a whole. To some degree, leading groups is a performance, in that the process works better when we present our most able and confident self to the group. This is not the same as 'acting' or 'being false.' Group members will sense falseness from a mile off, and reject it.

Containing the group's anxiety by predicting resistance We can take charge of potential resistance by anticipating it and in effect suggesting how the participant might resist. In introducing an exercise we might say, for example:

Group worker: *You may feel awkward or uncomfortable at the start of this trust exercise—stick with it and see how you cope. Pay attention to your thoughts and feelings, especially thoughts and feelings that may tell you this is too difficult. We'll talk about these thoughts and feelings when we finish the exercise.*

Phrasing our instructions in this way lets the participants know that we are aware of their potential bad feelings and that we will not set them up to 'lose face.' It also lets them know that they will have a chance to voice their concerns and that this will be treated as important to the process.

Normalising the portrayal of the opposite gender This is particularly an issue in men's or boy's groups, where there may at first be resistance to portraying women or girls. Bearing in mind the previous advice about anticipating resistance, we can take charge of this potential resistance by re-framing the portrayal of the opposite gender as a valuable opportunity for gaining insight and showing respect to others. We might say something like:

Group worker: *During this session we'll be creating some scene work where there will be both male and female characters. It doesn't particularly matter who in the group takes the roles first, because we'll be changing the roles around through the session, and everyone should have a chance to play both a male and a female character by the end of the session. Use this as an opportunity to expand your own awareness of what it's like from a male or female point of view. We're not going to ask you to raise or lower your voice or move in any special way 'like a woman' or 'like a man,' - in fact that will probably be unhelpful - but it will be important to respect the point of view of your character and try to get in touch with his/her thoughts and feelings.*

Empowering the participants Let the participants feel able to stop you and ask questions. Let them know they can opt out of an exercise if they feel it is too difficult for them. In this way you reduce the potential for resistance, as participants have a measure of control over how they participate. With this measure of choice, group members will still join in, but when they do it will be out of interest rather than feeling coerced.

Incorporating new members When a new member joins the group, encourage her to get actively involved in her first session. This will help reduce her sense of being an outsider, and helps the group members to include her.

Recognising the impact of our own behaviour Everything we do affects the group and gives them a message. If they see we are willing to participate, it lessens their feeling of being guinea pigs. They see that the group is a mutual process, not something being done *to them,* but *with them.* By participating in activities, we can also model a broad range of skills such as co-operation, communication and good teamwork.

It is also worth considering whether we as workers have a right to ask participants to do something we ourselves would not do, such as take part in a trust exercise or perform in a role play. When we try to facilitate an activity that we ourselves would not join in, there is a much higher risk of resistance, because the participants are likely to sense our anxiety. This is not to say that we must join in all of the activities; there are many times when it is important to stand back and act only as facilitator. The principle is, rather, would we join in the exercise under any circumstances? Indeed, have we done the exercise ourselves?

Leading by example This is similar to the previous point, and relates specifically to how we get the group members up and moving. When, for example, we ask the group members to 'push back your chairs and join us in a standing circle,' we say this WHILE WE ARE PUSHING BACK OUR CHAIRS and standing up ourselves. This is leading by example. It conveys a powerful subtext that 'I will not ask you to do anything I would not do myself'.

Avoiding moral arguments Be aware of the common trap of arguing a moral line or trying to force participants to change their attitudes. Offenders weigh up the pros and cons of anti-social behaviour just as we all do, and are just as likely to resist moral arguments. As an alternative, we can encourage the participants to engage in their own moral discoveries by using the strategy of leading from one step behind. This is sometimes called the

'Columbo technique' after the television detective. Using this technique places us in the position of the naïve questioner, from where we can ask honest, penetrating, yet seemingly naïve questions. For example, in considering a hypothetical *Frozen Picture* portraying a mugging, we might ask questions such as, 'Who else is the victim here?' or 'I wonder if he had any thoughts just before he decided to steal the purse. Can someone help me out? What thoughts did he NOT have?' This approach can be highly effective in encouraging participants to engage with the material, because it puts them in the position of experts on the subject matter. But this applies only if you ask these 'naïve' questions in a spirit of genuine enquiry and curiosity about what the participants think. If you are looking for them to fill in the blanks and give only the answers you expect, they will resist or tune out.

Being honest about our limits We should be willing to admit to participants that we know very little about them and what 'makes them tick.' We don't need to present ourselves as experts, but rather as having some useful tools to offer the participants should they wish to make use of them. This can help us avoid the temptation of making sweeping generalisations about the participants or trying to diagnose their problems by giving them a scientific sounding label. We also need to be aware that we bring all our history, needs, insecurities, strengths and weaknesses to the group, just as participants do.

Awareness of cultural differences There are times when particular instructions will clash with the cultural values or practices of some group members. Problematic instructions may involve, for example, shaking hands in greeting, the general use of touch, or using eye contact. When we anticipate that this will be an issue for a group member, we generally adapt the instructions to incorporate different cultural practices. It is often useful to explicitly acknowledge that the group contains people with different cultural backgrounds, and that this may mean that people respond differently to the exercises. With either strategy, there is much positive potential to open up respectful discussion about cultural differences.

Handling generalisations Participants will often make generalisations, such as, 'All women/ men are out to get is ...' or, 'Some 12- or 13-year-old girls get all dressed up so they can trap an older man,' or 'in my area everyone steals to survive.' While on the one hand such a generalisation may represent an honestly held view, we avoid getting into a debate on general issues, because it would be fruitless. Rather, after hearing such a comment we tend to steer the generalisation back to the specifics of the individual. We might intervene and ask, 'So how does that apply to you specifically? Has this happened to you personally? Let's not talk about generalisations because we could be here all day and not get anywhere. So, specifically, which women/ men are you referring to? Which girls specifically are you referring to? Is that why *you* steal, to survive?'

Challenge and rapport As workers we need to encourage participants to respectfully challenge each other. At the same time, we also need to promote an atmosphere of empathic concern and rapport among the group members. There needs to be a balance between empathic concern and scepticism/challenge, as there can be no effective challenge without genuine rapport. Challenge without rapport often leads to resistance.

Expecting the unexpected When leading an exercise, if we take the attitude that each time is the first time, we stay alive to the possibility that a group member will find a completely new way of solving a problem and a completely new way of interpreting an exercise. This is one of the great benefits of using experiential exercises; participants actively discover and make their own connections. The danger is that we become jaded and try to cleverly manipulate the exercise to get the same response as last time. In doing so, we may overlook or cut across the genuine interest of the group members, and so lose our rapport with them.

Letting the group members do the work As group workers, we can sometimes fall into the trap of trying to do all of the work for the group, in the hope that if we run enough exercises, make enough clever observations and just generally dance fast enough, then the participants will learn a great deal. If we are not careful, what happens is that we end up exhausted and the group members remain unmoved. It is easy for participants to reject a worker who is doing a song and dance, and much more difficult to reject a session in which they have made an investment.

Trust the group Bearing in mind all of these observations, the bottom line is that the problems we face with a given group are not just our problems, they are the group's problems as well. So make the problems explicit, and take them back to the group. Trust that the group will be resilient enough to cope with honesty.

A strategy such as this demands good judgement, and is not a licence to air all personal anxieties and difficulties. The issues raised should be directly related to the group process and should relate to an issue that group members can remedy either individually or collectively. For example, in an offending behaviour group a contentious issue creates a heated debate with everyone talking at once. As a worker you may intervene: 'Does the group notice what is going on here? Are we getting anywhere? Is there some other way we can handle this debate?' (Note the use of 'we'—indicating that the problem is a collective one, belonging to the worker as well as the participants).

ENCOURAGING DEEPER COMMUNICATION

As group leaders, it is important that we attend to the group dynamics and the quality of the interactions between the group members. Very often, the best strategy is to discuss openly the communication process in the group. In order to help facilitate deeper communication, trust and respect among participants, it can be useful to take some time to consider with participants the varying levels of communication (Ringer and Gillis, 1995). The levels can be divided into:

- **Small talk/ritual cliché** This is the most superficial level of communication, and helps us decide whether we want to get to know someone better. An example of small talk might be discussing the weather when we meet someone for the first time. Small talk can also take the form of banter (e.g. about football, drinking, sexual exploits) which can serve a positive purpose but which can also get out of control. At times, groups may need to be reminded that banter must be held in check when the group is in session.

- **Facts and information** This is equivalent to casual acquaintances at work who might need to exchange information in order to do their jobs. An example would be two work colleagues discussing a new job order.

- **Ideas and judgements** This would be the level of communication for good acquaintances, and includes some personal disclosure.

- **Feelings and emotions** At this level, individuals are able to share sensitive and emotional issues with each other in the expectation of tolerance, support and honest feedback. Groupwork functions well at this level because group members will be more able to discuss personal feelings, attitudes and experiences.

- **Close rapport** The level of greatest intellectual/emotional closeness between people. There are occasions when groups will engage in deep emotional connections, especially when dealing with difficult or painful issues that are relevant to everyone present (e.g. the sense of being a failure, dealing with rejection, struggling to come to terms with the pain caused to others). Such deep levels of communication can be highly beneficial for participants, particularly if they have no other opportunities to communicate deeply or feel so well understood.

Once the levels are made explicit, it may be useful to check in from time to time to see how the group members rate their level of communication. By being conscious of how they are communicating, they can make a more conscious decision to 'go deep' or to remain superficial. As facilitators, we can prompt deeper communication by making suggestions such as (assuming 'Brian' has just made an important disclosure about his feelings), 'I wonder if we can pay more attention to what Brian just said. This feels important. Does anyone else feel the same way? Let's show some respect to Brian by relating something from our own experience to what he has just told us.' In this example, the facilitator has asked the group to first pay deeper attention to Brian's statement and then to share personal thoughts, feelings or experiences with him. Both of these strategies will tend to deepen communication.

In the course of a session, groups will move up and down the scale of openness as part of a natural process. Nevertheless, it is important to let the group members know that deep level communication does not 'just happen'; it results from people taking risks and revealing personal thoughts, feelings and experiences. By making the levels explicit, we also make it the group's responsibility, and not just our own, to make their time together meaningful.

It is worth noting that with some groups it will be better to keep the levels of communication implicit rather than explicit. Some groups function better by remaining task-focused and resist when asked to focus on their own process. This will always be a judgement call for group workers.

COMPETITION

Most of the games and exercises in this handbook are non-competitive. A few, such as *Pulse Train* and *Hand/Face Progression*, involve a degree of competitive spirit. Where we can confidently establish clear boundaries around touch, safety and non-violence, we have found it beneficial to occasionally introduce competitive exercises. Very often, particularly with younger groups, competition gets participants involved more keenly and with sharper focus. Competition also provides much material for discussion and processing. For example, we can examine the competitive nature of an exercise and draw connections to the competitive nature of society and how people feel they need material goods, greater strength, more money or better clothes to compete with the next person.

The great drawback in using any form of competitive activity—aside from health and safety concerns—is the potential danger that the session reinforces the social distancing which often comes from negative competition. A participant may fear losing face and being seen to be inadequate or a 'loser.' This is one reason why so many people don't like to get involved in what they see as 'kids' games,' because they equate games with being made to feel stupid. By emphasising the co-operative nature of games, and avoiding the win-at-all-costs philosophy, we can help ensure that there is no negative competition in the sessions. On the other hand, there are many situations where these risks are far outweighed by the positive 'buzz' of a good game well played. This is particularly the case when the group members are able to enjoy healthy competition and the energy and co-operative team spirit that it can generate.

NON-VIOLENCE AND PHYSICAL TOUCH

Violence is never allowed in our work. However, it is often necessary and useful to examine scenes where violence is represented. This requires the use of theatrical conventions.

In any presentation where violence is portrayed, it is important for the facilitator to specify what theatrical conventions will be used. For example, we often specify that characters 'freeze' just before the point of violence. Where needed, we will teach and practise with the group members how to stop their own punch by drawing their fist back but never allowing it to move forward. This avoids the possibility of injury while still portraying all the useful material related to the build-up to the violence. We may then ask the group to present the scene that took place immediately after the violence. This excises only the violence itself, in order to focus on the options before and the consequences after.

Another option is to instruct participants that all violence will be portrayed in slow motion. This works with some groups, but for others it may have a comic effect undercutting the seriousness of the material.

With regard to physical touch, we recommend making concerns explicit, so the group can set the limits. When giving instructions for an exercise, we can be highly specific about what touch is allowed and not allowed, for example: 'As you lead your partner around, hold him gently by the wrist. This will be the only contact between you.'

As a general rule, we would recommend that, if you touch participants at all, you touch only their shoulders, hands and arms, and do this only when in full view of the group. However, even this minimal touching may be inappropriate for some groups and some situations. We must use particular caution when working with young people or any other group of people for whom even minimal and brief physical touch could be distressing. If any touch will be used, find out first from the participants and the agency within which you are working what touch will be acceptable, and stick to those limits.

Moreover, when participants work *in role*, it is crucial to be specific about what touch is allowed. For example, in a *Frozen Picture* portraying violence, we might ask the group member playing the aggressor in the scene to hold his fist well back from the victim's face. In any scene where two characters of different status (e.g. offender/ victim) are ostensibly in direct physical contact we would pay close attention to the nature of the contact and the possible discomfort of the participants. Most often, we can address the problem by having the participants move slightly apart. This 'telescopes' the contact by allowing a gap of several inches or even several feet. We can still imagine that the characters are in contact.

USE OF MATERIALS

In general, there is no need for complicated or expensive materials when using the methods in this book. Materials can often be more of a distraction, keeping the participants from interacting with each other. The main materials we use are masks (see *Chapter 9*). These being a rather specialised tool, we have included only exercises which demand minimum or no materials. Whatever you use, try to ensure that the focus remains on the human interaction, and not on the props, cameras, materials, etc.

Blindfolds For similar reasons, we don't use blindfolds either, because using them deprives us of the tremendous processing value in talking about the impulse to OPEN our eyes. We can ask participants what they do to overcome this urge. Alternatively, we can ask participants where they 'gave in' and opened their eyes momentarily. For example, in *Trust Walking* we would ask who wanted to open their eyes, and what thoughts they had which helped them to keep their eyes closed. Similarly, we might ask those who 'peeped' how they were able to continue the exercise with their eyes closed most of the time. We might ask, 'What thought did you have, or what did you say to yourself, which helped you close your eyes again and keep them closed?' We would then encourage the participants to see the connection and realise the potential they already have to intervene and control their thoughts and actions, even in the face of strong impulses toward self-protection. This can be a useful learning point, especially for participants who claim their behaviour happens only on impulse and without thinking.

Audio-visual playback If you have the resources for video or computer audio-visual playback, this can be a great incentive. Some groups will enjoy video recording and playing back their dramatic work, role plays and other forms of group work. A recent example is a group of residents in a hostel who created a video guide to their hostel in the form of a 'day in the life' of a resident. Other examples: Young offenders creating and performing in their own issue-based films; Role plays played back on video for feedback to the role players; Young people at risk of offending going into the community to interview shopkeepers and people in the street about their experiences of crime.

While audio-visual playback can be enticing, it can also be a distraction, so it must be carefully thought out and integrated into an overall package. In addition, some group members will object to being anywhere near a camera. In some groups, such as sex offender groups and domestic violence groups, there is likely to be a great deal of resistance to working in front of a camera other than for reasons to do with an agency's requirements to record sessions.

CHAPTER 3

Guidelines for Structuring Drama-based Work

This chapter outlines a systematic approach to structuring drama-based work. It contains:

- **Four Guidelines for Structuring Sessions**
- **Note of Caution Regarding Personal Work**
- **Planning, Co-leading and De-briefing**

FOUR GUIDELINES FOR STRUCTURING SESSIONS

We offer the following four guidelines to help you ensure that your sessions are properly structured and that the participants feel able to work at a productive and psychologically safe level. The guidelines are intended to be taken as a whole and used in balance with each other, so we recommend you become familiar with all four guidelines rather than focusing on one to the exclusion of others. For guidance about how to use these principles to structure an entire programme lasting from three days to many months, see *Appendix B*. We also offer a range of sample session outlines in *Appendix C*.

1. DEGREE OF DISTANCE: ONE STEP REMOVED AND PERSONAL LEVEL WORK

The first distinction to make is whether we are operating on the level of *one step removed* or on the *personal level*. These terms represent different levels of distance from directly personal material. They can be seen as two ends of a continuum, with one extreme representing very distant, fictional material (i.e. *one step removed* content) and the other end representing highly personal material (i.e. *personal level* content).

One Step Removed means that the content is not a direct recreation of the life events of anyone present. The content can be based on purely hypothetical events or on real events reported, for example, in the news. The work can be addressed directly or through metaphor. In one step removed work, we look at 'a scene of a robbery' rather than 'the scene of my robbery.' Generally speaking, working at one step removed is safer than the personal level of work because the distance allows participants to acknowledge their connections to the material at a pace they can regulate themselves.

It is important to bear in mind that there is a continuum of closeness versus distance in one step removed scenes. Some one step removed scenes will closely reflect the life experiences of the participants, and others will be more distant. Because of this, one step removed does not necessarily mean that the work is somehow 'lighter' or less serious. Often, it is indeed *because* the issue is 'close to my life' as opposed to 'my life,' that many participants choose to get deeply involved, as each extracts personal meaning from the scene without the encumbrance of 'historical accuracy.'

Working at one step removed also has the advantage that everyone's interpretation of events is equally valid, because everyone present has equal information about the fictional or news-related event. This contrasts sharply with personal level work (below), where the person who actually lived the experience is present in the room and must be the final arbiter of different interpretations about what happened and why.

The concept of *one step removed* also applies to discussion as well as to scene work. When a participant discusses the general theme of high risk behaviour, for example, this could be considered to be a one step removed discussion. As soon as he begins discussing his own risky behaviours, the discussion becomes personally focused. As workers, we need to be especially mindful of how we help participants to negotiate and maintain boundaries around the limits of personal disclosure (see *level of focus* and *readiness levels*, below).

Personal Level means that the discussion or drama activity focuses on direct personal connections and disclosure. At this level, the participant may discuss her personal thought processes, behaviour patterns, life experiences and personal beliefs. For example, a trust building exercise may lead into a discussion of 'who are the people I trust?' Participants might then talk about situations in their own lives where they broke trust, or when someone broke their trust.

Another example would be when a participant presents a recent event in his life (e.g. an argument) or rehearses an upcoming conversation in a role play. Be aware that scenes based directly on the personal life of someone present in the room (whether or not they are actively involved in the scene) must be handled with great sensitivity and caution because of the potential to tap into powerful emotions and traumatic issues. Please read the note of caution on p.33 before facilitating such work.

In practice, throughout a session we may move back and forth between one step removed and personal level work. What is important is that we are aware when the material is crossing into the personal level, and to facilitate the session so that everyone present is ready to work at the distance of one step removed before focusing on personal material. Our clarity about the extent to which confidentiality applies will be crucial, particularly as participants will often spontaneously disclose personal material almost without being aware of it. For example, when we ask for a fictional character's age, name, family background, number of siblings, types of crimes, etc., we often find that the suggestions coming from the group are directly autobiographical.

2. LEVEL OF FOCUS

The second factor to bear in mind is the level of individual focus placed upon anyone in the group at a given moment. In general, groups work best starting with low focus activities, gradually moving toward higher focus work in moderated stages.

- **Low Focus** means that the whole group is not looking at any particular group member for longer than a brief moment. It may also mean that participants are working in pairs or small groups.

- **Medium Focus** means that there may be a large number of people looking at a particular group member, but he shares focus with a number of others, for example while showing a small group *Frozen Picture.*

- **High Focus** indicates that all or most of the group are looking specifically at one group member for more than a fleeting moment, for example if he is the only one talking or if he is co-presenting a two-person scene to the group.

We also need to consider whether the focus is **Passing**, meaning that it briefly passes from one person to the next. If, for example, during a name game, person A catches the ball and the whole group watches her as she briefly says her name and throws the ball to person B, this would be passing high focus. Although all of the group members were looking at her, this lasted only a second or two, and she knew it would.

3. READINESS LEVELS

How do we decide the level of focus the group should work at, and whether it is appropriate to cross the border from one step removed into personal material? Likewise, how do we decide in a given moment of the session whether or not to pursue a particular piece of work focusing on one participant? We would suggest using as a guide the **Readiness Levels** of all concerned, and the 'contract' we have with the group. Using the readiness levels as a reference point can help us to run sessions that are neither too easy nor too threatening, but rather provide an optimum challenge for participants. The readiness levels are as follows:

Readiness of the facilitator Taking into account training, preparation, physical and mental health, awareness of personal position in relation to the issues and support from colleagues, are you ready to facilitate this piece of work?

Readiness of the co-workers Will they be able to join in the facilitation? Will they support the method of working?

Readiness of the participant who may become the focus of the group Is this the right time, and will she be able to assimilate this work? Is the participant motivated to do the work?

We also need to remember that some individuals are simply not suited to groupwork, and may instead benefit from one-to-one work. Exercises that are suitable for adaptation to one-to-one work are listed in an index at the end of the book. (p.221).

Readiness of the other group members Is the group able to handle this level of work without becoming overly anxious (being aware that sometimes we can confuse our own anxiety with the anxiety of the participants)? Will the group members support the participant who has the attention of the group?

The readiness of the group is also influenced by the **Contract** we have with them. The contract, whether written or verbal, is the agreement we have with the group regarding what kind of work we will ask them to do. This contract may have been set individually with the participants during their assessment for the group, or it may be established during the group itself, as part of rule setting. During assessments, we can discuss the nature of the programme, including the fact that it involves drama and active participation. This will provide ample notice for prospective attenders. Upon agreeing to the terms of the group, the participant may be asked to sign a written agreement to abide by group rules.

A written contract is only one part of the process. At the start of the group, a verbal contract must also be established between all involved. At times, a verbal contract will be the only contract there is. This is particularly the case in single session workshops such as those we frequently run during single day visits to prisons, where there is no formal assessment or screening process. To establish a verbal contract, we might use a short series of questions such as (adapted from Dryden, 1999):

- What do you, the group, expect from us?
- What do you expect of yourselves and each other?
- What do we expect from ourselves?
- What do we expect from you?

Most group members, especially offenders and young people at risk, expect little or no say in how the group is run. The first two questions invite such a contribution to the process. The second two questions allow the group workers to share their expectations with the group.

As an alternative, we might ask the group members to form pairs or groups of three and think of one rule and one expectation that they share in common. These can then be reported back to the whole group.

Having these verbal agreements about the nature and content of the work allows for modifications as the group progresses. For example, if, during the early phase of the group, the participants do not feel able to work on the personal level, it is perfectly acceptable to work entirely at the level of one step removed and, at a later stage, to re-negotiate the verbal contract. Assuming all of the readiness levels are taken into account, you might then proceed with more personally focused work.

The readiness of the agency Whatever form of contract we work to must correspond with the general expectations of the agency we are working within. For example, if the agency is offering an informational programme for those convicted of driving while intoxicated, and we turn the programme into a therapy session addressing deeply personal issues, the likelihood is that the group participants will not be supported after the session and neither will the group workers. This has obvious dangers. When in doubt, ask yourself the question, 'who will support this participant if he needs some special help after the session is over?' If the answer is 'no one,' this has important implications for how you manage the intensity of the session and, in particular, the closure of the session.

Similarly, the agency should be ready to support our use of drama and experiential methods. If that support is not in place, the facilitator using drama-based methods can easily find herself isolated for using what are often misunderstood as outlandish or unpredictable methods. This form of undermining can be insidious and highly disempowering to otherwise enthusiastic workers. Similarly, if logistical and administrative support is lacking, or if there is inadequate supervision for you and your co-workers, this may imply that the agency is not ready to properly support the work.

4. THE FOUR AREAS OF INVOLVEMENT

The last guideline helps us to distinguish between the areas of involvement in drama-based work. We suggest a model based on four identifiable groupings, or areas (see *Figure 3.1*), with each successive area tending to involve participants more extensively in different roles. This model is not intended to represent a hierarchy of difficulty or significance, because all of the areas have an equal potential to engage participants powerfully and memorably in the work. However, the model does represent a general chronological progression; as *Figure 3.1* indicates, groups will usually start with *Games and Exercises* or *Interactive Observer* scenes, and later move on to *Frozen Pictures* and *Role Plays*.

Games and Exercises This book describes the two main types of games and exercises that we use: those that are **general**—meant to encourage co-operation, confidence and general interpersonal skills; and those that are **offending-focused**—meant to directly address offending behaviour and related themes.

In some cases, we use a game or exercise simply as a warm-up to energise and focus the group on a certain topic. They help participants to 'break the ice' and to become more spontaneous in their participation in the group.

Most often, we will *process* a game or exercise when it is finished, in order to draw connections and talk about participants' thoughts and feelings during it.

Often, a game or exercise may provide the basis for an entire session. For example, the exercise *Tin Soldiers* may lead into a discussion about responsibility and self-control, which may then lead on to a series of personal examples where participants gave up control or took control of their lives. Continual reference might be made back to the controller and the 'tin soldier' in the exercise, asking participants to consider whether they are their own controller, whether they feel they are controlled, and indeed whether or not they prefer to have their decisions controlled by others.

The main distinction between games and exercises and the next three areas of involvement is that at this early stage the participants are not involved in a dramatic or 'as if' framework. With only a few exceptions, in games and exercises no one is asked to take on a character or role other than themselves. This type of involvement should feel familiar to the participants, as it is most reminiscent of team sports or schools games, though with the important difference that these exercises all have a specific aim related to the group process or an offending behaviour theme. This is an important point to stress with group participants, who are often concerned that whole group activities may just be 'silly games.'

Games and exercises are described in *Chapter 5.*

The Interactive Observer At the most basic level, the term Interactive Observer simply describes a group member who actively comments on and responds to a dramatic character or situation.

In Geese Theatre's approach, Interactive Observer scenes are usually the first time group members engage with dramatic situations and characters. We often use these techniques before *Frozen Pictures* and *Role Play* because they are generally *low focus* but they still encourage a high degree of involvement from the group members. Where appropriate, Interactive Observer scenes can serve as a stepping stone to the higher focus next levels, *Frozen Pictures* and *Role Plays*, where the participants create and improvise their own characters and scenes.

When using Interactive Observer techniques, we devise dramatic characters and situations in order to promote challenging debate about relevant themes. These characters and situations are always *one step removed*, and are presented in one of two ways:

- **Participants on stage** In techniques such as *The Two Person Exercise* and *Narrated Scenes,* one or two participants may be asked to represent the onstage role, but they will not be asked to dramatise the role. Only rarely, for example, would we ask a participant to speak in role during an Interactive Observer scene. In general, group members will be instructed to just stand still or perform a series of simple actions, while the facilitator and the rest of the group generate the dramatic content and debate the pros and cons of the scene.

- **Worker on stage** In the *Worker in Role* techniques, we present the scenes and characters ourselves, inviting the rest of the group to interact with the characters we present. This gives us total control over the action and allows us to shift focus and emphasis as the need arises.

Chapter 6 describes Interactive Observer techniques

Frozen Pictures Frozen Pictures, also known as sculpts, are static images of real or imagined situations and characters. They can be realistic or highly stylised and metaphorical. When creating Frozen Pictures, participants are encouraged to enter into the mind and feelings of the characters they present.

The beauty of Frozen Pictures is their infinite adaptability; you can use them to focus on any theme. When used in conjunction with the *processing techniques* covered in *Chapter 4*, Frozen Pictures serve as the simplest way to get group members actively involved in dramatic situations. Because of their adaptability, Frozen Pictures often feature at the heart of our groupwork sessions.

Frozen Pictures are described in *Chapter 7.*

Role Play Role Plays usually come after *Frozen Pictures* because they are quite high focus and demand spontaneous enactment, within role, in front of the rest of the group. Using Role Play, the participant can, among other things:

- illustrate a typical problem he faces and how he copes with it;
- improve his self-awareness, challenge his own thinking and increase his empathy for others;
- explore alternative solutions to difficult situations;
- practise and test new skills.

Role Play is described in *Chapter 8.* If you intend to facilitate role plays focusing on personal material, please read carefully the following note of caution.

NOTE OF CAUTION REGARDING PERSONAL WORK

Ethics and safety - an ongoing process We have included in this book descriptions of the whole range of drama-based methods that we use, from low focus name games to very high focus personal work such as the *Offence Reconstruction.* We have done so based on the assumption that the reader will act responsibly. Because the options and methods within drama are so broad, we should never feel the need to work beyond our own professional skill level and training.

Within Geese Theatre Company we continue to debate the methods we use and where our approach lies in relation to other fields. This acts as a safety net and improves our practice, because through constant debate we remain vigilant about the appropriateness and the limitations of these methods. Training from those within the therapy professions has also helped us to maintain safe boundaries, as we are primarily theatre practitioners and not therapists. We feel it is an absolute requirement that anyone leading drama-based work maintain such an ongoing debate about safe and constructive practice.

Maintaining non-oppressive practice using one step removed and personal level work Because drama-based methods are often highly spontaneous, we should be particularly mindful when we raise issues or facilitate activities that may be traumatic or emotionally volatile for participants. This applies most particularly to work focused on *personal level* issues.

Working on the personal level demands particular sensitivity and awareness on the part of facilitators because participants are likely to feel more vulnerable and, as a result, the general group anxiety will be higher. Asking directly personal questions about an individual's offence or past experiences, for example, or basing a role play directly on a personal incident in his life, is extremely high focus. If you choose such a route, be prepared at every stage to moderate the pace so that the participant who has the focus is left with the option of continuing or stepping back.

This spirit of collaboration is essential, because directly personal work always runs the risk of tapping into emotions which can provoke the participant's most powerful strategies of self-protection. This is where he can be at his most vulnerable. A participant in the midst of examining his own offence (e.g. in *Offence Reconstruction*) may experience powerful feelings of anger, hurt, vulnerability or shame (Jefferies, 1991). If asked to take the role of his own victim, he may also re-experience unresolved emotions (e.g. flashbacks to his own prior abuse). If this is not handled appropriately, he may be damaged by the work, react violently or reveal details that he later regrets disclosing. Afterward he may become blocked, suspicious or angry at the facilitator and the group.

Because the participant may be extremely vulnerable, we can inadvertently become cast in his personal drama in the role of persecutor, echoing earlier persecutors in his life. If we are not careful, we can react to this transference by becoming punitive and even abusive to him, even though we may not consciously intend to do so. It takes a great deal of personal insight to understand this process and to spot the ways in which we can fall into such a trap and become abusive. This is one reason why supervision and proper training are so important.

Moreover, we must beware of the trap of feeling that we must 'get results' in order to feel powerful, potent and expert. This common pitfall can lead to highly coercive practice where we try to force the participants to change, to cry, to 'be sorry for my victim,' or to say the right words in order to 'do well' in the programme. We must never allow the fact that the participants have hurt others to lead us to justify hurting them in the group session. This can be an even more difficult trap to avoid because many participants will consciously or unconsciously want us to punish them.

It is therefore crucial when undertaking work on the personal level that we do not 'trick' participants into revealing more than they are ready to disclose. This is particularly the case in work with young people, many of whom may still be in a highly vulnerable position in their personal lives. An essential strategy with young people is therefore to give plenty of options out at each stage of the work, and to place emphasis on situations and themes where they feel empowered.

Please see *Appendix D* for an illustration of how work on the level of *one step removed* can evolve into *personal level work* in carefully modulated steps

Using the areas of involvement to structure sessions As *Figure 3.1* shows, the four areas of involvement do not necessarily represent an orderly hierarchy or progression. The areas are suggested as a means of distinguishing categories of dramatic involvement and not as a prescription for ordering sessions. This diagram should be used as a general guide only; as you practise and your confidence grows, you will move fluidly between the areas in an instinctive way.

For example, group workers will find that some drama-based sessions begin more appropriately with *Interactive Observer* scenes as opposed to *Games and Exercises*. On rare occasions, sessions can start immediately with *Frozen Pictures* or *Role Play*, but this would happen only if all of the participants knew each other well and were experienced at drama-based work. As a general rule, therefore, we start with lower focus, more worker-led exercises and later progress to *Frozen Pictures* and *Role Play*, with the option of returning to *Games and Exercises* and *Interactive Observer* scenes when appropriate.

More than techniques In order to ensure safe practice, we need to be aware of the appropriate use of techniques and the theory behind them. It is often the case, particularly in the fields of drama and experiential therapy, that techniques get adapted, renamed and disconnected from their original source. The inherent danger in this is that techniques will be used simply because they are powerful or 'get results,' even though the practitioner may be only minimally aware of where the technique comes from, what the theory is behind it, or how it is intended to fit into an overall approach.

Bearing this in mind, it is important to note that in this book we use a number of widely adapted techniques from the field of psychodrama, such as *Role Reversal*. Where we use these techniques, we try to explain their appropriate use by non-psychodramatists. For those seeking more information about these techniques and the method of psychodrama, we would recommend Moreno *et al.* (2000), Karp *et al* (1998), or Blatner (1997).

PLANNING, CO-LEADING AND DE-BRIEFING

As you use the guidelines suggested in this chapter to structure your sessions, it may also be useful to keep in mind some of the following suggestions regarding planning, co-working and de-briefing.

Planning Some of the factors to bear in mind when planning sessions:

- What is the theme of the session, and which exercises will best address this theme?
- How much *focus* does each exercise place upon individuals in the group?
- How does the session plan take into account the *readiness levels* of the participants?
- Should we run the exercises at *one step removed*, on the *personal level*, or alternate between the two?
- Are we confident that we know our 'script' for introducing the exercise? If not, we can practise with colleagues first.
- What feelings are we as workers bringing to the session?

When these factors are taken into account, we can be confident that we know why we are using each exercise and what themes we want to highlight. We ordinarily divide up leadership of the exercises among the group workers, with the understanding that we need to be flexible. During the session, we may decide to leave out an exercise, or develop an exercise in an unanticipated way that still focuses on the same overall theme.

Figure 3.1: **Geese Theatre: Four Areas of Involvement in Applied Drama**

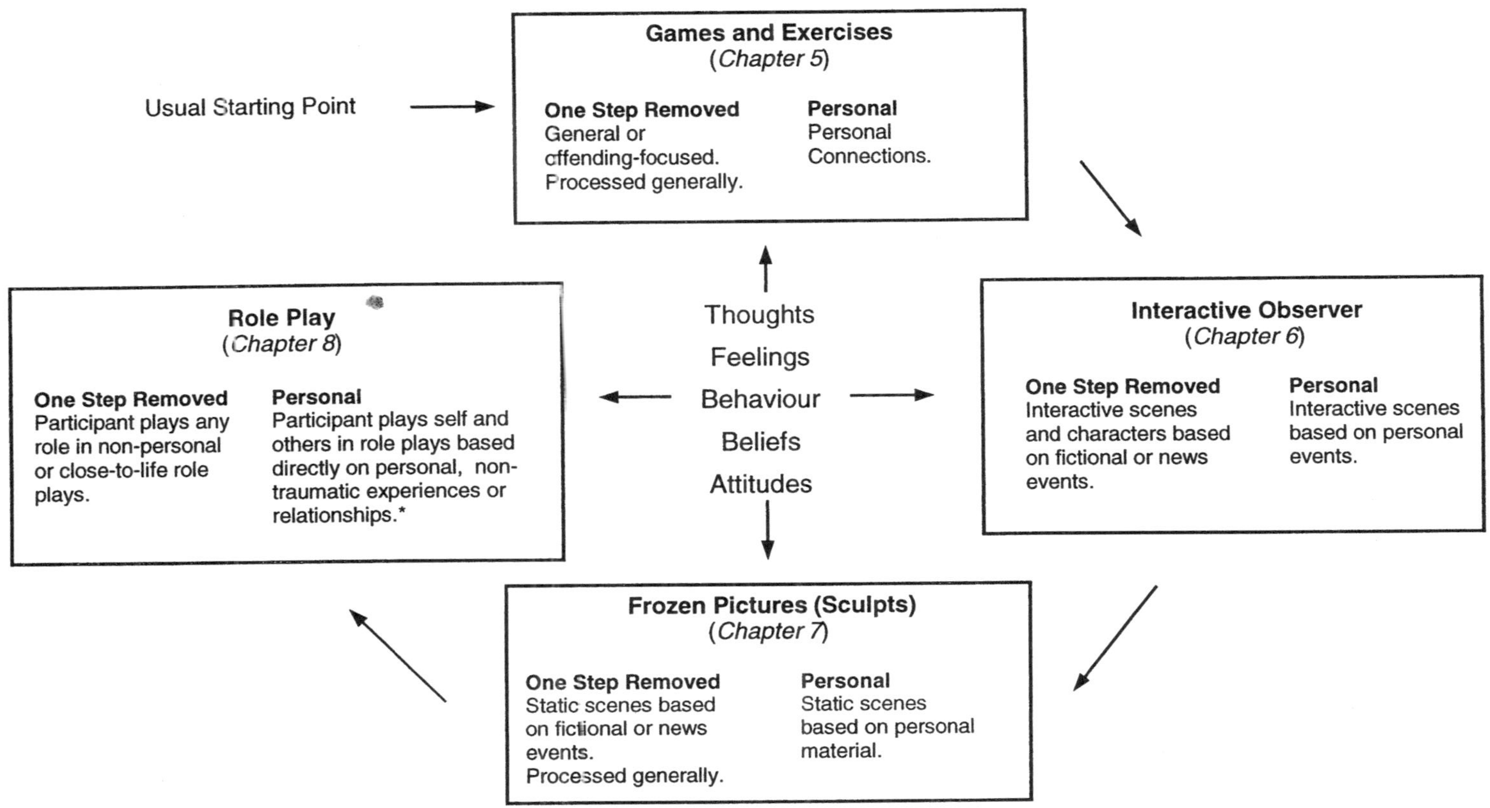

* Please read the introduction to *Chapter 8* before facilitating personal level role plays.

Co-leading Almost all of the work that we do is co-worked, and we highly recommend that you work in this way, too. A good co-working team can be highly effective in ways that an individual worker cannot, and can also provide an excellent opportunity for modelling co-operation skills.

During the session, it is vital that as co-workers we model co-operative behaviour. This means more than just smiling and nodding! For example, it is perfectly acceptable for co-workers to talk to each other during a session about the session itself. In front of the group worker A may say to worker B, 'I think it would be a good idea to shift what we planned in order to focus more on this issue, what do you think?' Worker B can then respond, and may offer a different option. Obviously, the idea is not to get into a prolonged discussion, but rather to ensure that the co-workers both know what the other is thinking without having to resort to hand signals and meaningful looks. This also provides a powerful model of co-operation, which is especially important if there are male and female co-workers.

Co-workers can also help each other by lending focus. To lend focus, we look at our co-worker when she is speaking, listening attentively and so helping to focus the group's attention on her. If we decide that we would like to add to our colleague's point, we may stand and 'take the floor,' in which case our colleague would move to the side and lend focus to us while we speak. When we finish, we return to our seat and our colleague continues.

We can also help our colleague by joining in exercises where appropriate. This may mean that we offer 'prompting' questions and comments when the group needs some help, or it may mean we actively join in a game or exercise in order to make up numbers or give the group greater confidence while taking part.

De-briefing After sessions, de-briefing is an important chance to improve our practice and to take good care of each other. In de-briefs, the emphasis should be on what we did *right*. It is not a time to beat ourselves up, *especially* when the whole session seems to have gone horribly wrong!

When discussing our own practice, it can be useful to follow a sequence of questions:

- What did I like about what I did in the session today?
- What would I like to see more of in my practice next time?
- What was helpful about what I did?
- What was less helpful about what I did?

Where desired, this sequence can be used to structure feedback from colleagues (e.g. 'What I liked about what *you* did in the session today,' etc.).

In addition to individual de-briefing, it is also important that colleagues consider their performance as co-workers. We suggest a standard three-step format, covering *content*, *underlying processes* and *feelings*. The steps need not be done in sequence:

- **Content** Here, co-workers discuss the overt behaviour of the group members and how the structure of the session was maintained. Co-workers can consider whether the right sequence of exercises was used, and if the exercises were appropriate to the group as a whole. Critical moments from the session can be examined and magnified. Consideration can be given to what methods and strategies might improve delivery of the content.

- **Underlying processes** Here, co-workers explore the dynamics underlying their interactions with each other and also with the group members. It is an opportunity for co-workers to have a respectful but frank discussion about their working relationship. While it is not a requirement that co-workers agree on all matters of professional approach, it *is* necessary for co-workers to be able to at least speak honestly with each other about issues related to practice. For example, it may be important for colleagues to discuss the impact of gender or racial differences on their co-working relationship and also on their dealings with group members.

  This is also a time for workers to explore the sub-text of the session, and to attend to any hidden processes which are affecting their behaviour towards group members. For example, it may be that a worker has highly persecutory feelings towards a particular group member, but needs help identifying why he feels this way.

- **Feelings** This part of the de-briefing is a time to discuss the feelings we had during the session and the feelings we are left with. It is particularly important to discuss negative feelings such as despair, powerlessness or vengefulness. Without airing these feelings and getting support, workers can be left feeling isolated and de-skilled—a recipe for burn-out. On the other hand, being in touch with our feelings and our vulnerabilities can be one of our greatest assets as group leaders.

CHAPTER 4

Processing Techniques

If you can learn a simple trick, Scout, you'll get along better with all kinds of folks. You never really understand a person until you consider things from his point of view, until you climb into his skin and walk around in it.

Harper Lee (1960) *To Kill a Mockingbird*

This chapter covers:

- **The Uses of Processing**
- **Processing Games and Exercises**
- **Seven Techniques for Processing Dramatic Scenes and Pictures**
  1. Opening Up Discussion ('What do you think is going on?')
  2. Inner Voice From the Audience
  3. Inner Voice from the Characters
  4. Lifting the Mask
  5. Interview in Role
  6. Role Rotation and Reversal
  7. Re-working the Scene

THE USES OF PROCESSING

The benefits of drama-based work derive not just from participating, but also from making the links with 'real life' outside of the group. We call this *processing.*[1] When used with *Games and Exercises*, processing helps clarify and integrate learning. Processing helps participants to 'see the point' of an exercise, which means they are more likely to join in. Through processing, we can help participants to describe their thoughts, feelings and behaviour during an exercise, and relate these to real-life situations (see example below). Finally, processing encourages personal disclosure, greater group cohesion and trust.

When used in conjunction with *Interactive Observer* scenes, *Frozen Pictures* and *Role Plays*, processing is also an excellent way to involve all group members, including those who are seated and watching. As workers using applied drama, one of the steepest challenges we face is what to do with a scene once it is presented. This is particularly true when the scene has very little detail and we need to develop its potential almost from scratch. We need effective processing techniques to make maximum use of this raw dramatic material.

It's all in the questions Whether processing a game or exercise or processing ideas about a role play, remember that 'it's all in the questions.' How we phrase questions, how we order them, which we include and which we leave out—these are all-important considerations.

When we ask questions, it is most important that we ask *open questions*, that is, *who, what, where, when, why* and *how* questions. These are questions that require more than a 'yes' or 'no' response. These should be *real* questions, not dead ones. A dead question is one that we already know the answer to. It's dead because it traps the listener into giving only one answer—ours. This is a sure way to break rapport with participants and cause resentment.

Far better to ask real questions, which are questions we don't know the answer to. Real questions capture interest and keep us as workers much more alive, as we will inevitably hear fresh responses. Examples of real questions are: 'If we go inside this character's head right now, what might he be thinking or feeling at this moment?', 'What might you do in his situation?', 'What might your options be?', 'What questions would you like to ask this character?'

Reminder: Processing scenes at *one step removed* and *the personal level* When working at *one step removed*, using the processing techniques

[1] The term 'processing' is sometimes used to describe the discussion and analysis of a session after it is complete. We do not use the term in this way; we call the post-session discussion a 'de-brief' (see *Chapter 3*).

allows for a general exploration of a scene where all opinions are equally valid. Because the scene is one step removed, it is open to a range of interpretations. Although there will be consensus on most opinions about the thoughts and feelings of the characters, there will also be some disagreement. At one step removed, we must often leave these disagreements unresolved. The participation of the group members and their exploration of different points of view is more important than everyone agreeing on the content of the scene.

By contrast, processing has an entirely different focus with scenes based on the *personal* experiences of a group member. Here, the person whose experience is being portrayed is the main focus of processing, whether or not they are 'on stage' in the scene. While we still use all of the processing techniques, the interpretations of the group members must be referred back to the teller of the story in order to assess their accuracy or usefulness.

Before leading processing on the personal level, please see our general note of caution about personal work on p.33.

PROCESSING GAMES AND EXERCISES

When we process games and exercises, we think of the exercise itself as the launch pad for group discussion around relevant themes. Because it is based on open-ended questions, processing may develop in unpredictable ways, depending on the group members' responses. Because processing demands a subtle approach, we offer here an example of what it sounds like 'on the ground' and eavesdrop on the thought process of the worker.

The group has just completed the *Trust Walking* exercise. In this example, the worker begins processing on the *general level* and - when appropriate - moves to *personal level processing*:

Worker: *What do you think the exercise was about?*
(Worker thinks: 'I want to get a range of responses and make sure I hear from the quiet people.')

Participants: *It was about trust ... About keeping your balance ... It was about not knowing where you are in the room ... It was about co-operating ...*

(Worker thinks: 'They're engaged with the process. They're interested. I'll ask a bit more to see if they want to make deeper connections.')

Worker: *Which did you prefer, leading or being led?*

Participant A: *Being led.*

Worker: *Why?*

Participant A: *It's easier. You don't have to look after the other person. You just follow.*

Participant B: *No, I'd rather be the leader, because then you're in control. I can't stand having my eyes closed.*

(Worker thinks: 'It's safe enough and the group is focused enough to go a little deeper now. I'll follow up B's statement with a personal line of questions. I'll leave A's comment for the moment because I don't think he is ready for a personal follow up question yet. I might come back to it.' Note: One of the tasks of the worker is to gauge the participants' different levels of readiness and ability, and to pitch the processing accordingly.)

Worker: *So, B, when you were being led around the room by C, did you open your eyes?*

Participant B: *No, I kept them shut, except for one time when I opened them for a second 'cause I thought there was a wall there.*

Worker: *Then did you keep your eyes closed after that?*

Participant B: *Yeah.*

Worker: *What did you say to yourself - what thoughts did you have - in order to be able to keep your eyes closed for the rest of the exercise?*

Participant B: *I thought it's alright 'cause C's not going to walk me into a wall or anything because you're watching.*

(Worker: decides to focus on the theme of 'thoughts controlling actions,' and opens up the theme to the whole group.)

Worker: *Did other people have this experience, that you had a thought which allowed you to keep your eyes closed even when you wanted to open them?*

Participants: *Yes, I wanted to open my eyes but I didn't ... The rules said we had to keep our eyes shut ... It was easy, because I knew where I was anyway because of where the light was coming from ...*
(Worker decides to summarise.)

Worker: *Now this is important. What you're all saying is that you proved that your thoughts can control your actions. Let's think about this: Some of you wanted to open your eyes, for good reason - you needed to be safe. But you kept your eyes closed because of a thought which was more powerful than the thought which said open your eyes. If your thoughts control your actions in this exercise, do they always control your actions?*

Participant A *Most of the time.*

Worker: *When don't they?*

Participant C: *When you're on drugs or when someone tells you to do something.*

Worker: *Something like what?*

Participant B: *Like getting in a fight. Sometimes you just do because your mates are in it.*

Worker: *So who's telling you to do it?*

Participant B: *You're telling yourself, because they're your mates and you don't just walk away.*

Worker: *So there's a thought there? What other thoughts are there?*

Participant D: *I shouldn't get involved because I'll get arrested again.*

As this dialogue shows, a 'simple' trust exercise can, with effective processing, move into highly focused personal offence focused discussion. This applies not just to trust exercises but to all of the activities in this book. Think of the exercises as 'feedback machines'; they are a starting place, a structure that encourages personal development and an opportunity for dialogue about important issues.

Note: Sometimes, we will use an exercise without any processing at all. An example would be when we use a quick energiser such as *Touchbacks* to get the group re-focused and invigorated after a break or after sitting down for a long time.

SEVEN TECHNIQUES FOR PROCESSING DRAMATIC SCENES AND PICTURES

What follows is a description of the seven basic processing techniques that we use primarily with *Frozen Pictures*, *Interactive Observer* scenes and *Role Plays*. Some of them can be adapted for use with *Games and Exercises* as well.

The techniques are listed in the general sequence in which we use them, but the sequence is not meant to be prescriptive; in practice, we move back and forth through the techniques based on the participants' responses. Sometimes we may use only one or two of the techniques to process a scene.

The seven processing techniques described on the following pages are:

1. Opening Up Discussion ('What do you think is going on?')
2. Inner Voice from the Audience
3. Inner Voice from the Characters
4. Lifting the Mask
5. Interview in Role
6. Role Rotation and Reversal
7. Re-working the Scene.

1. **Opening Up Discussion** ('What do you think is going on?')

The first processing technique applies to *Interactive Observer* scenes and *Frozen Pictures*, where at first viewing there is often useful ambiguity about the content. It can also be used in a more limited way to process *Role Plays.*

The first thing we can do to open up discussion is simply to ask the observers, *'What do you see?'* Very often there will be a wide range of interpretations. We can follow with open-ended questions such as:

> ***Who*** *might these people be?*
> ***What*** *seems to be going on?*
> ***What*** *do you think that gesture means?*
> ***What*** *does it seem like this person is saying at this moment?*
> ***Where*** *do you think this could be taking place?*
> ***When*** *does it look like this is taking place? Day or night? Past, present or future?*
> ***Why*** *do you think this person is looking at this person in this way?*
> ***How*** *do you think people are related in this scene?*

At this early stage of processing, we allow a wide range of interpretations. The observers may have been told the theme or title of the scene, but they may still have many different views about what is represented. This ambiguity acts as a powerful lure; it hooks the observers into the scene because in order to understand it they must, figuratively speaking, leap in and interact with the characters. In doing so, they begin to identify with the characters. This will be crucial as we use the rest of the processing techniques.

Example: The car crime

In an offending behaviour group for young male offenders, the themes of the session are 'The Pressure to Offend' and 'The Consequences of Offending.'

The aim of the session is to encourage the group members to think more deeply about the options they have to avoid offending and also the long-term consequences if they continue to commit crime.

Most of the group members have been involved in stealing cars. The group worker has asked several of them to create a fictional (i.e. *one step removed*) *Frozen Picture* looking at the moment just before a car is stolen. In addition, the group worker has given them a title to work with: *'The Outsider.'*

When the *Frozen Picture* is shown to the group, the worker asks the presenters to hold still while the other people look at the scene. To encourage involvement, the worker asks the observers to come up close to the image and walk around it in order to see the details.

The image itself shows a group of three people looking excitedly through the window of a car, which is represented by four chairs arranged as car seats. One of the three is pulling on the jacket sleeve of a fourth individual, who stands back, gesturing as if to say, 'I don't want to get involved.'

The worker gathers impressions of the scene: 'What do you think is happening?,' 'Who do you think they are?', 'What's their relationship to each other?', 'Why do you think this person is standing back from the others?', 'What does it look like this person is saying to others with that gesture?', 'Remember the title; who's the outsider in this scene?'

The worker encourages a wide range of ideas about what the image represents. Soon, a consensus emerges that it looks like a group of lads who are going to steal the car to go joyriding. The fourth lad looks reluctant, and probably doesn't want to get involved but feels he has to, 'or else he'll lose his mates.' He's the outsider.

(*Continued on next page.*)

2. **Inner Voice from the Audience**

Having begun to explore where the scene is set, who the characters are and what is going on, we now invite the observers to deepen the exploration of the thoughts and feelings of the characters by using the technique *Inner Voice from the Audience.* This technique allows individual members of the audience to enter into the psychological perspective of the characters on stage by temporarily speaking as if they were 'inside the head' of a character. This technique can also be used to support the onstage participants by helping them to speak when they can't find the words.

In this technique, an observer comes 'on stage' and stands beside the character of his choosing and speaks the thoughts and feelings the character might be having at this moment.

It is also possible to speak the inner voice from one's chair. To do this, the worker stands beside a given character and invites the observers to speak the thoughts and feelings of that character. This can be used to encourage shy group members to participate.

Example: The car crime (*continued*)

The group has named the outsider 'Lee' and one of the peers 'Dave'.

Worker: *Let's have someone from the audience come up and speak what this character might be thinking or feeling at this moment.*

(Observer 1 stands beside character 'Dave.')

Observer 1 (speaking for 'Dave'): *This is brilliant! Why is Lee being such a tosser?*
Worker: *And what's the feeling?*
Observer 1 (speaking for 'Dave'): *I'm buzzing!*
Worker: *And what about Lee?*
Observer 2 (speaking for 'Lee'): *I'm gonna get nicked. I want to get out of here.*
Observer 1 (speaking for 'Dave'): *We're gonna torch this car later. I can't wait.*
Observer 2 (speaking for 'Lee'): *I want to leave but I can't. They're my mates.*
Worker: *And what is Lee feeling?*
Observer 2 (speaking for 'Lee'): *I'm wound up.*

Note: The above could equally have been delivered by the observers from their seats.

Comments As mentioned on pp.37-38, there is a crucial distinction between using the inner voice techniques at *one step removed* as compared with the *personal level.* With one step removed scenes, anyone can speak the inner thoughts and feelings for any character, and everyone's ideas are equally valid because the scene is not a recreation of a specific offence or life event of anyone present. By contrast, with personal level scenes, the person whose scene is being presented must always be the final arbiter about the accuracy or usefulness of statements.

Source See *Glossary*.

3. Inner Voice from the Characters

After opening up discussion and hearing some ideas about 'what might be going on inside the heads of the characters', we can usefully move to the next stage of processing. To use the processing technique *Inner Voice from the Characters*, we place our hand lightly on the shoulder of each successive character and ask them to tell us—in the first person—what they are thinking, feeling or saying at this moment in the scene. Where it is inappropriate to touch a group member on the shoulder, we hold our hand just above the person's shoulder to indicate their turn.

Example: The car crime (*continued*)

The group members have discussed the scene and are confident that it looks like the three lads are about to steal the car with the one lad, the outsider, looking unsure. The characters in the scene give a range of responses:

Thoughts (Peers): *It's a turbo!; Yeah, let's do it!!!*
Thoughts (The outsider): *I'm in deep shit.*

Feelings (Peers): *I'm buzzing!; I'm brickin' it!*
Feelings (The outsider): *I'm wound up, feeling left out.*

Statements (Peers): *I'm saying to him, 'Come on, we're doing it now!'*
Statements (The outsider): *I'm saying, 'I can't do it, mate. I'm on licence, I'll get sent down.'*

Using this technique, we learn more about the characters in the scene and what is going on between them. When using this technique and the *Inner Voice from the Audience* technique, we continually draw the distinction between thoughts and feelings, a distinction that is often overlooked. Many participants have difficulty understanding their feelings and expressing them appropriately; *Inner Voice* techniques may help them develop a language for explaining their feelings.

Variations *Inner Voice From the Characters* may be used as the basis for creating a *Thinking Report* for any particular scene, be it a *one step removed* scene or a *personal level* scene.

Agreeing the content of the scene, and naming characters Assuming that we did not direct the scene ourselves, this is generally a good point to check with those presenting the scene to find out what they had intended. In most cases, this will be very close to what the observers were guessing. When we decide what the scene is 'really about,' it is important to stress the validity of interpretations offered by the observers. In general, however, we keep to the idea originally intended by those presenting the scene, unless everyone agrees that another interpretation is more useful.

At this point, we will also ask the people presenting the scene to give the characters names if they have not already done so. This draws a clear distinction between the group members and the characters they are portraying. In *one step removed* scenes, the names of the fictional characters should not be the names of anyone present, nor should they be the names of close friends or relatives of anyone present. This will avoid unnecessary distractions.

Once everyone agrees what the scene is about and what the names of the characters are, we can proceed with an in-depth exploration of the scene using the next processing techniques.

Inner Voice from the Characters can be usefully combined with the following technique: *Lifting the Mask.*

4. 'Lifting the Mask'

'Lifting the Mask' is an over-arching concept that applies across all of the processing techniques. We may 'lift the mask' at any point in order to deepen the impact of a scene or explore the motivations of characters. In general, however, we would wait until we hear some *Inner Voice from the Characters* before asking them to lift their mask.

The 'mask' is a metaphor for the way we present ourselves to others. *Lifting the Mask* allows us to contrast the public presentation of characters with their inner world. To do this, we use the phrase, 'lift your mask', which in effect asks a character to tell us what she is 'really thinking' or 'really feeling' at that moment. It is much like the theatrical convention of the aside to the audience, but differs in that it is purposely aimed at going deeper into the thoughts and feelings of a character and opening up the potential for dialogue with the audience.

You don't need actual masks in order to use this metaphor; it is enough to ask a character to lift his mask, and then to check with him whether or not his response was 'mask up'. Other processing techniques such as *Inner Voice From the Audience* and *Role Rotation* allow us to give our opinion about what is 'really going on' inside.

Lifting the Mask can be made more tangible by using simple actions to represent lifting the mask. For example, it may be useful to ask characters to take a step back or, if seated, to stand behind their chair, in order to signify they are lifting their mask.

Because the metaphor of *Lifting the Mask* provides such direct access to a character's private world, the technique must be treated with care, especially when working on the *Personal Level*. 'Wearing a mask' must not be seen judgementally as a negative strategy. We all wear different 'masks', and alter them depending on the situation. In order to be clear that 'wearing a mask' is not a term of stigma, we might first discuss with the group members situations where they feel the need to wear a 'mask' or put on a certain attitude. What 'mask' would they wear when stopped and questioned by the police, when in court or when out with friends? Are there times when we wear no masks at all?

When having such a discussion, we reassure the group members that the behaviours making up their 'front', or mask, are not under attack or being judged. However, if a mask is maladaptive—that is to say, if the mask once served the purpose of self-protection but now leads to negative consequences—the participant can make new choices about the masks he wears and the strategies he uses (Gergen, 1972).

See p.20 and p.183 for further discussions and examples of the uses of the mask metaphor.

5. **Interview in Role**

Interview in Role allows for active dialogue and debate between the observers in the audience and the characters on stage. We can ask questions of the characters, and those in the scene respond in role. Where appropriate, we may ask a character to share his inner thoughts and feelings by asking him to 'lift his mask' (see p.43).

Interview in Role has the added benefit that it helps those presenting the scene to get further into their role; they might not know much about their role until they answer questions as that character.

When working with *personal level* scenes, the group members can ask questions of the central person, the teller of the story, when he is in role as himself. This can be a very useful technique for the individual, as he will be speaking as himself at another point in time. This can help him check his progress over time.

Interview in Role shares much in common with *Worker in Role: Hot Seating,* one of the *Interactive Observer* exercises.

Example: The car crime (continued)
After listening to the thoughts and feelings of the characters in the scene, the group members ask 'Dave' what he is thinking about 'Lee':

Observer 1: *What are you thinking?*
Dave: *I'm thinking, what's he up to? Why's he backing off?*
Observer 1: *And what are you saying to him?*
Dave: *I'm saying, 'Come on, we'll have a laugh'.*
Observer 2: *Lift your mask and tell us what you're really thinking about him.*
Dave (Taking a step back to indicate lifting his mask): *What's he playing at? What's he trying to prove? He should fuck off if he's not gonna do it.*
Worker (Prompting): *I'm wondering if there's something else going on inside Dave. What else do you want to ask him about?*
Observer 2: *Yeah, lift that mask, too. Why do you think that way about your mate?*
Dave: *He's a tosser. He thinks he's better than the rest of us.*
Observer 2: *Yeah, but Lee doesn't want to do it. Why don't you let him go?*
Dave (Struggling to answer): *Just because!*
Worker (Returning to the technique *Inner Voice from the Audience*): *'Because.' Hmm. Any ideas from the group what Dave might mean by that?*
Observer 3: *You're shit scared too, aren't you? But you don't have the bottle to say it.* (To worker); *He's the weak one. Is that the point of us asking him questions?*
Observer 1 (To Lee): *And what are you thinking? Lift your mask.*
Lee ('Outsider'), (standing back to 'lift his mask'): *I can't do it. I'll lose my family if I get sent down again. But if I walk away, they'll think I'm soft. I don't know what to do.*
Observer 4: *They're not real mates. Real mates would understand.*

Comments This example demonstrates the principle that *the challenge comes through the role* (see p.21). By allowing the dramatic situation and the characters to take the main focus, the group members themselves do all of the challenging. As workers we stay neutral, although we can still make interventions, as the example shows. By withholding our judgement, we avoid moral debates which tend to reinforce the us/ them division between workers and participants. Being neutral does not, however, mean that we collude with pro-offending attitudes. On the contrary, as facilitators we ask questions and orchestrate scenes to ensure that all points of view are represented and that participants themselves challenge pro-offending attitudes. The key distinction is that we as facilitators do not do the explicit challenging when we use this strategy.

6. Role Rotation/Role Reversal

Role Rotation and *Role Reversal* are perhaps the most efficient techniques for challenging our distorted perceptions about other people and learning to empathise with other points of view. The techniques work so well because of our basic human tendency to believe that we are right and justified in our own actions. When we respectfully enter into another person's role, we may re-think our perceptions of that person and more fully understand their own reasons for feeling they are in the right. In a nutshell, *Role Rotation* and *Role Reversal* move us beyond the 'habitual limits of egocentricity' (Blatner and Blatner, 1988, p.175).

ROLE ROTATION

Role Rotation allows participants the complete freedom to move from one role to another in any type of scene, be it an *Interactive Observer* scene, *Frozen Picture* or *Role Play.* The technique generally applies to *one step removed* scenes and not to *personal level* scenes. The initiative to rotate roles can come from workers or from participants. Sometimes a role rotation will involve only a single substitution. At other times it might mean several simultaneous role exchanges. The aim is to get a number of different participants involved in playing each role, and also to ensure that those participants who may benefit from a particular role perspective are strategically offered such an opportunity.

Example: The car crime (*continued*)

Through a series of role rotations, the participants playing the roles of 'the peers' each have the opportunity to take on the role of 'Lee', the outsider. Likewise, the participant playing 'Lee' has the opportunity to take on the role of one of the 'peers'. In addition, group members who have been observing now take the opportunity to play the various characters in the scene.

During this process, one of the observers dismisses Lee's actions as 'soft' and 'weak.' The worker suggests to this group member that he take Lee's role in order to more fully understand Lee's dilemma and to better gauge what 'strength' and 'weakness' mean when facing such a high risk situation among peers. The group worker encourages the participant to find a way to identify with the role and to insist as Lee that he be respected and heard. This calls for strong leadership, and the worker does not allow Lee's feelings to go unspoken or ignored. She tells the participant newly in role as Lee, 'Your feelings matter here. Tell us what it's like for you. We can see you're trying to pull away from the others.' While in role as Lee, the participant who previously insulted Lee now experiences how difficult it is to 'stand up to your mates'. This leads to a de-brief where group members discuss the pros and cons of continuing to offend, and the challenges of 'going straight'.

ROLE REVERSAL

In *Role Reversal,* two key figures in a scene physically change places and take on each other's role. This allows for direct experience of one's own behaviour from the other's point of view. It also allows the participant to in effect answer his own pressing questions by asking in one role and reversing roles to answer. Role reversal is particularly suited to scenes involving two people in dialogue, where one person would benefit from reversing roles in order to gain insight into the other person's point of view. Just like *Role Rotation, Role Reversal* encourages us to re-think our perceptions of other people and to change our behaviour in relation to them.

Example: A group for men who have been violent to their partners

In a *one step removed* role play based loosely on his own abusive behaviour, participant Jim plays the role of a husband (given the fictional name 'Tony') who is verbally abusing his wife 'Sandra' (played by another group member) because he thinks she is spending too much money. After shouting for several moments, Jim reverses roles. Now the participant who played Sandra is in role as Tony, and Jim is Sandra. Jim experiences first hand what it is like to try to deal with a loud, hostile and potentially violent man. After resisting being in Sandra's role for several moments, Jim allows himself to acknowledge what he has so far denied: that he habitually uses his size, voice and strength to completely dominate and control his female partners. Jim and the rest of the group move on to have a wider discussion about their own violence and their use of power and control tactics, comparing and contrasting their behaviour with Tony's.

Comments It is important to bear in mind that role reversal works quite differently on the level of *one step removed* as opposed to the *personal level* (see pp.37-38). Remember that, regardless of whether a scene is *one step removed* or on the *personal level*, it can still have a powerful and unexpected effect on those involved. This applies not just to the central role player but also to those playing the other roles. In the example above, the group member who first plays Sandra may have his own powerful reaction to being in this role. This is why it so important to discuss scenes when they are completed, in order to allow those directly involved in the scene as well as the observers a chance to process their experience.

A common problem when using role rotation and role reversal is that participants may fall out of role. Falling out of role means that they refer to their character in the third person ('He doesn't want to steal the car', rather than 'I don't want to steal the car'.) or otherwise speak as themselves. When this happens, we acknowledge that they have come out of role and encourage them to re-phrase their statement in the first person. In most cases, a few reminders will be all that is needed.

Occasionally, a participant is resistant to speaking in the first person as a particular character. When this happens, it is usually because the participant is defended against feeling empathy for the character or the real life person who is represented by the character. For example, a racist attacker may strongly resist speaking in the first person as someone from the race he targets. If so, it may be useful to discuss the difficulty he has taking on the role and showing any respect for another point of view. Another strategy might be to ask for another volunteer to take the role for awhile. By gradually increasing the amount of general tolerance in the room, we may reach the point where the man who has committed the racist attack is willing to speak respectfully in role as someone from another race and, if all goes well, as someone from the race he targets. While he is in the role, we would encourage the group to ask him questions about what it feels like to be targeted by racists, and how this has affected him.

Source See *Glossary*.

7. Re-working the Scene

Re-working the Scene is not so much a single technique as an umbrella term for the range of related techniques that together give us total control over the action. When we re-work a scene, we can do virtually anything to shape the drama in order to evoke useful material and provide a constructive challenge for the participants. These techniques can be used with *Interactive Observer* scenes, *Frozen Pictures* and *Role Plays.*

Some of the basic options we can use to modify scenes:

'Go' Starts the scene or presentation.

'Stop' Stops the action. This is a crucial control to practise, particularly where scenes could involve simulations of violence or sexual activity.

'Crossfade' Crossfades the action, so that one part of a scene can be heard and seen more than another. This can be extended so that at various points one part of the stage is in action and the other part is frozen.

'Come to life' E.g. 'For ten seconds only'. Used with still images.

Other useful options: 'Instant replay'; 'Freeze frame'; 'Skip forward in time'; 'Skip backward'; 'Slow motion'; 'Volume up'; 'No volume'; Add or subtract characters.

Other options can change the dramatic tone of the scene and the characters:
Play the scene as if you are assertive/passive/aggressive.
Play the scene as if you are having a bad day/ a good day.
Play the scene as you would in real life/ the opposite of how you would in real life.
Play the scene the opposite of how it should be done/ play it how it should be done.
Play the scene with greater intensity/ less intensity.
Play the scene with more conflict between the characters/ less conflict.
Play the scene with one or more characters gender-reversed (i.e. a male character becomes female, or vice versa).

You can also use dramatic and film conventions to create new scenes related to the ones presented: Flashback; Dream sequence; 'Meanwhile, back at the ranch...'; End credits (e.g. a scene far in the future showing what became of the characters. This is useful for prompting discussion about the consequences of behaviour for self and others).

With these options in mind, if we go back to consider the car crime example that has been used through most of this chapter, we might want to 'flashback' to earlier in the evening when Lee first met the other boys. Likewise, we might want to see the 'end credits' and flash forward in time to see the consequences of the crime for Lee, the other boys, the victims and the boys' families. Finally, we might want to use the concept of 'meanwhile, back at the ranch ...' in order to see what it might be like for Lee's family when the police show up at their door looking for him.

Finally, re-working the scene offers the opportunity to multiply scenes and interchange characters: For example, ask several small groups to each devise their own *Frozen Picture* with the title 'The Argument,' then compare and contrast their differing interpretations of the title.

Comments Encourage participants to devise new techniques to re-work scenes. Among other benefits, reworking scenes reinforces the notion that it is possible to stand outside (metaphorically or actually) an interaction, weigh up alternative strategies and consider other possibilities. By re-working scenes to examine differing outcomes, we make the concept of determining our 'life script' real and tangible.

PART II

Exercises and Drama Structures

Deathbird, from *Lifting the Weight*

Photo: iD.8 Photography

CHAPTER 5

Games and Exercises

'What's this got to do with my offending?'
Participant in an offending behaviour group, while playing *Grandmother's Footsteps.*

This chapter covers:

- **About Games and Exercises**
- **The Limits of Categories**
- **Setting Up Exercises**
- **The Common Template for Descriptions**
- **General Games and Exercises**
- **Offending Focused Games and Exercises**

ABOUT GAMES AND EXERCISES

As outlined in *Chapter 3,* games and exercises come in two varieties: *General* and *Offending focused.*

General games and exercises are suitable for most settings. Their main focus is on generic rather than offending behaviour themes, although you can, where appropriate, highlight connections to offending during *processing.* The general games and exercises are divided into the following sub-sections according to their primary aim:

- Learning names; Group building pp. 54-58
- Inviting personal disclosure pp.59-64
- Promoting trust pp.65-66
- Problem solving and co-operation pp.67-71
- Energising the group; Practising concentration pp.72-86
- Communication; Assertiveness; Emotional awareness pp.87-91
- Imagination pp.92-94
- Drama skills pp.95-96
- Closure exercises; De-roling; Relaxation pp.97-100.

Offending focused games and exercises directly address offending behaviour themes and may have some 'general' applications as well. They can also be adapted for use with people at risk of offending and with other, non-offender populations, because many 'offending behaviour' issues are issues common to everyone. In this handbook, however, the offending focused games and exercises are explained with reference to offenders and people at risk of offending. They are grouped as follows, according to their primary aim:

- Power and control; Empathy; Victim empathy pp.101-108
- Relationships and gender issues; Responsibility; Locus of control pp.109-110
- Goal setting; Motivation to change pp.111-114
- Offending cycles; Offending tactics; Risk taking pp.115-120
- Perspective taking; Thinking distortions; Handling conflict pp.121-124
- Relapse prevention; Self control; Self-talk; Dealing with pressure; Options out of offending pp.125-129
- Controlling thinking and fantasy p.130.

THE LIMITS OF CATEGORIES

All systems of classification have their limits and are to some degree arbitrary. Although we have divided the exercises into categories according to their main aim, these are by no means strict categories. Indeed, most exercises have three or more listed aims; the categories are for convenience. Nevertheless, we have divided the exercises into categories to help you select appropriate activities and devise session plans. We hope you find ways to apply them that we haven't yet discovered.

SETTING UP EXERCISES

The rule of three rules When introducing games and exercises it can be tempting to explain all of the rules and aims before starting. This can be confusing and distracting for the participants. In most instances, a gradual introduction is better. A useful guide is the rule of three rules: when giving instructions, do not give more than three at a time. If there are more than three, phase them in gradually.

When we introduce exercises little by little, it allows us to make a swift start. The group members find themselves doing the exercise despite their anxieties. With any luck, they find it's not so bad as they thought it would be.

More importantly, by explaining only the minimum amount necessary, we do not pre-empt discoveries or predict the 'meaning' for the group members. If we give too much away or try to explain the purpose in too much detail, the group can lose interest; they have no need to invest in the process. The minimum information is therefore best. It allows participants to make their own discoveries through live experience and then make their own links in the processing at the end of the exercise.

One note of caution when using the rule of three rules: When we use this quick start approach, group members may feel the need to ask, 'Why are we doing this!?,' 'What's this got to do with my offending?' or similar questions during the exercise itself. This is usually because they are anxious. In response, we might suggest broad aims such as 'This is about problem solving' or 'This is about building trust in the group.' Yet we still keep our 'predictions' to a minimum. Often it is best to reply, 'See what happens and we'll talk about it at the end.'

Forming pairs and small groups It is often difficult for group members to form pairs, particularly early in a group. They may feel it is too risky to choose partners or express preferences. We can help overcome the awkwardness of choosing by making arbitrary suggestions such as 'choose someone who is wearing a similar colour to you,' 'choose someone who is roughly the same height,' 'choose someone whose first name has a letter in it that your first name has in it,' or 'choose someone who was born in a different month.'

Another, more direct option: We can decide for the group members by designating the pairs.

In large groups, a further option is to play ***Groups of ...*** In this exercise, people begin by milling around the room. When the leader calls a number, for example, 4, group members quickly get into groups of that number and signal that they have done so. Those left outside of a group can form another group. The leader can specify whether groups are to be mixed, for example including one leader in each, or more experienced and less experienced group members. The last number called should be of the group size and mix that you want in the next exercise.

There are many criteria you can use to play *Groups of ...* For example: Get into groups of people born in the same year/ decade; groups who have the same star sign; groups born in the same season of the year; groups who have the same favourite continent that they have visited or would like to visit; groups who have the same number of syllables in their first and last names put together. Use your imagination, but be aware that the groups should be formed based on non-controversial subjects that will tend to increase the sense of group bonding and togetherness as opposed to highlighting differences. In some circumstances, of course, you may *want* to form groups specifically to highlight important differences (e.g. 'Groups of the same sex,' 'Groups of the same ethnic background,' 'Those who want to be here and those who feel they were forced to come'), but that is obviously a very different process and would need sufficient time for discussion and working through.

THE COMMON TEMPLATE FOR DESCRIPTIONS

The following template describes the common layout of the exercises:

Title of Exercise

Aims Most exercises list three or more aims, with the most commonly applied aim listed first. Participants will inevitably discover new 'aims' for the exercises by interpreting them in unexpected ways. In most cases, one or more of the aims is featured in the processing questions (see the section on *Processing*, below).

Level of focus The level of focus on individuals during the exercise. *Low, medium, high,* or *passing focus.*

Suggested group numbers The optimum number of participants in a given exercise. Most exercises have a fairly broad range.

Time needed The approximate time needed to run the exercise *with adequate time for processing.*

Worker participation Based on the assumption that there are at least two co-workers leading the session, we provide several suggested levels of leader participation. The suggestions still apply if there is only one group worker:

- **'Yes'** Where 'yes' is indicated, we suggest that all of the workers participate in the exercise, although it is understood they are involved to assist the exercise and will not generally answer processing questions.
- **'One stays out, others optional'** We suggest that at least one worker stays out to run the exercise, usually for reasons of safety. Other workers have the option of joining in.
- **'No'** Where 'no' is indicated, we suggest that none of the workers join in, other than to demonstrate the exercise.

Method The exercises are described in two ways: in step by step fashion and/ or with a 'script' of the worker's instructions. With the scripted instructions, we suggest you *do not* try repeating the script verbatim. The script is there to learn and then forget. Use it as a starting point, then modify it as you see fit.

Comments/concerns Where needed, this section has general comments and safety concerns, especially those related to working with young people or vulnerable participants. It may also note particular skills you will need in order to safely carry out the exercise.

Processing: General level and Personal level In most exercise descriptions, we provide a range of sample questions that are meant to open up discussion on the general level and/or the personal level. Where appropriate, we connect processing specifically to aims listed at the top of the page (not necessarily the first aim). For guidance about how to process exercises, see p.38.

Variations In this section we suggest variations of the exercise that you may wish to use in order to better suit a particular aim or because it would better suit the group dynamic.

Sources Where possible, we identify a specific source for the exercise. However, because experiential exercises are often the result of collaboration and adaptation, and have been handed down through generations of practitioners, it is notoriously difficult to ascertain an original source. Where we have not indicated a source, we welcome readers' feedback about original sources if known to them. We will include such attributions in future editions.

GENERAL GAMES AND EXERCISES

Name Game Progression

Learning names; group building; co-operation skills
Low to passing high focus
For groups of 5 to 30
Time needed: 5 – 20 minutes
Worker participation: yes

Method

1. (Optional first step): The group members arrange themselves in a circle, alphabetically by name. Or, they arrange themselves by date of birth (day and month only, not the year), the distance they travelled to get here, the time it took, etc.

2. Group standing in a circle: *This is an exercise to help us remember each other's name. We'll go around the circle this way. When it's your turn, simply say your name loud and clear. I'll start. My name is …*

3. After a round: *This time it's a bit different. We'll go around the other way and this time when we come to you say loudly and clearly 'my name is' and then say your name. Then the whole group will energetically say 'hello (blank)!' It's a way to learn names and also gives us a good welcome, so I'll start with me: 'My name is …'* (ensure group responds energetically).

4. After another round: *All right, I think we have a good idea of names now, so I'm going to stand in the middle and when I point to someone in the group, the whole group will say that person's name, and everyone's name will be remembered. Let's see how it works …*

Group worker stands in the middle of the circle and points one by one at each person in the group, in any order, occasionally pointing to himself or herself as well. Make sure everyone's name is remembered. This sequence should be done with energy, confidence and humour, as there are likely to be several little 'mistakes' along the way. These can be breezed over and considered 'part of the exercise.'

- ***Variation: I'm sorry I forgot your name*** (this can be added as a fifth step to the exercise). *Take a moment to look around the circle and check if there are any names you are not quite sure of. It's OK to ask that person their name. In fact, let's make it a group rule that it's OK to forget each other's names, just to take the pressure off. So if we forget someone's name, we can ask them their name and not have to pretend we remember it. Let's all do a quick practice of 'I'm sorry I forgot your name …'* (All go around introducing themselves to each other, saying, 'I'm sorry but I've forgotten your name.')

Another variation: Have each person say their name in the form, 'My name is …' and then the whole group say in unison, 'My name is …' putting in the name of the person who just spoke. It would sound like this: (Eddie): 'My name is Eddie'. (All): 'My name is Eddie'.

Throwing Names

Learning names; dealing with pressure (relapse prevention); concentration
Low to passing high focus
Groups of 5 to 20
Time needed: 5 – 15 minutes
Worker participation: yes

Method

The group stands in a circle, worker with a ball:

This is a way of learning each other's names. I'll start by holding the ball up and making eye contact with someone else in the circle. It works best if it's someone roughly across the circle from me. Once I have eye contact with them, I say my name, then 'to', then their name, as I throw the ball in a nice easy arc so they can catch it easily. So it sounds like 'Joe to Mark, Mark to Tracy, Tracy to Andy, etc.'

Once the group members are more familiar with each other's names …

Now let's miss out our own names and just say the name of the person we are throwing it to. Let's try to quicken the pace a little.

Add in a second ball, then a third. If the participants are just throwing the ball in any direction, without heeding the receiver's ability to catch, pause the exercise and ask the group to suggest strategies to make it run more smoothly.

Personal processing: *dealing with pressure* (relapse prevention). *What did it feel like when you forgot a name or dropped the ball? In what other situations do you feel like that? What pressures would 'overload' your coping system? What have you done in the past to bring your system back into balance? Did it work? Would you like to try something else? If so, what?*

Variations

- Where throwing and catching may be a problem, try throwing 'invisible' balls.
- A good variation involving walking rather than throwing balls is ***Cross Circle Switch:*** The worker begins by demonstrating how people are to cross the circle by saying their own name and the name of the person they are walking toward. While the first person is walking toward the second person, the second person makes eye contact with a third person, says their own name and the third person's, and walks toward that third person. And so on. It should sound like, 'Marcy to Wendy, Wendy to Ian, Ian to Irene', etc. When everyone knows the procedure, the leader initiates the next stage, where there are two people walking across the circle at any one time. If the exercise is going well and the group is large enough, the leader can add a third or even fourth simultaneous cross, so that at any one time three or four people will be crossing the circle.

This variation works in a similar fashion to *The 'Yes' Game*.

Introductions

Group building (including setting group rules); personal disclosure, communication
Low to passing high focus
Groups of 6 and up
Time needed: 5 - 10 minutes or more
Worker participation: one stays out, others optional

Method

1. Group standing in a circle: *To start, everyone crosses the circle and shakes hands with everyone else. Don't speak, just shake hands. Try to end up in a different place in the circle. Go.*
2. When step one is complete: *This time we cross the circle again, and this time shake hands with everyone else in the room and exchange names. Go.*
3. When step two is complete: *We cross the circle again, and this time find someone you don't know or don't see every day, and get into a pair. In your pairs, learn the other person's name and share three facts about yourself, nothing too personal, such as a favourite film, or a place you have visited. If you want to, you could also tell us something you are proud of, an accomplishment of some kind. Each person in the pairs will then introduce their partner to the rest of the group and report on those three facts.*
4. Give time for people to exchange facts and then go round the circle with each person introducing their partner by name and feeding back the three facts. Check with the partner is the details were fed back accurately. Everyone is thanked.

Option: Instead of, or in addition to, telling each other three facts about themselves, the people in the pairs discuss and agree *one common aim* they have for themselves in the group and *one group rule* they both agree is important. These are reported back to the whole group.

General processing *How did the group cope with meeting each other and learning a bit about each other? What do you think is the purpose of an exercise like this?*

Personal processing: *personal disclosure* *What was it like talking about yourself? In life generally, who do you talk with closely and who do you keep more distant? Do you ever feel shy? How do you cope with the shyness?*

Variations

- When introducing their partner to the group, each person reverses roles and speaks in the first person as their partner.
- Step one is expanded, so that people cross the circle 'as if' they are shy but still aware of and looking at people, then 'as if' curious but cautious, then 'as if' very friendly.
- Find three things you and your partner share in common.
- Find out what brought your partner to this course or group.
- Find out your partner's name. What does his name mean? Who gave him his name? How does he feel about being called by this name? Is there a name he'd prefer to be known by in this group? (This can be done as a whole group discussion rather than in pairs).
- A light and fun variation: When introducing themselves to their partner, each person must tell only lies. The lies are reported back to the group verbatim.

Meet and Greet

Group building; communication skills; learning names; energiser
Passing high focus
Groups of 5 to 20
Time needed: 5 - 10 minutes
Worker participation: yes

Method

Everyone standing in a circle:

This looks complicated at the start but it should soon become clear. As you know, my name's Steve. Now what I'm going to do is look across the circle and make eye contact with someone, in this case Jason. Hello, Jason.

Now I walk over to Jason and I introduce myself as if I'm meeting him for the first time. We'll probably shake hands, too, because we'll imagine it's a formal occasion and I'm a good host. Hello again, Jason, I'm Steve, how do you do? ('Hi, Steve').

Now this is the complicated part: When I've introduced myself to Jason, I take him to meet SOMEONE ELSE in the circle. After all, I'm a good host and I want to make sure everybody gets introduced. So, Jason I'd like you to meet Lou, Lou this is Jason. ('Hello, Jason, nice to meet you.' 'Hello, Lou.')

After Jason meets Lou, HE now takes HER and introduces her to someone else in the circle. Meanwhile, I go back to my original place. After Lou is introduced to a new person, Jason goes back to his original place, and Lou carries on and introduces that new person to someone else, and so on. Let's give it a go. If any of that was unclear, we'll remind ourselves as we go. We'll keep going 'til everyone has had at least one go.

Comments/concerns Remind people that it is perfectly OK to ask someone what their name is (see *Name Game Progression*).

With some groups it will be important to build the exercise in stages. For example, for some groups shaking hands may be quite a big step. It may also be that some group members do not ordinarily shake hands for cultural or personal reasons. This can become a topic for discussion; the group can consider the different types of cultural greetings, what signals different types of greeting give, etc.

General processing *Did you find this exercise difficult, and if so, why? What feelings did you have and how did you cope with those feelings?*

Personal level processing: *communication skills* *How do you feel when you meet people in everyday life? What situations do you find difficult or easy to introduce yourself in? Does assertiveness play a part in this?*

Variation A more energetic and *lower focus* version is ***Birthday Party*** (Weinstein and Goodman, 1992): The group members are told that today is their birthday. They have invited all these people to the party and are determined to be a great host. On the word 'Go!' all group members leave their space in the circle simultaneously. Their task is similar: they act as a good host and greet everybody they meet and then introduce that person to someone else. They all do this at the same time. When a group member has met and greeted every other member of the group, they return to their original place in the circle. This version can be quite loud and energetic.

It is often helpful to give highly specific instructions such as, 'Try to make eye contact when you are shaking hands with someone, and repeat their name when you hear it. If you are normally a shy person, try being a very proud and assertive host just for the next two minutes. This is a BIG birthday!'

Dangerous Places

Group building (rules and safety); relapse prevention (high risk situations); personal disclosure
High focus or passing high focus
Group size: any number
Time needed: 5 – 20 minutes
Worker participation: yes

Method

Ask the group members to quietly walk around the room and identify areas and objects that could be dangerous, for example during an active exercise.

After a few moments, ask the members of the group to stand by one of these dangerous places or objects. One at a time, they tell the group what the dangerous place or thing is, and why.

Encourage them to use their imaginations and go beyond the merely practical. For example: 'This flipchart is dangerous because I could trip over it but also because I could write something on it so intelligent and amazing that everyone's brain will explode when they read it.' Or: 'This space in the middle of the room is dangerous because I am all alone here and everyone is looking at me.'

Concerns/comments For health and safety reasons, this is a crucial exercise to put in at the start of a group using active movement such as drama games. If group members miss some of the important hazards in the room, you can identify and explain the hazards yourself.

General processing *If this object is dangerous, what can the group do to make sure that no one is hurt? Do we need any special rules to take this into account?*

Personal processing: *relapse prevention* (high risk situations). *What is a dangerous place for you? Name one dangerous place that you avoid. Or it may be a person. Why do you avoid it, or them? When do YOU become the 'dangerous place'? Who would consider you to be dangerous?*

Variation You can make this part of a name-learning sequence by asking people to repeat their name when they are explaining their 'dangerous place.'

Dangerous Places is an ideal warm-up to *Map on the Floor.*

Map on the Floor

Personal disclosure; group building; goals; relapse prevention
Low to high focus
Group size: any number
Time needed: 5 – 30 minutes or more
Worker participation: yes

Method

Let's start by having everyone spread out randomly around the room … Alright, now I'd like you to imagine that we have spread out on the floor a huge map of the UK (choose appropriate map location and size) *and Ireland. This will be north, this will be south, east and west. So, where I'm standing now would be, let's say, Dover, and here would be Wales, here would be Ireland, north and south, here's Scotland, here's Newcastle, East Anglia and London. Everyone have a pretty good idea of what's where? If you don't, that's OK, someone will help you. This isn't a geography test! Now I'd like you to please put yourself on this map according to where you were born. … If you were born outside of this map, stand against the wall in the direction of the place you were born. Talk to the people nearby to you, to see where they are in relation to you. Explain to them where you are.*

Comments/concerns Be aware that the question of where they live or even where they were born might be too threatening for some group members. It may set up rivalries in some groups, and it may not be information they wish to share with each other. If this is the case, use a suggestion from the list below.

Variations Other criteria for placement on the map might include:

- Where I once had a good time or a good day out.
- Where would I most like to visit in the whole world? (*Go there now and tell us about it*).
- Where is my best friend?
- Where is the place I would least like to go to again?
- Where do I feel most competent?
- Where does my family come from?
- Where is a place I like to be / a place I like to go?

Questions on issues related to offending or high risk:

- Where is the place that would be a high risk place for me to go?
- Where have I lapsed or offended in the past?
- Where is a safe place for me to be?
- Where am I most vulnerable?
- Where can I go if I feel high risk?
- Where are the people in my support network?
- Where have I caused the most harm/hurt?
- What prisons have I been in?
- Where is a place I am afraid to go/ person I don't want to meet?

Connections

Personal disclosure; group building; communication; handling conflict
Low to passing high focus
Groups of 6 and up
Time needed: 2 – 20 minutes
Worker participation: yes

Method

The participants and group workers create a three dimensional picture of the connections that exist between the people in the group. Those who know each other well get near to each other, and those who have never met before place themselves apart from each other. Particularly strong connections can be represented by, for example, a hand on the shoulder, standing back to back, or whatever spontaneously emerges from the people who know each other well. Encourage the participants to make the sculpt as accurate as possible, so that the result is a good picture of the underlying connections in and among the group members.

Comments/concerns This is a particularly good exercise to do in those groups where there is a rolling intake, where the older members of the group can take the initiative of welcoming the new group members. It is also a useful exercise to do in the first session of a new group, where the worker is aware that some of the group members may have previous connections to each other. The exercise is in this case useful for making explicit what would otherwise be hidden alliances.

If this exercise is done in the first session of a group, you may get a 3-d picture of a group with very weak connections. If this happens, use the exercise as an opportunity to reinforce the importance of the group coming together. You can suggest that after one or two sessions, this exercise will be done again, to see if people feel more connected.

Processing: *group building* It can happen that there is a large part of the group with inter-connections, and one or two members who don't know anyone else present. In this case, use the exercise as an opportunity to acknowledge the importance of the 'in-crowd' welcoming the 'isolates'. You can ask the isolates what they may need to hear from the group in order to feel welcome. Often this will be nothing more than hearing that they are welcome to be part of the group. Likewise, the inter-connected people can be given the chance to welcome the isolates, either verbally or perhaps through some gesture, e.g. shaking hands. This should be sensitively negotiated on both sides.

Variations After the first phase, ask the group to make connections based on certain criteria that you want to make explicit. For example, you could ask the group members to: *Make a connection with the one person you know best in this group, and tell the group what the history of this connection is; Make a connection with the one person in this group who you feel you may have a problem or conflict with, and tell them and the group what this conflict may be* (be careful to ensure that this is done respectfully and as safely as possible. Be clear about why you would want to do this); *Make a connection with the person you know least well, and learn something about them.*

Another variation: Do *Connections* only verbally, with the group in a circle. Participants note their connections but do not demonstrate the connections physically.

Anyone Who

Personal disclosure; group building; energiser; co-operation
Passing high focus
Groups of 5-30
Time needed: 3 - 10 minutes
Worker participation: yes

Method

Preparation: The group sits in a circle of chairs, with the facilitator standing in the middle. There are no extra chairs in the circle.

I am in the middle of the circle and I want a seat. The way I find a seat is by saying something about me that I might share in common with others of you, such as 'anyone who wears a ring,' or 'anyone who has a brother or sister,' or even something more personal, like 'anyone who's ever tried to change a habit.' It can be almost anything, but it has to be true about me personally. Then, everyone who shares that in common with me changes seats. As you've guessed, someone else will be left standing in the middle, and then they do the same thing. Now remember, it's not a race, so you should NOT bump into anyone, and be careful not to tip over your chair when you reach it. This is a non-contact sport! Also, you can't shift to the chair either side of you, and you can't go back to the seat you came from (too easy). Finally, if you can't think of anything, say 'all change,' and we will all change seats at the same time.

Comments/ concerns This is one of our favourites. If you use it at the right time and with enough energy, groups will find it a good energiser as well as a good group builder. Be aware that this is a passing high focus exercise, meaning that for a brief moment all eyes will be on one person. This can be threatening to some, particularly if the group is very new. It should be run in a brisk manner, as one of the factors making it less threatening is if people know they will only be 'in the spotlight' for a few seconds.

Anyone Who has a lot of rules, so prepare your introduction.

Variation A lower energy but equally useful variation is ***Things We Have in Common:***

All stand in a circle. One at a time, any group member can step forward and say something about himself or herself, e.g. 'Join me in the middle if you like music' or 'Join me in the circle if you're trying to change something about yourself.' The others who share this in common step forward *if they wish to.* Those who step forward acknowledge their common link and perhaps discuss a few particulars. This can be quite a gentle and supportive exercise. It may be more suitable for those groups that are resistant to more energetic activities or anything resembling a 'game'. It is also far less potentially threatening, as the group members volunteer to step forward and there is no chance of getting caught in the middle.

This variation is particularly useful for 'taking the temperature' of a group, because the level of disclosure in the exercise will reflect the degree of safety and bonding felt by the group members. If the level of disclosure is minimal, encourage personal disclosures by stepping forward yourself or asking the group, 'What sort of statements do you think you might make if we were to do this exercise in three months time?' Again, group members must be allowed to set their own limits. Discuss the importance of safety and confidentiality in the group. Encourage the group members to share on a deeper level, perhaps on a theme related to the purpose of the group.

Continuum

Personal disclosure; group building; motivation to change; relapse prevention; any theme
Medium to high focus
Group size: any number
Time needed: 10 - 20 minutes or more
Worker participation: one stays out, others optional

Method Draw an imaginary line on the floor, the ends representing opposites, e.g. agree/disagree; like/dislike; me/someone else; every time/not at all. Participants place themselves on this continuum based on their responses to questions/statements:

Anger/ Violence
How many times per week do I get angry?
How many times per week do I get violent?
(Compare responses to these questions in order to emphasise anger control techniques they already have)

Self-determination/ Self-esteem:
My life is going the way I want it to.
I can see a clear way forward.
I am in control of my behaviour.
I am in control of my thoughts.
I control the direction my life is going.
I am responsible for the decisions I make.
I am motivated to change.

Offending and risk:
How responsible was I for my offence?
How responsible was my victim?
How much do I want to not re-offend?
How dangerous am I?
How often do I fantasise about . . . ?
How much power and control did I exert over my victim?

Relationships:
How much do I agree with the statement (insert belief about women, men, gender, stereotypes, etc.)?
Who should initiate sexual contact? ('Me' / 'My partner')

Denial/ Relationship to group:
How honest do I feel I can be here?
No one here sees me as I really am.
I can express my true opinions here.

Comments/concerns A good general disclosure exercise. Very adaptable, for any group. Can be low, medium or high focus, depending on how we process. Continuums can often be used as a warm up for role-plays or other work.

It can be highly beneficial to ask the participants to place themselves on the continuum according to their response at various points in time, past, present and future. You can use this to support changes they have already made, and for goal-setting.

It is important to allow individuals to explain why they placed themselves where they have. In a large group you can ask for responses from only a representative sample of each continuum. When short of time, ask participants to share their response with one person near them.

Variations Introduce the idea of continuums by asking the group members to arrange themselves alphabetically by name, by year or date of birth, or other simple criteria.

Another, potentially very powerful technique is where group members to take on the role of their partner or close family member to answer the questions in reference to themselves but from that person's point of view. Example: (Group member in role as his girlfriend): 'I'm Richard's girlfriend Bernadette, and I would say that he raises his voice to me in anger this many times (standing on the continuum) in an average week.' It can also be useful to ask group members to place *each other* on the continuum. This can open up a wide range of feedback between group members, e.g. 'I put you there on the continuum because I know you well enough to say ...' Finally, you can generate useful debate about masculinity by forming a continuum of, 'Who is the toughest person in the room?' Process with questions around, 'What is toughness?', 'Is it internal or external?', 'What is true strength to you?'

Opening Questions

Personal disclosure; group building; warm up to any theme
High focus or passing high focus
Group size: any number
Time needed: will vary according to group size
Worker participation: yes, where appropriate

Method The purpose of an opening question is to warm up the group members to explore the issue raised in the question. It is meant to directly relate to the theme of the session.

- **Start of a new group: motivation and goal setting**

1. One thing I would like to get from this course/workshop. Also, how able am I to do this now, in percentage terms? (e.g. If the goal is 'to control my violence,' the participant may say for example that he is 40%, 60% or 95% able to control his violence now. It is useful for the participants to register that they are building on already existing skills rather than having to start from scratch. Have them set a goal for what percentage it will be at the end of the course.).
2. What brings you here? What have you given up to be here?
3. One reason you don't want to be here, and one reason you do.
4. Let's go into the future: If at the end of the group it has all been a great success for you, what session made the difference for you? What was discussed or explored, and what insight did you have that made all the difference?
5. Something you want to achieve this week/by the end of the course/this year/in life.
6. Who will benefit from you being here and making progress toward change?
7. One thing you are good at and one thing you're not so good at that you'd like to improve.
8. What internal strengths do you have that will help you in this programme (e.g. honesty, being hard working, desire to change, helping others)? Who are the people in your life who give you strength? What accomplishments are you proud of?
9. Something that might hold you back in the group (e.g. tiredness, conflict with a group member, ambivalence about change, reluctance to be here).

- **The group process; denial; responsibility for own change process**

10. What do you think you have in common with the other people here?
11. What is helpful/ less helpful about this group?
12. What topic do you find difficult to talk about in this group? Before coming to the group, what did you decide you wouldn't talk about?
13. What questions should the group be asking you?
14. What are the most important questions you should ask yourself? Ask them, and try to answer.

- **Power and control**

15. A situation where you had power and used it well / where you misused power?
16. An area of life where you have power / have no power?

- **Anger management and violence**

17. When was the first time you were violent?
18. What is the smallest thing that makes you angry?
19. When you are angry, what do you do to stop yourself being violent?

- **Thinking about thinking: self-talk, self-control and responsibility**

20. Do you control your thoughts or do they control you?

21. What actions are you responsible for and not responsible for?
22. When are you likely to convince yourself that you are not responsible for your actions (e.g. when feeling bad/using alcohol)?
23. How do you deal with the bad times?

- **Core attitudes and beliefs about self and others; self-esteem; self-disclosure**

24. What messages have been given to you that have discouraged you from achieving what you wanted to? (e.g. 'You'll never amount to anything.' or 'You should know your place.')
25. One rule you live by/ What is your personal motto?
26. What one quality would you like your child to have?
27. What is the hardest thing you've ever done?
28. Where does your name come from? Does it have a meaning? What do you think of it? What do you want to be called here?
29. Who was your first friend?
30. What will be your epitaph?
31. If you could be talented in something you are not, what would it be?
32. Something that no one here knows about you that you are proud of.
33. Name someone you admire/respect; someone you consider to be a hero or heroine.
34. Who has had the most impact on your life?

- **Relationships/gender training and beliefs**

35. When did you become an adult?
36. What did your father/mother teach you about being a man/woman?
37. In a relationship, a man/woman should ...; In a relationship, partners should ...

- **Family, and early learning**

38. What were the unspoken/ spoken rules in your family when growing up?
39. What are the spoken and unspoken rules within your home now?
40. What did you get from your parents that you wish you hadn't / are glad you did?
41. Your favourite memory of playing as a child.
42. Tell us about your favourite/ least favourite teacher.
43. What was the first time you were punished? What lesson did you take from that?
44. Describe your relationship with your family when you were young. Might it get in the way here in the group, which is after all a bit like a family? Can you separate out the two?

- **Victim empathy and awareness**

45. If my victim(s) were here, they would say about me...
46. Who has been directly or indirectly harmed by your actions? What would you say to them if you had the chance, particularly about the fact that you are on this programme?

- **Relaxation; taking a time out; free time**

47. How would you decorate a room of your own?
48. What is your favourite place? Where would you most like to visit in the world?
49. Your favourite T.V. programme/ film/music/book/free time activity.

- **Relapse prevention and high risk situations**

50. What was the last high risk situation you handled well/ didn't handle well?
51. What would be your first indication that you are getting into an offending cycle? Who would you contact?

Trust Walking

Trust; responsibility; self-talk; group building; self-control; empathy
Low to medium focus
Groups of 4 and up
Time needed: 10 - 30 minutes
Worker participation: one stays out, others optional

Method In pairs, A and B: *This is an exercise about trusting the other people in the group and also about being aware of what's around us. Person A will go first as the person with their eyes closed, while person B leads you around the room. Before you do this, just a couple of things: First, this should be a completely silent exercise, so as soon as you set off, no speaking. Take care of the person you are leading. Let them enjoy using their other senses as they walk around. While you are walking around, try not to follow other pairs, and try to make it so that you never need to turn or stop suddenly. Think ahead so that all of the turns can be gentle. The person with their eyes closed can tell their partner if they feel uncomfortable. If at any time it becomes too uncomfortable for the person being led, they can open their eyes.* Allow each person to be led for two to five minutes, then swap around after brief immediate feedback.

General processing *What was the exercise about? What makes it run well or badly? What skills did you need to use? Is there anything in there that is important for us to remember as a group?*

Personal processing: *responsibility; self-talk* *What discoveries did you make when doing the exercise? Which did you prefer, leading or being led? Why? How does that relate to the world in general? Do you prefer leading or being led generally?*

Who wanted to open their eyes? Did you? If you did, did you close them again? Why? What thoughts did you have that told you to open your eyes? If you managed to keep your eyes closed, even though you wanted to open them, how did you do that? What thoughts did you use to control your impulse to open your eyes? In what other situations in life do you find that you need to use thoughts to intervene in powerful thoughts and feelings?

Variations One variation is ***Trust Trios,*** which works in the same way except there is one person either side of person with their eyes closed. This can add a greater measure of safety and control. It also involves co-operation and negotiation. In some groups, it is useful to have a worker in as one of the trio to encourage safe behaviour. However, that worker must be willing to take their turn in the middle.

Another good trust walking exercise is ***Wall Crash*** (Brandes and Philips, 1990). Two people act as a safety net at the far end of the room. One at a time, group members walk from the opposite end of the room with eyes closed. The two people acting as safety net stop them before they reach the wall. After everyone has a go, repeat with increasing speed, until people are RUNNING across the room knowing they will be safely stopped.

As a useful exercise in trust, self-control and spatial awareness, *Wall Crash* can be adapted so that the person who is walking or running with eyes closed must *stop himself* by counting or estimating the number of steps to the wall. The two people acting as the safety net will still be there 'just in case.' Process around the issue of 'stopping myself' and 'opening my eyes to keep out of dangerous/ high risk situations.'

Walking Trust Circle

Trust; self control; self-talk; co-operation; empathy; group building; responsibility
Passing high focus
Groups of 6 to 25
Time needed: 2 - 3 minutes per person, 15 minutes to process
Worker participation: yes, or, one stays out, others optional

Method Group members stand in a circle, about arms length from each other. Ask for a volunteer or use a co-worker to demonstrate. The volunteer comes to the centre of the circle and closes her eyes. The volunteer is now slowly turned once or twice, and asked to walk straight ahead, with her arms relaxed at her sides. When she reaches the edge of the circle, the person at that point in the circle stops her *by the shoulders*, points her in a new direction and gently sends her on her way. The volunteer crosses the circle until the same thing happens again and she is sent in a new direction across the circle. And so on. Group members to do the exercise silently, making every effort to take care of the person in the middle.

As the person is crossing the circle, add occasional words of support. Let her know that whatever pace she is walking at is the right pace, and there is no pressure. When you sense that the person crossing could benefit from a bit more of a stretch, encourage a faster pace if this is safe and appropriate.

After two minutes or so, repeat for other volunteers. Be willing to demonstrate the exercise yourself, as it can seem quite daunting for some groups.

Comments/concerns Remind participants that they should stop the person crossing the circle by gently but firmly taking hold of their shoulders. When this instruction is made clear, it should alleviate some the participants' anxiety about where they are supposed to touch each other. Pay close attention to ensure this instruction is carried out.

For safety, if it seems like the volunteer is heading between two people, have them make a decision about who will stop her, i.e. do not have one person touching one shoulder and another the other; this can lead to people 'falling through the gaps.'

General processing *What is involved in an exercise like this? What skills did you need as a group to make it work well? What skills are important to help the group function? Did you feel you took care of each other? If there were lapses of concern or sensitivity, what can the group do to help become more trusting and supportive of each other?*

Personal processing: *self-control*; *self-talk* *What thoughts did you have when you were crossing the circle? What feelings? How did you cope with these thoughts and feelings? Did you want to stop, or open your eyes. Were there some times you wanted to open them but didn't? What thoughts do you remember having that allowed you to keep them closed? What other strong impulses must we all regulate? How does this relate to the reasons you are in this group?*

Advanced variation: Two or more people cross the circle simultaneously.

Paper Not Floor

Problem solving; co-operation; group building; responsibility
Medium focus
Groups of 5 to 20
Time needed: 10 - 20 minutes
Worker participation: no

Materials: A large sheet of flipchart or newspaper. With large groups you may need two or three sheets. Place the paper on the floor and have the group gather around it.

You will see we have a large sheet of paper. Here's the task: Everybody must be in contact with the paper and not with the floor. Let's see a solution that fits that rule.

Most often, group members will gather in a huddle and stand on the paper at this point, as it is the most obvious solution. When the group comes up with a solution fitting the rule, congratulate them, repeat the rule, and reduce the size of the paper by half. Each time you do this, the rule is the same but the problem gets harder. Encourage the group to think laterally at each stage. Once they come up with a solution, encourage them to think of new ones. If they decide to use furniture, for example, allow that solution but then at the next stage you can rule out furniture.

Eventually, after five or six stages, the paper will be the size of a postage stamp. The ultimate solution is one in which each group member is touching the tiny piece of paper and the group jumps in the air. An alternative last stage solution is for the group members to pass around the piece of paper, jumping in the air one by one when they hold it (After all, there was never a rule about them all being in contact with the paper at the same time. They just assumed the rule was there. Likewise, there was no time limit set, so a brief jump in the air will suffice).

Comments/ concerns As the group attempts the task they are likely to have many questions and they might become quite frustrated. Keep reminding the group that there is only one rule ('Everybody must be in contact with the paper and not with the floor') and that you have no further information to give them.

A useful hint to give them: *Think about what I am saying and what I am NOT saying. You may be adding rules that aren't there.*

Another useful hint if they are really stuck: *You only need to hold your solution for a maximum of one second.*

Quite often the group will come up with solutions that they are unsure about. For example, they may ask whether they can use furniture or whether they can tear the paper. Again, stress that there is only one rule to this exercise and that the group is at liberty to interpret it as they wish. Encourage them to try any solution that fits the rule.

General processing *What is the exercise about? What skills did you use? Were any of your solutions used? Were any of your solutions not used? How did you feel about that? What can we do as a group to make sure everyone's ideas are listened to?*

Personal processing: problem solving *How does this exercise relate to your lives outside this group? What sort of problem could the paper represent? Although the paper got smaller you kept using the same solution for a long time. Why? At what stage did the solution have to change? Why? What connections can you make between the process you went through in this exercise and how you deal with problems outside this group?*

Source: Sue Jennings (1986) calls this the *Newspaper Exercise.*

You're on the Spot

Problem solving; self-talk; self-control; power and control
High focus
Groups of 4 and up
Time needed: 5 minutes per person, plus 15 minutes for processing
Worker participation: yes

Method A volunteer waits outside the room and is told that when he returns he will have to follow clapping clues (the equivalent of 'warmer/ cooler') in order to perform a simple action.

The group decide on an action for that person to do. These must be simple, physical and intuitive actions, as there will be no verbal instructions allowed. Examples: The volunteer must turn on the light switch; The volunteer must open the window; The volunteer must pick up a pen and draw a circle on the flipchart.

When the volunteer returns he tries to perform the action that is required, being led there only through louder or softer clapping from the group: louder means he is getting closer to the task. When he guesses successfully the rest of the group give a loud cheer. Repeat with other volunteers.

Comments/concerns Because the focus is so high in this exercise and the power/ information imbalance so great, it is possible for a volunteer to get quite distressed if he doesn't guess the action quickly. Be prepared to put a time limit on how long someone spends trying to guess the action. However, don't make it too short a time limit; a central feature of this exercise is letting participants experience and deal with frustration when they are 'in the spotlight.' It often works best when they have the opportunity to really persevere and try out a number of options to find the solution. Because the exercise can be frustrating, remember to process the feelings of the volunteer as well as the group.

Be aware that some group members might not be able to resist 'rescuing' the volunteer. If this happens, it can be useful to discuss with the whole group.

General processing *What thoughts and feelings did you have while trying to guess the action? Likewise, what was it like to know what you wanted and then try to communicate this to the volunteer? What thoughts and feelings did you have? Let's talk a bit about the power and control relationship? What was that like? Can you think of examples from life where one person has all the knowledge and the power, and the other is kept guessing?*

Personal processing: *problem solving; self-talk; self-control* *How did you decide what to do in order to guess the action? Could you have cracked it by just standing there? What stopped you trying certain things? Did you have any difficult feelings or negative self talk? How did you cope with this? What were your feelings when you guessed correctly and completed the task? What sort of positive challenges in your life may involve this kind of perseverance? What kinds of new situations will you need to negotiate?*

Variations The exercise can be used to explore the theme of *self-talk* and *empathy* by having someone walk beside the volunteer to give a running commentary of his thoughts and feelings as he tries to solve the problem. They can make supportive comments in the first person, such as 'I can do this. Let me stick with it and find the solution.' After the task is completed, the volunteer can let his helper know how accurate he was, and also whether the supportive comments were useful.

The Knot

Co-operation; problem-solving; communication; self-control
Low focus
Groups of 7 to 12 (large groups sub-divided)
Time needed: 5 - 20 minutes
Worker participation: one stays out, others optional

Method

The group stand in a circle, shoulder to shoulder, facing in. Each group member raises their right hand, reaches across and takes the right hand of someone else in the circle who *is not* standing next to them. If there is an uneven number in the group, there will be one hand remaining free. This will not affect the exercise, but that hand should remain raised.

Each group member then raises their left hand, and takes the hand of a *different* person in the circle, but again it *must not* be someone standing next to them. The group then lower their arms to a more comfortable height, keeping hold of the grip.

Now the group is in a knot, and the group members must work co-operatively to untie it. Give the instruction 'unravel this knot as far as it will go.' Group members must not break the links by letting go of hands even briefly, as this can make the knot impossible to untie. They can, however, alter their grip if they are twisted into an uncomfortable position.

The group decide when they think the knot has been fully unravelled. There are three end points to the knot: 1) A complete circle; 2) Two inter-linked circles; 3) A Gordian knot (a knot that cannot be unravelled without breaking a link). If the group get to the last two solutions, ask them if they would like to break a link in order to further unravel the knot.

Comments/concerns As it involves physical contact, this exercise demands confident leadership to contain possible anxiety. It will also be inappropriate in some groups.

General processing *What was the exercise about? Did you feel you co-operated? Did you need a leader? What were your expectations at the start of the exercise?* (Remind the group that you gave them the instruction, 'unravel the knot as far as it will go' and that they cannot fail at this exercise) *How might this relate to expectations in life outside of this group?*

Personal processing: *problem solving* *How did you feel doing this exercise? How did you feel when the solution did not come immediately? Did you want to give up at any point? Why didn't you? If the knot represents a problem in everyday life, what might it be? What kind of feelings does that problem generate in you? What do you normally do with those feelings? Did you deal with them differently here?*

Variations The group works in silence, or with eyes closed. Or: Send someone out of the room while the knot is tied. Then, when the knot is completed, this person can give instructions to the group in order to unravel the knot. Again, those in the knot could have their eyes closed.

An easier version: Group members join hands in a circle. Without breaking the links, the group now ties itself in a knot by having people walk through, over and under other linked hands. At this point, the knot can be untied using any of the variations.

Another variation with a similar aim is ***Circle to Square***: Group members stand in a circle and close their eyes. Instruct them to turn the circle into a square while keeping their eyes closed. Also try: *Circle to triangle.*

Groups wanting a bigger challenge can be given more difficult shapes, such as a letter of the alphabet, a household item such as a toaster, or a large structure such as a ship or an aeroplane.

Mirror Circle

Co-operation; group building; empathy; energiser; drama skills
Low focus
Groups of 7 and up
Time needed: 5 - 15 minutes
Worker participation: yes, or one stays out, others optional

Method Group members stand in a circle with enough room to swing their arms. If there are an even number of people in the circle, have each person observe the person who is standing three (or another *odd* number) places to their left. If there are an odd number in the circle, have each person observe the person who is standing four (or another *even* number) places to their left.

I want you to watch that person and to do exactly what they do. Don't add or subtract anything, just copy. Be very observant, and copy exactly what they do. This includes sounds and coughs and shuffling feet, everything.

Because everyone is observing someone else, theoretically very little should happen. However, invariably a movement will begin somewhere, and should quite rapidly progress through the group. As the movement progresses it often becomes slightly exaggerated and occasionally the group ends up rolling around on the floor, jumping up and down, etc. If nothing happens, remind the group that they should copy even the smallest movements they notice. Encourage the group to be as observant as possible.

Optional instruction: *Exaggerate everything you see that person do, and all the sounds they make.* When they get up to full exaggeration speed, which can be very exhausting, ask them to *subtract* a little from everything they observe. This will quickly bring the movement down to almost complete stillness.

Comments/concerns If it is too complicated to ask people to count a certain number of places to their left, you can just ask them to focus on someone who is roughly across the circle from them.

General processing *How did the group function? What connections might there be in there to how the group functions generally* (e.g. being sensitive and aware of each other)*?*

Personal processing *How did you feel during that exercise? Did you have any thoughts or feelings about observing someone else and also knowing that you were being so closely observed by someone?*

Variations Instead of focusing on just one person, each individual focuses on the entire group. This way, impulses and movements are passed and picked up by everyone at all times. The instruction would be: *Watch everyone. Everything you see, you do. Copy everything as soon as it happens. Work together, be part of the whole. Try to get it all working in synch. Don't add or subtract, just do exactly what you see anywhere in the circle.* When this works well, the whole group becomes one unit and moves together. This can be a powerful group-building exercise.

A good variation is ***Guess the Leader:*** A volunteer goes out of the room. A leader is chosen, who will lead a series of actions (e.g. moving arms slowly) that the whole group will follow as they all stand in a circle. The volunteer returns and tries to guess who the leader is while the entire group does the actions.

Make Together

Co-operation; group building; concentration
Low to medium focus
Groups of any size
Time needed: 5 - 20 minutes
Worker participation: one stays out, others optional

Method

The group members form pairs, and each pair has a sheet of plain paper. Ask each pair to make a paper airplane from the sheet of paper, each person *using only one hand.* Encourage them to work together and make it a shared project. When each pair has finished the task, have a 'competition' to see which pair creates the airplane that goes furthest, takes the longest to reach the floor, does the most loop-the-loops, takes the shortest time to reach the floor, etc. Having many categories of 'winner' ensures that the emphasis stays on the co-operative process rather than the end product.

General processing *How did your pair achieve the task? What made it work well, and what hindered it? Did one person or the other try to dominate? What did you do when this happened? What skills needed in this exercise are also needed in order for the group to function well together?*

Personal processing: *co-operation* *Are other relationships in your life similar to the relationship you had in this exercise? How? Do you tend to be aggressive or passive in situations where you need to work with others? Are you happy being that way? Do you want to change anything about the way you behave in situations like this, where you need to co-operate?*

Variations

- Follow the same process, this time having the pairs tie a pair of shoe-laces.

- Each pair shares one felt tip marker (or similar). Working together, they draw a picture of a house, making alternate strokes with the marker, but using no words.

- Think of other simple tasks for the pairs to accomplish using only one hand each. Or try variations, so perhaps one person can move but has their eyes closed, and the other person has sight but cannot move. Have the participants think of their own variations.

Touch Backs

Energiser; concentration; group building; co-operation
Low focus
Groups of 5 and up
Time needed: 5 - 10 minutes
Worker participation: one stays out, others optional

Method

1. Worker instructions: *Start walking around the room in any direction, milling around and filling up the whole space. You can say hello to people as you walk ...*

2. As they walk: *Now, here's the task: when I clap my hands, you touch one person on the back, and as you do this, you FREEZE. When I clap my hand a second time, walk again.*

3. Clap hands, quickly check they have done followed the instruction, clap hands again so group members are walking again. As they walk: *This time, when I clap my hands, you FREEZE touching TWO people on the back at the same time...*

4. Clap hands, quickly check they have done the task, clap hands again so they walk. As they walk: *This time, when I clap my hands, you FREEZE touching THREE people on the back at the same time. It CAN be done! No bunching in the middle. Spread out, keep walking and wait for the signal ...*

5. Clap hands, quickly check they have done the task by making contact with heads, hands, feet, etc. Then clap hands again so they walk. As they walk: *Now, when I clap my hands again, this time it's NOT a freeze. You must touch EVERYONE ELSE IN THE ROOM on the back but avoid your own back being touched. You can't lie down or stand against the wall...*

6. Clap hands. End the exercise when people are still enjoying the rushing around this last step entails, but before they get exhausted.

Comments/concerns A very active, low focus exercise. We use it a lot. Be aware that the last step includes people moving quickly in all directions, and can be dangerous.

Variations

- For added safety, ask the group members to do the last step in slow motion (show what you mean by SLOW), or, for a fun variation, running with their knees together.

- ***Pig's Tail*** is a similar exercise to the last part of *Touch Backs*: Each group member places a 'tail' in their back waistbands or pockets. The aim is to grab as many tails as possible without losing your own. This is highly energetic and competitive, so it is worth putting a time limit on it of 30 seconds.

Zip, Zap, Bop

Energiser; relapse prevention; communication; controlling thoughts and fantasies
Passing high focus
Groups of 8 to 30
Time needed: 15 - 20 minutes
Worker participation: yes

Method

The group stand in a circle: *This is an exercise called Zip Zap Bop! Each of these words has an action that goes along with it. Let's start with 'zip.' We are going to pass the zip around the circle - imagine that you are passing around a bolt of electricity. The zip will go around very quickly with loads of energy. The action consists of putting your hands flat together like this and turning to pass the electrified zip to the next person. As you turn, say 'zip!' It's important that the zip goes quickly, but don't pre-empt it. Wait until you actually receive it. Let's see how it goes ... Zip! ...*

Have a practice. When the zip is whizzing around the circle for a while, stop: *Right. Now this could get a little boring, so we're going to add the 'bop.' At the moment the zip can only go one way once it has started. The bop allows us to change direction. When a zip comes to you, you can now put both hands facing flat out in front of you to 'refuse' it or block it, at the same time as saying 'bop!' The person passing the zip to you must now turn and pass it back the other way. Let's practice ...*

Practice both instructions. On occasions the zip may get stuck between two people. Choose one of these occasions to add the last instruction: *Now, the bop can get stuck at times, so we are going to add the 'zap.' You can zap at any time. To zap, put your hands flat together just like a zip, but this time get eye contact with someone ACROSS THE CIRCLE and zap the electricity across - pointing at them and saying 'zap!' The receiver can now make a choice: they can either zip either side or zap someone else across the circle. However, here come two rules: You CANNOT BOP A ZAP and you can't zap back to the person who has just zapped you (that would be the same as a bop). Let's give it a go.*

Comments/concerns Some groups find the 'play' within this exercise hard to cope with. The high focus can be intimidating, particularly if the participants are anxious or get the instructions 'wrong.' So your facilitation should have a light touch, with an emphasis on how 'tricky' this exercise can be.

General processing *What skills were needed for the exercise to work? Which was your favourite action? Why? What was it like when you felt the zip coming towards you? If this exercise is about communication, then what is the zip, the bop or the zap?*

Personal processing: *relapse prevention* *If the energy pulse is a thought impulse, what is the bop? What is the zap? How do you to stop a thought? Is it possible to control our thoughts? What if the zip is a thought telling you to commit an offence? How do you stop that thought?*

Variations Try doing the exercise in silence—with gestures only—after doing it with the words. After the silent version, try doing it with turns of the head and facial expressions only: *What are the smallest or subtlest gestures you can make which will still allow the game to work?* With very skilled groups, try passing two or more 'zips' at once.

Keepy Uppy

Energiser; group building; co-operation; concentration
Low focus
Groups of 4 to 30
Time needed: 3 - 10 minutes
Worker participation: yes

Method

Materials: a light plastic ball about the size of a football.

Group members in a circle or spread throughout the room: *The object of Keepy Uppy is for the entire group to keep the ball in the air as long as possible by tapping it back up in the air if it comes to you. You can use hands, head, feet or any other body part to keep the ball in the air.*

The group members all count each tap out loud and try to reach as high a number of taps as possible. You can add the rule that if the ball hits the ceiling or a wall, that counts as a tap. Also, one person cannot tap the ball twice in a row. If the ball touches the floor, start over again.

Comments/concerns This is a high energy game. In the right circumstances it can really bring a group together because the live challenge builds great team spirit. *Keepy Uppy* has the advantage of being highly active and challenging but also being completely co-operative. To lessen the importance of the ball hitting the floor, make this a fun part of the game by having people either cheer or groan in an exaggerated way when it does. This takes the focus off the person who 'dropped the ball.'

The biggest benefit of *Keepy Uppy* is that you can come back to it many times during a programme. The group will enjoy the challenge of beating their last score. They can set targets for themselves. We've seen groups reach over a hundred taps.

Check for health problems among the group members before asking them to be involved in this; it's quite physical.

General processing: *group building; co-operation* *Keepy Uppy* (and *Piggy in the Middle*, below) can open up discussion about the rules we learn as children, such as co-operation and competitiveness. *How do you want things to run in this group? Does anything happen in the group currently which is like Piggy in the Middle?*

Variation

You might contrast the co-operative spirit of *Keepy Uppy* with the potential cruelty of ***Piggy in the Middle***. This well-known children's game involves two people either side of someone in the middle who tries to intercept the ball as the two pass it back and forth. It's a common game where children get teased on the playground.

Same Journey

Energiser; concentration; co-operation; goal setting; group building
Low focus
Groups of 5 and up
Time needed: 5 - 20 minutes
Worker participation: one stays out, others optional

Method

Ask the group members to walk around the room in any direction, randomly filling up the space. Ask them to stop walking when you clap your hands. When you clap, the group members should be randomly spaced. If not, repeat until they are: *Look at where you are in the room and try to remember where you are standing. When I say 'go!' I want you to touch all four walls, the floor, a table, something red, and something green (not anyone's clothing) and shake at least three people's hands, in any order, and then return to your spot.* (What you ask them to touch will obviously depend on the room). *This is to be done silently and as efficiently as possible. Don't bump into anyone. So again that's all four walls, the floor, a table, something red, something green and shake at least three people's hands, then return to your place. Remember your journey as you go. Ready? Go!*

After the first attempt: *Try the same thing again, repeating exactly the same journey. Go!*

After a couple of rehearsals: *Now think about the journey that you have just taken. Go through it in your mind and think about what problems you encountered. If you found that you were always cutting across the same person, think about how you might solve this. If you need to negotiate with anyone, do it now in order to make your journey as smooth as possible. This time I am going to time you.*

After this attempt: *Try again and let's see if you can improve your time. What goal do you want to set yourselves?* Give the group several attempts.

Comments/ concerns This is a great energiser and popular with most groups, especially young men, perhaps because it contains an element of competition. However, it can be quite exhausting, so keep an eye on how tired the group is getting. Also, be aware that this exercise involves a lot of rushing about and can result in some collisions. Stress that it is an exercise in efficient movement and AVOIDING other people in the room. Remind the group members that sometimes too much haste really does mean less speed!

General processing *What was it like to do that exercise? What did you like or dislike? What strategies made it work best? How did you negotiate with other people?*

Personal processing: *goal setting* *What goals did you set for yourself during the exercise? Did you meet them? What connections can you make between this exercise and your life generally? What did you discover about setting goals? How realistic were they? How did you feel about achieving/not achieving your goal? What were the obstacles? What might these relate to in real life? Is it inevitable that you will keep running into the same obstacles?*

Equidistance

Energiser; concentration; group building; offending tactics
Low focus
Groups of 7 and up
Time needed: 10 - 15 minutes
Worker participation: one stays out, others optional

Method
1. *This exercise comes in three stages. For the first stage the whole group needs to be spread around the room randomly, so please do that now. ... Good. Now I'm going to ask you to look around the room silently, and in your mind's eye identify two other people in the group, but don't let them know who they are. Leave me out of it, so no one should be picking me. When I say 'go,' I'd like you to move and stay equal distance from both of those people at all times, but at least two metres away from them. The tricky part is that they will be trying to do the same for their two people. Everyone clear? Be careful not to bump into people. Go!*

2. Move onto the next stage: *Well done. Now the next stage is a bit different. Can you spread yourselves around randomly again. This time, I'd like you to pick two new people in your mind's eye, but again don't let them know who they are. And again, leave me out of it. Now, in your mind, label those people A and B. Have you done it? Good. This time, your job is to keep person A between you and person B at all times. Distance is not a factor. Again, be aware of the space, and don't grab or bump into anyone. Go!* These instructions will lead on to a challenging series of bobbing and weaving movements, as group members try to get into the correct positions. This step should normally not last more than about 20 seconds. When you stop them, you might like to check who has stopped in a 'correct' position with a Person 'A' between them and their 'B.'

It may be worth noting in your description of stage two that it works the same as the well-known game *Bombs and Shields.*

3. When this is done: *Good. Now for the third variation. This time, I'd like you to pick two new people, again leave me out. Label these two people A and B. This time your job is to make sure that you are as close as possible to person A, without touching them, and as far away as possible from person B. Be careful not to grab or force anybody, and again, no bumping. Don't run, but you can walk quickly. Go!* This quite often results in a slightly madcap sequence. Stop after 30 seconds or so.

Comments/concerns This is a high energy game, and in very new groups can put some people off as it can seem a bit silly. Use this exercise only after you have tried other high energy exercises such as *Anyone Who*, *Same Journey* or *Group Juggling.* It is important to use the labelling of persons A and B as the basis for stages two and three, as this eliminates the possibility of people thinking that someone has deliberately tried to get near them or far away from them. You can make this even more clear by instructing mid-way through stages two and three that each person should switch in their mind the roles of A and B. So if they were trying to avoid B, they are now trying to get near to B.

Personal processing *The second step is like the game Bombs and Shields; What would be a 'bomb' for you, or something to avoid? What sort of power does that 'bomb' have over you? Do you have a 'shield?' What is it? How do you protect yourself, or get protection?*

Variation *Who's Tracking Who?*: *Walk around the room keeping track of just one other person, not letting that person know you are tracking them.* After a while, allow people to try to name their 'tracker.'

Captain's Coming Aboard and Wild West

Energiser; group building; drama skills
Low to high focus
Groups of 8 and up
Time needed: 10 - 15 minutes
Worker participation: one stays out, others optional

Method The leader introduces a series of commands that have associated sounds and actions:

1. 'Captain's Coming Aboard': Snap to attention, salute and whistle the Bosun's Call.
2. 'Sharks!': Place one hand vertically on head as a fin and stand on one leg while doing the theme from 'Jaws.'
3. 'Seagulls Overhead': Cower, hands covering head, and give high pitched yell.
4. 'Scrubbing the Decks': Kneel down and scrub the decks, making scrubbing sounds.
5. 'Man Overboard!': Wave goodbye and say 'Bye!'
6. 'Climb the Rigging': Mime motion of climbing the rigging.
7. 'Hornpipe': Cross arms on chest and do a sailors' jig while 'la la la'-ing an appropriate tune.
8. 'Sea sick': The obvious gesture and sound.

When everyone has practised the commands, call them out one by one. The whole group must energetically perform the appropriate action with as quick a response time as possible. Keep this going for a few minutes. Then, the slowest members of the group are weeded out to judge the others. (Optional: those who are slow *on purpose* may be kept in!) Play until only two people are left. (Optional: Give the last remaining two a new sea-faring instruction, e.g. 'Tidal wave!' to which they must improvise a sound and action. The most creative wins the game.)

The cowboy version is ***Wild West***. The procedure is the same but the calls are:

1. 'Quick Draw': Draw two pistols, fire, blow away the smoke, twirl the guns and re-holster.
2. 'Lasso': Swing mimed lasso around head and then throw it as if roping a calf.
3. 'Gold Nugget!': Spot nugget, pick it up and raise it above head with a cry of 'Yeehah!'
4. 'Gravedigger': Mime digging with suitable digging sound effects.
5. 'Hoe Down': Grasp one's lapels and dance a jig, humming 'Yellow Rose of Texas'.
6. 'Whiskey Barman': Pour a shot of whiskey while saying 'glug glug glug,' then slide it down the bar with a 'whoosh'.
7. 'Spittoon': Mime spitting into a spittoon, including the 'ping' as it hits the side.
8. 'Ride 'em Cowboy': Ride a galloping horse while 'dum da da'-ing the *Lone Ranger.*

Whittle down the players until two remain, then give them a Western themed new command. Whoever does the best interpretation is pronounced Sheriff. Example of a new command: 'Show down'; 'Camp fire'; 'Saloon doors'.

Comments/concerns Because there is a high 'silliness' factor to both of these exercises, they work best with groups who have been working together for a while. If the group members really enjoy this game, encourage them to invent their own theme and to create the commands. One of the best we've seen was a version created by a group in Scarborough and called, as it happens, 'Scarborough!' The group created their own inventive commands related to their seaside town: 'Bingo'; 'fish and chips'; 'carousel'; 'promenade'; 'sand castles', 'trawler man,' etc.

General processing *What is the value of playing a game or having fun? Why is it that we get the message when we grow older that we must stop playing? Do you think you would have played this game in your first week in the group? What's different now?*

Self-supporting Structures

Energiser; co-operation; problem solving; group building
Low to medium focus
Groups of 5 and up
Time needed: 5 - 20 minutes
Worker participation: one stays out, others optional

Method

Group members split into groups of five to eight: *You must make a structure using all the people in your group. However, the structure must be self-supporting, which means that it has to hold itself up. Here's an example of self-supporting: If Camilla and I stand a few feet apart like so, take hold of each other's hands and lean back, that's self-supporting, because if we let go, we fall over. If we weren't leaning back that wouldn't be self-supporting, because if we let go, nothing would happen.*

Now, as well as being self-supporting, the structure must have a certain number of points of contact with the floor. Points of contact are hands, feet, head, back, bums, knees and elbows, which all count as one point each. Let's do a test run. Can you make a self-supporting structure with eight points of contact with the floor? Make sure it's safe for everyone to be a part of, and make sure it includes everyone.

When a group has completed a structure, check that it can be held for a couple of seconds and give them a new number of points of contact for their next structure. You can keep decreasing the number (some groups can get down to two points) or give them a mixture of lower and much higher numbers (e.g. 6, 23, 4, 38, 3). If you are going for high numbers, you can give groups more scope by saying that each finger or toe counts as one point of contact with the floor. Ask the groups to choose their favourite structure and show it to the larger group.

Comments/ concerns A very physical exercise. It works particularly well with young people, who enjoy the physical challenge and often build impressive and sometimes precarious structures! Stress physical safety.

General processing *What skills did you need in order to do the exercise? How did your small group work together? Did different people take on different roles in the group? What messages might there be in the exercise about how the group can function better or worse?*

Personal processing: *co-operation* *Did you tend to lead or follow during that exercise? Is that typical for you? What thoughts and feelings support that typical pattern for you? How would you like to be in this group? Do you want a chance to do it differently?*

Variations A similar exercise is ***Household Appliances***: By linking together, groups create household appliances as you call them out. Ideas to call out: Start with a few letters or numbers, then move on to kitchen appliances such as a toaster, a food mixer, a washer/dryer or an electric kettle. If they are still enjoying the exercise, move on to other structures such as a ship, an airplane, a crane, a bridge or a football stadium. Where appropriate, ask the groups to move as their structure, and even give it sound.

Monuments (see p.147) works on the same principle: groups are asked to form themselves into sculptures, or monuments, depicting a current or historical event, or a famous world building/ structure, e.g. Eiffel Tower, Stonehenge or the Leaning Tower of Pisa.

Source: *Gamesters' Handbook* (Brandes and Philips, 1990).

Knee Tag

Energiser; co-operation; concentration; risk-taking
Low focus
Groups of 4 and up
Time needed: 5 - 15 minutes
Worker participation: one stays out, others optional

Method

Group members divide into pairs. The object of the game is for each person to try to lightly tag their partner's knees as many times as possible without letting their own knees get tagged. Remind the participants that they must not be rough with each other; it is a game of stealth and strategy, not strength. Give them three 30-second rounds (or any variation which promotes friendly competition and not too much exhaustion). Each pair keeps their own score.

Vary the rules as appropriate. For example, you can make the exercise slow motion and ask the group members to exaggerate their movements so it becomes a sort of underwater or martial arts exercise. Or, you can break the groups into threes, so that each pair always has a referee who keeps score, disallows points for unsafe behaviour and gives 'yellow' and 'red' cards. Alternate players so each person is referee.

General processing *What was the role of co-operation in that game? Was there anything unsafe going on during the exercise? Why might that have been? What messages do we get about competition when we are young? Do you agree with them? Are there any exceptions to these rules?*

Personal processing: *risk taking* *What did you focus on more, the tagging or the getting tagged? What's more important to you, getting what you want no matter the consequences, or thinking about the consequences? Is one easier to focus on than the other? Why or why not? Where in life do you take risks? What are your rules about winning?*

Variations

A closely related exercise is ***Pig's Tail*** (see similar variation in the description of *Touchbacks*), where the same rules apply but instead of tagging knees, each player tries to pull out a cloth which their partner has tucked into his belt at the back. The cloth must be removed to count as a point. Vary the rules so that at any one time one person is in pursuit while the other defends. This avoids highly lop-sided scores.

A calmer - but still competitive - variation is ***Zen Wrestling***, in which two people stand facing each other and join hands, or have finger tip contact only. Their task is to try to make their partner move one of his feet: *If your partner moves one of his feet even a little bit, you win that round. We'll play several rounds.*

A non-competitive variation is ***Equilibrium***, in which two people in a pair push and/or pull each other using designated parts of the body (e.g. hands, backs, arms/ shoulders) and must constantly move but stay balanced in equilibrium the entire time. This variant leads to important processing around the theme of co-operation and keeping balanced in life.

This exercise, particularly the latter two variations, work well in tandem with *Staying Balanced.*

Random Chairs

Energiser; co-operation; concentration; group building
Low focus
Groups of 8 and up
Time needed: 3 - 10 minutes
Worker participation: yes

Method

Start with all group members seated in chairs, spread randomly around the room. All extra chairs are put away or turned to face the wall, as they are out of bounds. Leader stands in the middle of the room:

I have no chair and I would like to have one, but the only way I can get a seat is if one of you moves. The only way you can move is if you make eye contact with someone else and then silently agree to swap places. Everyone should be looking to each other to change seats at any time. While you change seats, I may nip in and take a seat, so be quick. BUT IT IS A NON-CONTACT GAME. No one should ever touch anyone else during this. If I sit in a seat, obviously someone else will be left looking for a seat, and so on ... Alright, when I say 'Go,' everyone start looking around and try to find someone to change seats with. Oh, and I forgot the most important rule: No one can stay seated for more than ten seconds, otherwise your chair will explode. Go!

Comments/ concerns This is meant to be a light, energetic exercise, but it can get frenzied, so you may wish to run it in slow motion or make it quite short. Really stress that it is a non-contact game and that people should not rush into a chair so quickly that they fall over.

How Many Walking?

Concentration; co-operation; energiser
Low to passing high focus
Groups of 8 and up
Time needed: 10 - 20 minutes
Worker participation: one stays out, others optional

Method

1. Group spread randomly through the room: *When I say "go" one person will start to walk around the space without touching any of the people standing. No one knows who that person will be but there can only be one person walking. The person who starts walking can stop at any time. When they stop, someone else must start to walk. No one should speak and you can't give each other signals. Only one person can be walking at any time.*

2. When the group members are comfortable with this procedure, give further instructions: *Now see if we can have two people walking. You will have to be even more focused now, as you have to concentrate on two people not just one. If you haven't walked yet try to do so.*

3. As the group gets more skilled at this, build up the number of people walking. Eventually it will become obvious that the group needs a system in order to succeed, usually when there are between four and six people trying to walk. You can either let them decide a non-verbal system straight away or you can add this instruction: *I'm going to go out of the room and while I'm out I want you to decide on a non-verbal signal. When I come back in I want you to continue the exercise with* (n) *people walking and I will try to guess what the signal is.*

4. Let the walking continue and try to guess the signal. Whether or not you guess correctly, eventually bring the number walking down in stages until everyone is standing still.

General Processing: co-operation *What skills did the group need to make it work? How did you decide which signal to use? Why is it important that this group develops ways of working together through exercises like this? Where else might people need to use the skills used in this exercise?*

Variations

Vary the ways in which the walking is 'handed on.' For example, you could add the rule: If someone else wants to walk then they can start and the person who is walking must stop. Or there could be a rule that either person, the walker or the one who wants to walk, can take the initiative.

A good variation is to work this exercise in the opposite way so that at any given moment (n) people are *not* walking. In this variation, most of the group will be walking and will stay focused on those who are not walking. The same rule variations can be tried regarding whether the walkers or those standing determine who will walk next.

A non-walking version is ***Four Up*** (Weinstein & Goodman, 1992): Group members are seated randomly through the room. At any time, any person can stand, but they can only stand for a count of five. The whole group must work together to make sure that at any one moment only four people are standing.

Group Juggling

Concentration; energiser; group building; co-operation; problem solving
Low individual focus
Groups of 6 to 20 (divide larger groups)
Time needed: 15 -45 minutes
Worker participation: yes

Method

1. You will need a number of soft juggling balls or similar objects, almost as many as there are group members. Begin with the group standing in a circle and throwing a juggling ball to someone roughly across the circle in an easy-to-catch arc. The person who has just received the ball does the same, throwing it to someone roughly across the circle from him. He then folds his arms to let other people know not to throw the ball to him again. In this way the ball will be thrown to each person only once, then back to you. You should be the last to receive it. This is now the set pattern of throws for the next step.

2. Ensure that each person is clear who they are throwing the ball to and who they are receiving it from. The ball is now thrown in the same pattern again, until people are comfortable and confident about the sequence. Now, one by one, add in as many juggling balls to the sequence as the group can tolerate without dropping. It should look like a big juggling ring. (Option: After doing the group juggle, collect all of the balls and have the group follow the same juggling sequence, but this time with imaginary juggling balls. *See how fast we can get the juggling going when the juggling balls are invisible.*)

Comments/concerns Stress the need for easy throws.

General processing *What was involved in each task? Did you feel you achieved each task? What helped or hindered you as a group?* Focus on concentration, co-operation and trust. Ask the group to reflect on the skills and adjustments necessary to achieve a group juggle. How might this apply to their work as a team over the next period of time? What will they be 'juggling' in the course of the programme? Can they use any of their understanding about this exercise as the basis for some group agreements on working together? *How does it feel to have things thrown at you when you're not ready? How is this like situations in the real world? What can be done to ensure someone is ready to receive information / support/ a new skill?*

Variations

To emphasise group building and problem solving: Introduce the overall goal and give the group control over how they achieve it - e.g. how to remember who is throwing to who, how to manage the throwing and catching so that people don't drop the ball, etc... Hint: The key skills that people need to identify are: only throw a ball when your partner is ready to receive it, and keep your attention on the person who is going to throw the ball to you.

To encourage the group to take complete ownership of the problem, skip the above steps and simply give the group a selection of objects to juggle such as juggling pins, balls, soft cushions, etc. Set a time limit in which they have to practice and perform a group juggling display using any of the available items. A successful juggling circuit would include each chosen object passing through each person's hands at least once / twice without dropping.

Pulse Train

Concentration; self-control; relapse prevention; controlling thoughts and fantasies
Low to passing high focus
Groups of 8 to 30
Time needed: 20 - 40 minutes
Worker participation: one stays out, others optional

Method

Group split into two equal teams, seated in two lines, facing each other one metre apart. On an extra chair at one end is placed a towel or other easy-to-grab object. It is within easy reach of both of the players who are in the last chairs of their respective teams. The leader is at the other end of the line with a coin. Members of each team are asked to join hands with each other behind their chairs in order to create an 'electric circuit.'

I am going to throw this coin in the air and if it lands on 'heads' I want the two people nearest me to squeeze the hand of the person next to them. They in turn squeeze their neighbour's hand and a 'pulse' will be sent down the whole line. When it reaches the two people at the end, they must try to grab the towel first. The team that gets the towel wins a point.

However, there is a complication! Everyone except the two people nearest to me must have their eyes closed. The two people at the other end can open their eyes as they grab the towel.

If the coin lands on 'tails' you must not send the pulse. If you do and your team grabs the towel, the other team wins a point. So you must control your impulses! If you send the pulse accidentally and try to stop it by shouting or something like that, again the other team wins the point.

Other rules: If both teams grab the towel at the same time, no points are awarded. When a team wins a point, the person who grabbed the towel walks to the other end of the line and takes up the position closest to the leader and everyone else moves down one chair. The team that manages to move everyone round so that they end up in their original position, wins the game.

General processing *When the coin came up tails and the pulse was passed along anyway, what was going on? Why do you think the pulse was sent? In general, how do people control their impulses? Are there some impulses you can't control?*

Personal processing: *self-control; relapse prevention* *If the pulse is an internal thought or desire, what might this thought or desire be for you? Who controls it? Can it be controlled? Relate these thoughts and feelings to your own pattern of offending. How do you typically deal with powerful thoughts and feelings? Is this a conscious process?*

Variations A far simpler exercise incorporating some of the elements of *Pulse Train* is ***Pass the Pulse***: The group members stand in a circle holding hands and a 'pulse' (brief hand squeeze) is sent continually round the circle. The object is to see how fast it can travel. The exercise can be done with eyes closed or open. ***Catch the Pulse*** is another variation, where a person standing in the middle must 'catch' the pulse as it travels around the circle. The pulse is caught when the person in the middle grabs a set of hands at the precise instant that the pulse hits there. The group is not allowed to vary the pace of the pulse. This exercise can open up discussion around, for example, self-control and thought-stopping, e.g. *How do you stop a thought? How do you catch your own thoughts and change them?* Encourage the participants to 'break the mould' and find creative ways to stop the impulse racing around.

Footsteps

Concentration; perspective taking
Low to medium focus
Groups of 4 to 40
Time needed: 10 - 25 minutes
Worker participation: one stays out, others optional

Method

The group members stand randomly around the room. Explain that in a moment you will ask them all to close their eyes and not open them again until you give the instruction to. Explain that after they close their eyes you will begin walking around the room, weaving in and out of the participants. After a while, you will come back to the spot where you are standing now, the participants will open their eyes, and as a group they will have to try to piece together the path you took through the room. Try not to make the path too difficult, as you must remember it too.

Depending on how the exercise is going, you may wish to take it to the next level. This sequence runs along similar lines, except that you instruct the participants that as you are walking around, you may quickly tap someone twice on the shoulder. This is the signal for them to open their eyes, walk around for a moment or two, then come back to you, at which time they stand still again and you continue walking. It is important that they do not reveal that they have been walking. You can instruct them to keep their eyes open or closed when they return; each variation will alter the exercise. When you have given three or four people a chance to do the walking, walk back to your original spot, and ask the participants to open their eyes. The group as a whole must now work out who walked, and also retrace the path taken by the walkers.

Comments/ concerns This exercise follows on nicely from *How Many Walking.*

General processing *What senses did you use to track the walkers? What did you notice? What sort of feelings did you have when someone was walking near you? What is it like for people right now, knowing that some people here know they walked but aren't saying? It may also be that some people here saw others walking, but aren't saying. What is it like seeing the others try to guess what you already know?*

Variation

Have group members retell the path the walker took by 're-enacting' his walk and narrating it in the first person. This provides practice in role reversal and perspective taking.

Source

We have adapted this exercise from one suggested by Rawlins and Rich (1992).

Walk Means Run

Concentration; energiser; self-control
Low focus
Groups of 5 and up
Time needed: 5 - 15 minutes
Worker participation: one stays out, others optional

Method

Ask the group members to walk around the room. As they are walking, instruct them to run. After a few seconds, ask them to walk again. As they walk this time, tell them that, 'from now on, walk means run and run means walk.' Then instruct them to 'walk,' at which point they should run. After a few seconds, tell them to 'run' (meaning walk) again. As they are walking, introduce further paired instructions in the same way, first with the normal meanings and then with the meanings reversed. Examples: 'Stop means jump and jump means stop.' 'Smile means frown and frown means smile.' 'Whisper your name means shout your name and shout your name means whisper your name.' Etc.

Add the instructions in gradually. Combine them to create a very challenging and fun warm-up.

General processing: concentration and self-control

How difficult was it to remember the instructions? How did you cope? How did you manage to control or block the automatic response in order to follow the new instruction? How does this relate to the theme of self-control? How easy or difficult is it to control automatic thinking or automatic actions? What are other examples of thoughts or actions that are automatic, and may need more paying attention to?

Source

Thanks to Adrian Jackson who taught us this exercise.

Paranoia

Concentration; co-operation; offending tactics
Low to high focus
Groups of 7 to 20
Time needed: 15 - 30 minutes
Worker participation: one stays out, others optional

Method

The group is in a circle, standing or sitting. Group members draw numbered slips of paper from a hat, so that at the start of the game they each have a unique number. If there are ten group members, there should only be the numbers 1 - 10. If 15 group members, you would make 15 slips of paper and number them 1 - 15, etc.

One group member comes to the centre of the circle and calls out two numbers within the range present. For example, in a group of ten, he may call out, 'three and ten' (he does not call out his own number).

He now begins looking intently to try to find out who has those numbers.

The two people whose numbers have been called furtively look around the circle trying to identify each other *without letting the person in the middle know.* This is why the exercise is called 'Paranoia,' as the person in the middle quickly becomes very paranoid about what is going on behind his back. When the two people have identified each other, they make a silent agreement and then, when they think they can make it, they quickly change places. The person in the middle tries to take one of their places while they exchange. If he doesn't get there in time, he starts over and calls out another two numbers. He cannot repeat the numbers he has just called. If he succeeds in getting a chair, the person who was caught out is now in the middle and must call out another two numbers. Encourage new numbers to be called so that each member is given a chance and to prevent the caller from anticipating who will move.

After a few rounds, have people exchange numbers, as by this time their number will have been identified.

General processing *What feelings were around during that exercise? What was it like being in the middle? What was it like when your number was called, and you were looking for the other person? How did you make contact, and agree to change places? What feelings did you have about the person in the middle?*

Personal processing: *offending tactics* *Did you prefer being on the outside or in the middle? Why? How did you feel? What about just before you changed places? What was it like for you in the middle? What connections are there between this exercise and life outside this group? How does this exercise connect with offending? Are you good at not getting caught? What's it like, having to avoid detection? Do you care whether you get caught?*

What Are You Doing?

Communication; drama skills; offending tactics
Passing high focus
Groups of 5 to 25
Time needed: 10 - 15 minutes or more
Worker participation: yes

Method

Group stands in a circle, worker in the middle: *I am going to mime a simple repetitive action. Once I have established my mime and you are pretty sure you know what I am doing, any one of you can step forward and ask the question, 'What are you doing?' At this point I will LIE to you. If I am miming brushing my teeth I may reply to you that I am flying a kite. Whatever I say, you then must come in to the middle and mime that action, and I go back to my place. When you've done your mime for a few seconds, another group member steps forward and asks, 'What are you doing?' YOU then have to lie and say something that is not what you are actually doing. The exercise will go on like this until everyone has had at least one or two goes in the middle. As a group, if we try not to completely set somebody up, the exercise will run more smoothly and be more enjoyable. So try not to name something that would be embarrassing if you were asked to do it, even if it's tempting to.*

Where groups need more structure, move from person to person around the circle rather than waiting for volunteers.

Comments/concerns Stress that no one is allowed to suggest something that is beyond an individual's physical capability or may be considered indecent or offensive by other members of the group.

General processing *What skills were involved in that exercise? Think about what you were doing in terms of drama. How was that like drama?* Discuss mime, action, being on stage, imagination, allowing others to see what you have imagined, etc.

Personal processing: *offending tactics* *What is a lie? What's the difference between a lie and a falsehood? In what situations might you lie about what you are doing? Are there any situations in life where you feel lies can be justified? If so, why? Does anybody lose from these lies?*

Variations

- ***Add to the Scene*** When one person begins miming an activity, for example building a brick wall, as soon as the mime becomes clear, others join in the action, so that eventually the whole group is involved in the scene, building a wall or doing other activities related to wall-building. Let the scene continue until it finds a natural end. As an option, add words or sounds.

- A much more elaborate exercise focusing on miming is ***Chain Mime*** (Brandes and Philips, 1990): Five people leave the room, and the remaining group members decide a mime sequence for them to do, e.g. packing a backpack, changing a car tyre, setting up a camera and tripod. The first person re-enters and is told what to do or shown by a group member. The second person then comes in and watches the first do the mime. The third then comes in and watches the second, and so on, until the fifth person performs the mime for the whole group. The fifth person usually ends up doing something quite different from the original mime. Process by asking each what they thought they were doing, then looking at the original.

Take Me On A Journey

Communication; imagination; trust; drama skills
Low focus
Groups of 4 and up
Time needed: 10 - 60 minutes
Worker participation: one stays out, others optional

Method

This exercise normally works better if the group has already done *Trust Walking*. The group members divide into pairs and label themselves A and B. The leader demonstrates how A should guide B around: standing to the side and holding one arm by the wrist and elbow gives secure support.

In your pairs, A is going to lead B around the room while B keeps her eyes closed. As you guide your partner around the space, you are going to describe their journey to them. Use your imagination; you can make it as fantastical as you wish. Maybe you are at the bottom of the ocean or in the middle of a jungle or on the moon. You can travel to different places as well, so if you start at the North Pole you can finish at Birmingham New Street. As you pass things, you may like to investigate them with your partner. For instance, a chair leg might become part of a shipwreck. If you are being led, enter into the imaginary environment as fully as you can, using all of your senses and imagination. Be a good 'guest' on the journey, and ask questions as you go. After about 5 minutes you will swap over. If you are the guide you must take care of your partner and don't allow them to crash into anyone or anything. Give them a positive and memorable experience, and remember at all times to be respectful.

Option: Same as above, but with eyes *open* not closed.

General processing: *communication; imagination* *How did it feel to be the guide or follower? What were the imaginary landscapes like? What was happening there? Was it a place you would like to go? Could you see the objects and places in your mind? Were there any surprises? What feelings and thoughts did you have while doing the exercise? What skills do you need in order to do this exercise? When you were leading, how did you keep the story going?*

Variation

A useful variation is ***A Place That I Know***: Partner A takes partner B on an imagined tour of an *actual* place or environment that he is familiar with. It should be a place of positive memories, such as a good day out that he remembers, or a playground where he once played. Or it might be his back garden from childhood where he has good memories of playing. As person A gives the tour, he and his guest actually move around the room as if they are in the actual environment. This will help person A remember the specifics of the environment, and will make the tour more real for person B. The idea is that person B listens, asks questions and becomes an attentive and respectful 'guest' on this tour of person A's world. After ten or fifteen minutes, swap over. Process by discussing the importance of these places and memories, and what it was like for the participants to gain such insights into each other's lives.

This exercise calls for a high degree of group bonding and respect, and can help foster deepening levels of communication in the group.

Environment Sculpt

Communication; imagination; drama skills; relapse prevention
Medium focus
Groups of 4 to 30
Time needed: 20 - 40 minutes
Worker participation: one stays out, others optional

Method

The group splits into two equal halves: Group A leaves the room, and group B thinks of an environment that they will put group A into. Examples: Surface of the Moon; a football match; a traffic jam. It must be an environment where everyone has a role. Group B decides who from group A will be placed into each role, and also who from their group will sculpt which person from group A. Group A returns and close their eyes. Each person from group B then goes to a person from group A and sculpts them into a distinctive position. Speaking to each other with their eyes closed, group A will then figure out where they are and what they are doing. Be brief with this process, as some people may be in awkward physical positions. When they are happy with their conclusions, they can open their eyes and check it out. The exercise is then repeated with group A sculpting group B.

Comments/ concerns There are two main methods of sculpting. The first is physical sculpting, where the person being sculpted remains still but pliable while the sculptor moves his or her body into position. The second method is verbal sculpting, where the sculptor describes the exact moves she wants the person being sculpted to make.

General and personal processing: communication *What thoughts and feelings did you have as you tried to communicate your part in the larger picture? Did you feel understood? What other situations in life are like this? What was it like having responsibility for sculpting someone else?*

Variations

- The group who have been sculpted can - with their eyes still closed - mould the sculptors into the position they think they were originally sculpted into. They then open their eyes to look at the sculpt.

- The 'sculptees' can be given simple repetitive actions to perform, or even sounds.

- A more active version is ***Who Am I?,*** in which one or more people leave the room while the rest of the group decide on an environment, choose roles for themselves, and decide which roles the person or persons outside the room will have. One by one, the people outside return to the room. As they enter, the main group enact their roles and talk to the newcomer as if they are already a part of the scene and should know what to do. The newcomer must try to fit in and enact the appropriate role as quickly as possible. Example: The group decide that they are all here to practise scuba diving and the role of the person outside is that of scuba diving instructor. As soon as the outside person walks in, the main group go into role and ask scuba diving related questions and ask for assistance and instruction with their scuba gear. The outsider must try to quickly assume the role of a scuba instructor. It doesn't matter at all if they know nothing about scuba diving; the important thing is that they *assume the role* of an instructor. This variation can be very useful in training individuals to be 'ready for anything that comes my way,' one of the most important 'going straight' (relapse prevention) skills.

The 'Yes' Circle

Assertiveness; dealing with pressure; self-control; concentration; communication
Medium to high focus
Groups of 8 to 20
Time needed: 10 - 20 minutes
Worker participation: yes

Method

The group members stand in a circle. One is nominated to start the 'Yes' circle in motion. This person must make eye contact with another person in the circle. The person they have made eye contact with should respond by saying 'Yes.' The nominated person then starts slowly walking towards the person who said 'Yes.' The person who just said 'Yes' must then make eye contact with someone else in the circle and repeat the process. Their aim is to have started moving before the other person has reached their place. The important rule in this exercise is that you cannot move until you have received a definite 'Yes.'

Comments/ concerns This exercise can take a while to get going. It appears simple at first, but actually requires a number of skills including concentration, self-control and the ability to make clear eye contact.

One of the biggest obstacles that group members must overcome is being able to wait until they have received a 'Yes' before they move. It may be useful to take time during the exercise to discuss with participants where the difficulties lie and how they can improve the smooth running of the circle. If you have time, it can be very rewarding to work towards there being more than one person moving across the circle at the same time.

General processing *What skills were you using to make the exercise work? What thoughts and feelings did you have during the exercise? What parts of the exercise did you find difficult?*

Personal processing: *assertiveness; dealing with pressure; self-control* *What are the consequences of saying 'Yes' in this exercise? What comparisons might you make between these experiences and experiences where you've felt pressured? When was the right moment to move? How do we decide upon the right time to act in real life? If the 'Yes' in this exercise represented a signal that action had to be taken, what sorts of signals do we receive in life that make us feel we should take action? When do we feel good about making decisions and taking action? When do we not? What do we need to do and feel before we feel confident about making a decision or taking action?*

Variation

Another variation of *The 'Yes' Circle* is ***Frankenstein.*** In this variation, as you walk across the circle, you walk with your arms extended in the style of Frankenstein's monster. The person you are walking towards does not want to be 'got,' and they escape by making eye contact with someone else in the group, who frees them to move with a nod of the head or by saying their name (you can use the latter option as a name game).

The 'Yes' Circle has a format similar to *Throwing Names* and *Cross Circle Switch.*

Guess the Feeling

Emotional awareness; empathy; drama skills
High focus
Groups of 4 to 20
Time needed: 15 - 30 minutes or longer
Worker participation: yes

Method

There are several forms of this exercise:

1. ***Feeling Sculpts*** Divide into groups of four to six. The small groups name as many feelings as they can, and then focus on one. Each group presents their chosen emotion in the form of a sculpt or short sound and movement sequence to the other groups, who try to guess which one it is.

2. ***In the Manner of...*** A volunteer waits outside the room while the group decides on a feeling adverb, such as 'sadly,' 'happily' or 'curiously.' The volunteer returns and asks individuals or the entire group to do simple actions 'in the manner of the feeling.' Example: 'Tie your shoe in the manner of the feeling.' The volunteer tries to guess the feeling.

3. ***Guess the Feeling*** Individuals go out of the room and re-enter in the manner of a feeling. The other members guess the feeling. Or: The group members stand in a circle. In turn, each person mimes a simple action conveying a feeling. The group tries to guess the feeling, and may ask the person to do several other actions in order to guess.

4. ***Help or Hinder*** One person expresses to another a pressing need, e.g. 'Help, my finger is trapped in this lift door,' or 'I'm only six years old and my dog has just been run over in the street!' The other person must try to help - or alternatively, hinder - the person in need. Where they try to help, the focus should be on matching the level of need. Option: Instruct participants to try giving slightly *less* help than needed, then slightly *more*, then, finally, the appropriate amount. Process around the theme of empathy and how we deal with our own and other people's emotions.

General processing *What are common emotions, and what are uncommon ones? How can we tell how someone is feeling? What do we look for and listen for? What are examples of good feelings, of bad feelings and of painful feelings? What causes them? What do we need to happen when we feel strong feelings? Are feelings useful or not?*

Personal processing: *emotional awareness* *What do you do when you're feeling good or bad? What causes you to feel good or bad? What role do feelings play in your offending? Are you in a certain mood before offending? During offending? After? How do you think your offending affects the feelings of others? Should we care about your feelings and what causes them (I think we should)? If that happens, is it then fair to ask you to think about others' feelings? Do you want to get better at recognising and naming your own feelings? And respecting the feelings of others?*

Soundscapes

Imagination; communication; drama skills; closure/ relaxation
Low to passing high focus
Groups of 4 and up
Time needed: 20 - 40 minutes
Worker participation: one stays out, others optional

Method

For this exercise, the larger the room the better.

1. One or more volunteers wait outside the room. While they are out, the group decides on an environment rich in recognisable sounds. Examples: a fairground, a seaside town, a harbour, an old fashioned steam railway station or a jungle. They then create a soundscape of that environment using just their voices and simple percussion. They should not use actual words, although they can represent language through garbled mumbling. Encourage the participants to think about what can be achieved with tone, pitch, rhythm, etc. How can they make the room as atmospheric as possible? Ask them to place themselves around the room in order to give maximum effect when the volunteers return.

2. The volunteers return and are led around the room, listening to the sounds as they go. This can be done with eyes open, although it works better if they have their eyes closed. Can they guess where they are? If the room is small, instead of leading the listeners around, ask them to sit in a tight circle, facing out, with their eyes closed. Ask the group who are creating their sounds to slowly circle them while creating their sounds. The groups then swap over.

Comments/ concerns This is meant to be an enjoyable, imaginative experience. Encourage the participants to be inventive. Where relevant, stress that this exercise helps build basic drama skills.

In large groups, subdivide the group and have each group create a soundscape for the others. Groups of four to ten work best.

General processing *How did the group arrive at decisions? Were people able to guess the environment being created? What sounds made the most impression on you? Did you notice sounds outside of the room?*

Personal processing If people are willing to share their memories, the exercise can be a useful way of focusing on emotional memory and how memory works.

This exercise works well in tandem with *Environment Sculpt.*

Block of Air

Imagination; drama skills; communication; empathy; closure
Passing high focus
Groups of 4 to 20
Time needed: 5 - 25 minutes
Worker participation: yes

Method The group members stand in a circle. The leader demonstrates taking a 'block of air' and, using exact movements, shaping it into an object of any size or type. It may be a pair of glasses, cricket bat, violin or hang glider; it could be anything. Once the leader shapes the object, he or she briefly mimes how the object is used or interacted with, e.g. playing the violin. The group members then guess what it is. When the correct guess is made, the leader takes the object and passes it to the next person, who takes it and then claps his or her hands to create a new 'block of air.' This person then shapes the block of air into some other object. And so on. Do one or two full rounds.

Comments/concerns Block of Air can be done silently or you can encourage participants to create sound effects that go with their object. This exercise is often used as the first introduction to drama skills. If group members start to freeze up with anxiety, use gentle prompts, such as suggesting they think of a favourite sport, or a musical instrument, an object found in the kitchen or an actual object of theirs (past or present).

At times, some group members will create 'objects' or mime explicit actions related to sex, drugs or violence. You can rule out these themes at the start of the exercise, or allow all themes and trust the group to set their own limits. In general, it is best to leave the rules quite unstructured, because any 'object' that the participants create can be a useful lead into discussion about what is important to them. Give them further opportunities to create objects with greater imagination after they have 'used up' these initial responses.

General processing *You've all just proved that you can create theatre. You see something in your mind, and you present it so that others can see it too. That's theatre. What kinds of objects were created? We'll do another round, and this time really let your imaginations go.*

Variations

- When a person creates an object and starts using it, everyone instantly starts doing the same thing. Or: First person makes a simple movement, such as giving a thumbs-up. Next person gives a thumbs-up and does a second action, such as throwing a ball. Third person does thumbs-up, throws ball and does another action. Continue adding around the circle.
- ***Object Transformation*** Pass around an everyday object such as a clipboard, a rolled up newspaper or a clothes hanger. Each person uses it in a different way. Example: a clipboard becomes a steering wheel, then a dinner tray, then an oar. A follow-on: divide into small groups. Each group has a prop around which they develop a scene.
- ***Closure and departure variations*** At the end of a session, group members shape a positive object and present it as a gift to the person on their left or right, or to the group. Similarly, if someone is departing the group, each person can shape an object that conveys a positive message of support (e.g. a photo album to remember the sessions; a good luck charm; a tape recorder to remember the feedback from the group). They present their object as a gift to the departing person.

Word at a Time Story

Imagination; concentration; group building; victim empathy
Passing high focus
Groups of 6 and up
Time needed: 20 minutes or more
Worker participation: yes

Method

Group standing or seated in a circle. Working together with concentration, the group members tell a story, each saying only one word as they go around the circle in turn. The story can be completely unstructured, or there can be a theme. The story may naturally come to an end. If not, ask the group to wind up the story if it goes on too long.

Comments/ concerns This is an exercise to do once the group members are familiar with each other; in new groups, participants may be inhibited by feeling 'not clever enough.' One of the keys to the success of the exercise is for group members to stay open to the constant shifting of the story, and to try not to force their ideas onto it. Remind the group members that simple is best, and that it is OK just to say a little word like 'and' or 'of.'

General processing: *group building* Ask the group how they did. Were they listening to each other? Were they trying to take too much control of where the story went, 'forcing' their ideas on the others? Can they see any connections between this exercise and the process of the group?

Variations

- Give time limits to the stories. Add structure by giving a narrative form, such as 'Dear diary...' or 'My apology to my victim' (this can be a powerful victim awareness exercise for the whole group).
- Instead of one word, people contribute as much or as little as they like. Stories are best passed on in mid-sentence, e.g. 'And then ...' or 'At that moment ...'
- Other story telling exercises include ***Tell Me About ...*** and ***No You Didn't.*** These are both quite short and snappy improvisation games, and are both played in pairs. In *Tell Me About ...* , person A tells any story, fictional or real, with great energy and speed. At any time, person B can interrupt and refer to something person A just said by saying, 'Tell me about ... (e.g. 'the traffic jam,' 'your Aunt Irene,' 'the police helicopter'),' at which point person A immediately changes course and tells about that person, object or part of the story.
  Similarly, in *No You Didn't,* person B interrupts A at any point in the story and says, 'No you didn't,' at which point A agrees, backtracks and 'corrects' herself. Example: 'Then I went to the space shuttle launch in Florida...' 'No you didn't.' 'No I didn't do that, I actually went to Margate Sands and got stung by a jellyfish and got rushed to hospital.' 'No you didn't.' etc.

Slow Motion Race

Drama skills; imagination; co-operation; self-control
Low focus
Groups of 6 and up
Time needed: 10 - 15 minutes
Worker participation: one stays out, others optional

Method

With the centre of the room cleared of chairs and obstacles, everyone lines up along one wall. Tell the group members that they are about to start an *ultra slow motion race* to the far wall and back, and it's 'each man for himself' as they are allowed and encouraged to 'cheat' as much as they can. They can trip people, push them, distract them or throw other people in their way, but everything must be done in ultra ... slow ... motion. Show what you mean by ultra slow. Encourage the 'runners' to add sound effects, too, again in slow motion. So a shout becomes eeeelooooongaaated as if the audio tape has been slowed.

To really drive home the point about it needing to be in slow motion, say that although they must look like they are playing to be *first* across the line, the 'winners' will be the people who come in *last*.

Comments/ concerns *Slow Motion Race* is meant to be light and fun. When done at the right time, it can be a sort of breakthrough exercise where group members realise that they can be completely at ease and even silly with each other as part of the overall serious work of the group. When groups can go to this extreme of imagination and absurdity and still feel safe with each other, it is a great sign of health, and the group members will sense this.

This exercise is also an introduction to being 'in role,' because the players will in essence be following a prescribed role given by the leader; in order to play this game they must play the role of 'ruthless cheater'—but in good fun rather than in its destructive real life equivalent.

General processing *What were your thoughts and feelings during the exercise, and how do you feel about it now? What does being able to do the exercise together say about you as a group? In this race, who was first across the line didn't matter at all. What do you think about the issue of competition and cheating? What are alternative ways of looking at survival?*

Variations

- If the group members enjoy the game, run the race again but this time make it a slow motion race where they must run *backwards.*

- Alternatively, run the race as before but have the group members form teams with imaginative names. Each team works together to trip up the others. Again, this is all done in ultra slow motion.

Fool Factors/ The Room That Fought Back

Drama skills; locus of control; relapse prevention
Medium to (voluntary) high focus
Groups of 4 and up
Time needed: 15 - 25 minutes or more
Worker participation: one stays out, others optional

Method

Group members divide into groups of four to eight. Each group works for five to ten minutes to create a room in a house in which all of the appliances, furniture or other objects 'fight back' at the occupant. For example, two people form a comfy chair that seems fine at first, but then collapses and swallows the person who sits down on it. Or one person could become a shower that seems to run fine until it splutters to a stop and ejects the shower-taker. All of the objects should be appropriate to the room created; no toasters in the bathroom or beds in the kitchen.

After the groups have time to rehearse, send one of the co-leaders or a group member from another group into each 'room,' one at a time. Alternatively, each group can designate its own 'guinea pig' to go through the room. Once in the room, the person goes to each object or fixture and uses it appropriately until it fights back, at which point he reacts and moves on to the next item.

Comments/concerns This is an excellent exercise to introduce the idea that group members can create scenes very quickly, without props or sets.

The exercise is also relevant to offending behaviour and *locus of control* (our sense that we are in control of our own decisions and actions). To make this link, we use the metaphor *Fool Factors* to represent things that can go wrong that are outside our control, as distinct from difficulties that are *within* our control to prevent. For example, a group member may say that he was late for the group because his alarm didn't work. This may or may not be a Fool Factor. If he forgot to set his alarm, that is not a Fool Factor because he could have remembered to do that. However, if it is an electric alarm clock and there was a power cut in the middle of the night, that was outside his control and so it *is* a Fool Factor. The question is, 'how do we manage and cope with Fool Factors in our lives?'

General processing *Have you ever experienced days like this? There is a difference between things that go wrong that we can control and things that go wrong that we can't. We'll call the second type 'Fool Factors' because it's like there's a Fool somewhere taking great delight when our day turns into disaster. Let's have some examples of other Fool Factors and also some mishaps that we CAN control.*

Personal processing: *locus of control; relapse prevention* *To what degree were your offences influenced by Fool Factors or by your own decisions? What about potential future offences?*

Variations

- Create any imaginary setting and invite group members to add Fool Factors to the scene. For example, try adding Fool Factors to a probation hostel scene, a prison landing, a public bus or an everyday street scene. Encourage experimentation and problem solving.
- Where appropriate, move into personal level role play to allow group members to practise coping strategies for dealing with their own, real life Fool Factors.

These two variations share much in common with *Forum in Reverse*.

Closure Exercises

Closure; goal setting; empathy; communication; group building
Low to high focus
Groups of all sizes
Time needed:15 - 30 minutes
Worker participation: varies

It is important to take time at the end of sessions to process the work with participants and to ensure that everyone is leaving in a contained state. This is a time for participants to identify how they felt about the session, how it related to or affected them and what they feel they have learned. Discussing the work also makes it more memorable.

For someone who has played a role, it can give them the time and space to fully integrate how the role might relate to them. It also helps to de-role participants, effectively 'closing the role' they have played.

Ideally, closures should last between 15 minutes to half an hour, depending on the size of the group. Try to ensure that everyone has a chance to speak. As the group members grow accustomed to this part of the session, they may feel more willing to share their feelings and insights.

Closure 1: De-roling

When one or more group members has taken on a role during the session, it is always worth de-roling them in order to increase their ability to observe their own process and also to reinforce learning. Sometimes, people can also be left with uncomfortable or negative feelings after playing a role, and de-roling can help them to leave the role behind while retaining the learning.

There are two types of de-roling, reflected in the examples below. *Overt de-roling* makes direct reference to the characters portrayed and asks group members to consciously step out of their roles. *Covert de-roling* generally occurs when people become involved in a starkly contrasting activity such as *Balloon Explodes* or a more prolonged, relaxing exercise such as *Soundscapes*. *Covert de-roling* can also occur simply in an end-of-session round of statements (see *Closing Questions and Statements*).

Overt de-roling:

- Make a sound to describe the way you're feeling as opposed to the way your character was feeling.
- Make a facial expression or other gesture to show how you're feeling as opposed to the way your character was feeling.
- Re-introduce yourself by name and do either of the above.
- Say one way you are similar and one way you are different from the character you played.
- Ask the entire group to stand and vigorously brush themselves down in order to 'brush off the role.'

Covert de-roling:

- Any brief, fast-paced game, or a group concentration or relaxation exercise.
- Processing exercises and scenes.
- End of group discussion.

Closure 2: Closing Questions and Statements

- One thing I want to remember from today.
- One thing I will share with my partner, family, or other person close to me, about the work I have done today.
- A goal or challenge I have set myself for the coming week.
- One message for the group as a whole and one thing I want to remember about the session.
- Leader starts off: 'Something I have learned today'; 'Something I wish to do with my life'; 'Something that I would like to say to the group is...' (Each person completes the sentence. No one is allowed to comment on what someone else says).
- 'What I like about this group is ... And what I don't like about this group is ... (Each group member completes both sentences. They can say 'pass' or 'There's nothing I like or don't like' if they wish but the leader should be careful that this does not just become an easy way to opt out. No one is allowed to comment on what is said, although the leaders should obviously take note of the important feedback that will come with these statements).
- 'I am ... I feel ... I need ... I want ...' (Each person completes the sentences).
- Each person says how they felt at the start of the group compared to now, using the form: 'From .... to ...' Example: 'From nervous to curious.'
- Quick closure: (Each person gives word/sound/gesture to describe their feeling. No comment should be passed).
- Feelings can be elicited by each person placing themselves on a *Continuum* from very positive at one end and very negative at the other. If the continuum is done both at the start and end of a session, any shift in feeling is concretised.
- Exit introduction: (Each group member 'introduces' herself at the end of the group using the structure: 'Who am I, why I'm here, how much of me was here, and what I got from today.'
- 'Something positive I'll do just for me this week in order to take care of myself, and something positive I'll do for someone else even though I might not be thanked for it.')

Closure 3: Rain Forest

All stand in a circle. The worker instructs: *I am going to start off an action. The person on my left will copy it and when they do the person on their left will begin and so on around the circle until we are all doing the same action. I will then change it and the new action will go all round the circle, and so on. Don't change until the person on your right does, and don't stop until they do. If it all goes according to plan, we should hear the sound of a rainstorm in the forest.*

The sequence of actions:

- Rubbing hands briskly together (wind blowing through the trees)
- Clicking fingers (first rainfall, or, crickets)
- Patting hands on thighs (heavier rain)
- Pattering plus stamping of feet (torrential rain and thunder)
- Stamping stops, pattering continues (back to heavy rain)
- Clicking of fingers (the rain is ceasing)
- Rubbing of hands (the wind drops)
- The Worker stops and the actions cease one by one around the circle (when the last person stops, that is the last breeze of the storm).

Closure 4: Balloon Explodes

The group members stand in a circle facing inwards: *I want you to imagine that we are all part of a big balloon which is going to be inflated. We'll start with our hands joined and our arms down low. I'll be the start of the breath, and the breath will travel around one by one making a louder and louder "shhhushhh" sound as it goes and as it goes round we get louder and louder and lower and lower until it comes around to me again and we all explode with a great "POW!" and jump together into the air. And that will be the end of the session!*

Variation The breath and balloon can be replaced by a 'hissing' fuse and a firework, ending in, 'Boom!' or 'Pow!' Or: A 'whoooosh' sound can build to a crescendo and end in a bigger 'WHOOOOOSH! and a group jump. Think of your own variations.

Closure 5: Relaxation

The group members are seated or lying on the floor. If the group members are sitting, ask them to ensure both feet are on the ground and their hands are resting on their laps. If they are lying on the floor, they should lie on their backs.

Ask the group to focus on their breathing. Ask them to count silently from one to ten, each complete inhalation and exhalation counting as one. If they find that they lose count ask them simply to go back to the beginning and start again. The group should not worry about losing count. This does not mean they are doing it 'wrong,' but rather that the mind will inevitably drift at times as we practice relaxation. Once they reach ten, they should go back to the beginning and start again.

As they concentrate on breathing, ask the group to allow their arms and shoulders to relax and to feel the tension begin to diminish.

Variation On inhale count 'one,' on exhale count 'two' and so on up to ten.

Closure 6: Group Count

The group members stand in a circle facing inwards. If there are more than twelve in the group, divide into two equal size groups: *As a group I want you simply to count from one to ten. Sounds easy... however, only one person must say each number. If two or more people say a number at the same time then the group must start counting again from one. The numbers must go in the correct order, you cannot create a 'system' like simply going round the circle, and no one person can say consecutive numbers. Let's give it a go...anyone can start.*

Comments/ concerns Because this exercise can take a long time, it is important to leave enough time for completion, as failure to finish the task can leave some groups feeling let down. If the group members are finding it difficult, you can stop the exercise and talk about why it's not working (It is often simply that they are rushing). The sense of achievement felt by groups when they do complete the task after many attempts is a good way to end a session.

Variations

- If the group completes the task quickly, move on to counting to 20 or even 30.
- Group members close their eyes while they count.
- Return to the exercise week after week in order to set higher challenges.
- If there are domineering members, add the rule: no one calls more than one or two numbers.
- Have several teams working on the task at the same time and in competition with each other. First team to 20 wins a point.

Closure 7: Guess a Minute

This is a good exercise to focus a group at the close of a session: All group members stand and, at the leader's signal, close their eyes and estimate the passing of a minute. When a person thinks a minute has passed, she sits down and opens her eyes. The leader gives feedback about the accuracy of responses. This can be briefly processed around the theme of time, and time passing.

Closure 8: Positive Feedback

Variations

- Everyone milling around. Each person goes around to all of the other people and gives them a positive message such as, 'I think you tried really hard to join in today.' (Option): The only response the receiver is allowed to say is 'I know.'
- Everyone milling around. When you see someone you want to give some positive feedback to, send them that message via someone else. Example: 'Would you tell Sarah thanks from me for helping me with the obstacle course last week?' Source: (Brandes and Philips, 1990).
- Each person improvises a brief 'Dear Me' letter in front of the group, talking about how they did in the group, what they want to remember and the goals they have for the immediate future.
- Similarly, the group can compose a 'Dear Me' letter using the *Word at a Time Story* exercise.
- The group members pass a 'thank you' handshake, smile or hug around the circle. Obviously the hug option may not be appropriate in some groups.

Offending-focused Games and Exercises

Cup, Table, Chair

Power and control; gender issues; empathy
Low to medium focus
Groups of 4 and up
Time needed: 10 - 30 minutes or more
Worker participation: no

Method

Ask the group to form an audience. Randomly place a cup, a table and a chair on the 'stage.'

In front of you is a table, a chair and a cup. I would like you to come up one by one and arrange these three objects in a hierarchy so that one is the most powerful, one is in the middle in terms of power, and one is the least powerful.

Group members come up individually and arrange the objects. As they do this, stress that there is no right or wrong and that each individual's interpretation is valid. After each group member has completed his arrangement, ask him to explain why a particular object achieves power in the arrangement.

General processing: *power and control* *What makes something or someone powerful? What does it mean to be powerful? What kinds of power are there? Is power only physical? Are men more powerful than women, or vice versa? If someone wants power, what sort of things can they do to get it?*

Personal processing: *power and control* *If we were to relate your arrangement of the objects to a situation in everyday life, who might the table/chair/cup represent? How do you feel about power? How do you try to get power? How do you use power with other people? Where do you feel powerful and where do you feel you have less power than you want?*

Variations Use a variety of objects to sculpt other relevant themes, such as 'family,' 'freedom,' 'victim,' 'institution,' 'police' or 'job centre.' Use more chairs if they are available. Invite people into the image to develop the theme. This in effect becomes a *Frozen Picture* and may even move into *Role Play* (see following chapters).

This exercise is followed well by the exercise *Barriers to Change.*

Source Augusto Boal (1992)

Hand/Face Progression

Power and control; co-operation; self-control; gender and relationships
Low focus
Groups of 4 and up
Time needed: 15 - 20 minutes
Worker participation: one stays out, others optional

Method

Group divides into pairs, A and B. This exercise has three stages.

1. Person A holds one palm flat and facing out vertically. B follows the palm, keeping his face about 6 inches from it at all times. Person A is to lead reasonably slowly so B can follow, but may move his palm up, down, around or wherever he wishes. CAUTION: Stress that sudden smacks into the face with the palm are *not allowed.* Person A must lead in such a way that person B can follow without injuring himself. Person A leads for a short period, then B leads. After this phase is completed, move on.
2. Person A holds out one wrist. Person B reaches with his hand as if he is about to grab the wrist, but he must maintain a distance of about six inches from the wrist at all times and is *not allowed* to grab it. This time person A may make it as difficult or as 'easy' as he wishes (Person A will quickly discover that it does not matter whether he moves his wrist slowly or quickly, because person B cannot grab it). Person A leads then B leads. Allow about thirty seconds for each, then move on.
3. Same as the previous step but B is now allowed to grab the wrist. If he is successful, A and B swap and keep going. They swap each time someone successfully grabs the wrist and keep their individual scores. Set a time limit of about two minutes maximum. This stage is quite active and competitive, so make sure there is plenty of space for each pair to work in.

Comments/ concerns Because stage one can be intimidating, it can be useful to stress that B is following A's palm rather than that A is leading B. Stages two and three are quite energetic so remind group members to be safety conscious.

General processing *What are these exercises about? Which did you prefer? What situations in life are like these? Who gave their partner a difficult time? Who gave them an easy time? Why is that?*

Personal processing: *power and control; self-talk* *In the first part, which did you prefer, leading or following? Why? How does leading or following relate to your offending? In the second part, how did you feel about not being allowed to grab the wrist? When else do you feel like that? What is the link between this exercise and your experience of frustration/anger/violence in the world outside?*

What feelings did you have about the exercise? Did anyone refuse to do it or stop mid-way? Why? When you feel like that in other situations, what do you usually do? How about those of you who wanted to stop, but didn't? What did you say to yourself to help you to stay involved?

Variations The first section can be expanded. A and B can be far apart, for example. Or, everyone in the room focuses on one part of a central volunteer's arms, legs or head. As the volunteer moves, the entire group moves too, each person moving in relation to a part of the central person. Experiment with one person leading two, or chains of people so that A leads B who leads C, etc.

Source: Augusto Boal (1992)

The Mirror

Power and control; co-operation; empathy; relationships; locus of control
Low to medium focus
Groups of 2 and up
Time needed: 5-20 minutes or more
Worker participation: one stays out, others optional

Method

Group members in pairs, A and B: *In your pairs, find a space in the room and stand opposite each other about a meter apart. When I clap my hands, person A begins a movement, and it is the task of person B to act as the mirror image of A, reflecting this movement as accurately as possible. This is not a competition. You are working together to create a movement and its accurate mirror image. Concentrate on the details, the rhythm and the speed of the movement. I recommend that A starts with some fairly slow simple movements, possibly with the hands, and then gradually you can increase the speed and complexity until you are moving around the room.*

After several minutes, swap the roles over so that B is leading and A provides the reflection. Emphasise that this exercise requires concentration and so it is best done in silence.

When B has led for awhile, get the pairs to start again but this time there is no designated leader—in a sense they are both leaders and followers, so the leadership should swap between them. Emphasise that it is essential that no one person tries to force the other person to copy her all the time, but that the exercise is most effective when the pair are working together and continually negotiating who is leading and who reflecting. The pairs should work so well together that someone on the outside would not be able to say who was the leader and the who the reflection.

Option: If the group members are working well together and the room is large enough, encourage them to move very far apart and continue the mirroring.

General processing *What skills were involved in the exercise? What made it work well or not so well? With one leading and one following, what sort of a relationship was that like? What was the power and control balance in the first part as opposed to the second part, when the two sides of the mirror moved together with no leader? What sort of relationship is that like?*

Personal processing: *relationships; locus of control* *Which did you prefer, leading or being led? Why? In what situations in life do you lead or are you led? What's easier? Does the issue of leading or being led have anything to do with your offending? For example, were you alone or with others when you committed your offence? Did the others have an influence on you? How do you feel about that? What about in relationships? Who takes the lead? How easy or difficult is it to share power in a relationship?*

Variations

- A more challenging variation is to do the exercise with two pairs mirroring each other in typical situations calling for close interaction between two people, e.g. hairdresser and customer, tailor and customer, shoe fitter/ shoe shine and customer.
- ***The Puppeteer*** Person A is the puppeteer, and person B is the puppet. The control mechanism is person A himself: We imagine that there are strings running from A's feet to B's feet, A's hands to B's hands, A's head to B's head, etc. The two place themselves far apart, and A leads in exaggerated movements. B makes every movement to correspond as if tied by the strings. After a while, swap over. In processing, stress the power and control theme, e.g. *Are there real-life relationships like this?*

Get Them to the Corner

Power and control; handling conflict; co-operation; motivation to change; communication
Low focus
Groups of 4 and up
Time needed: 10 - 20 minutes
Worker participation: one stays out, others optional

Method The group divides into pairs, A and B. The exercise has three stages:

1. Person A is given the instruction to *physically push* person B into one corner (or one end) of the room. B is told to do the same to A, but to the opposite corner, so the two will be working in direct opposition. Before the signal is given, everyone does a trial attempt at safe pushing (e.g. hand to shoulder or shoulder to shoulder), and agree on a safe method. Give the signal to begin. Stop after 30 seconds or less (often, just ten seconds will suffice to make the point).
2. Person A is then told to get B into the corner using *argument, threats and bullying,* but no physical touch. B is told to do the same with A at the same time, so once again they are working in direct opposition. Run for thirty seconds to a minute.
3. Persons A and B must both accomplish the same goal, but this time they are to use *conversation and compromise.* No physical contact.

   In stage 3, several outcomes are possible (discuss these after the exercise):
   - A and B go together to one corner then the other;
   - A goes to B's corner and B goes to A's, so both accomplish their task simultaneously;
   - A goes to B's corner with B but B then refuses to hold up to the bargain; or
   - Neither compromises, and neither accomplishes the task.

Comments/concerns Because stage one involves a great deal physical contact, it is important that people are physically warmed up and feel comfortable with each other. Remind the group about the dangerous places in the room, e.g. chairs, tables. If anyone feels uncomfortable, they must be allowed to stop. In general, try to form pairs of people with relatively the same height and build. Don't pair men and women together. With young people, extra care and attention should be paid to safety. When in doubt, step one may be safer in slow motion. Or, you can ask everyone to use only 50% of their actual strength; the point about physical force will still be clear.

General processing *How did it feel to be pushed and argued with, then to try compromise? How did it feel trying to get the other person to do what you wanted in each of the three ways? Who accomplished their task? What connections might there be to working with other people, or with relationships? What situations in the world are like this exercise, for instance conflicts between nations or cultures? How do you move from fighting to arguing, or from arguing to conversation and compromise?*

Personal processing: *motivation to change* *How does this exercise relate to your life? How does it relate to your process of change, and the changes you are currently trying to make? If the corner represents a change, who is doing the pushing or pulling? What do you need to do before change will happen?* Use this exercise to make the point that in this group no one can be forced to make a change. A person will only 'go to the corner' or make a change if they can see the sense in it. This can reassure group members who may feel that the groupwork process is designed to remove their control or 'mess with my head'.

Source Thanks to Pete Harris for teaching us this exercise.

No Rule

Victim empathy; power and control; gender issues; problem solving
High focus
Groups of 6 to 20
Time needed: 20 - 40 minutes
Worker participation: no

Method

Whole group at one end of the room. Four chairs set out randomly in the centre of the room:

One at a time, each person will make their way to the other end of the room. There is a way from your end of the room to the other, and I have it in mind. Once you start, I will say 'no' if you go wrong and you will have to try a new direction (or, as an option: *you will have to go back to the start*). *You must each complete the task individually but can make attempts in any order, one at a time.*

The leader should have a particular route in mind. It may involve sitting on, standing on, crawling under or walking around the chairs. Once one person has crossed the room, the others usually assume they can follow the same route. At this point, the leader should *change the route* she has in mind and begin saying 'no' according to this new route. The leader should not enter into discussion with the group about whether she has changed the rules or 'got it wrong,' and should encourage each group member to complete the task. (There will be some confusion and frustration at this point. Some group members can get quite agitated and angry about the seeming arbitrariness of the leader's decisions.)

Once the route has changed several times, the leader stops having a route in mind and begins to make completely arbitrary decisions about whether someone is right or wrong as they cross the room. Some people will get straight through, others will be sent back. It should be random. Again, the leader should not engage in discussion around the rules until everyone is across.

Comments/concerns *No Rule* usually generates powerful emotions, often frustration and anger. Because of this, it is vital that you have good rapport with the group and feel confident that you know when to stop the exercise and how to let people opt out without seeing this as sabotaging the exercise.

No Rule can also be used to explore the experiences of victims, particularly those of domestic violence, where 'not knowing the rules' is terrifying and debilitating.

Personal processing: *power and control* Ask the group to relate their experience of 'not knowing the rules' to life situations where they may feel they are not in control. Explore any strong feelings aroused, e.g. anger at the leader, powerlessness, unfairness, feeling stupid.

With men who have been violent to their partners, you may want to explore how 'changing the rules' or having arbitrary rules affected their partners and how they, the offenders, may have used this as a tactic for maintaining control.

Ask the group members how important 'rules' are for them, what happens when someone breaks their rules, and how it feels to break or keep others' rules.

The Silent Hunter

Victim empathy; power and control; offending tactics; self-control; self-talk
High focus
Groups of 6 and up
Time needed: 20 - 30 minutes
Worker participation: one stays out, others optional

Method

The group members form two equal teams and line up against opposite walls, facing inward. These two lines of people now represent the boundary lines.

Two volunteers come into the centre of the room and decide who is A and who is B. They go to opposite ends of the room and face each other, with the boundary lines to their left and right. Both close their eyes. The object is for person A to reach the other end of the room without being touched or tagged by person B. They may both wish to remove their shoes in order to be silent as they walk. The only way person B will be able to find person A is by using strategy, listening closely and using her other non-visual senses. Instruct all present to be silent, so that the two players in the middle can hear. Do a number of rounds, with different people in the middle.

As a safety measure—and to keep the rest of the group involved—those forming the boundary lines are given the task of redirecting the two players in the middle if they stray out of bounds. The redirection is given with two firm, silent and quick taps on the shoulder of the person who is walking out of bounds. The two taps tells them to head toward the central area again. The two players in the middle should be told to expect the two taps if they stray out of bounds. The reason for two taps instead of one tap is so that person A does not mistake an 'out of bounds' tap with a 'being caught' tap (i.e. being caught by person B).

General processing: *self-talk* *What strategies did the people in the centre use? What thoughts and feelings did you have when you were the hunter or the hunted? Did you want to open your eyes? Did you do so? If not, what thoughts stopped you from opening your eyes? Can you control your thoughts and feelings?*

Personal processing: *victim empathy* *Which role do you prefer, hunter, hunted, or boundary referee? Why? When you are the hunter or the hunted, what is it like for the other person? Are you concerned with the other's predicament? What situations in your life resemble what takes place in this exercise? How might victims of crime feel similar to the 'hunted' in this exercise? How does committing crime make you like the hunter/ the hunted? What would happen if the exercise was changed, so that one had their eyes open and the other didn't? What situations in life resemble this?*

Variation A close variation is ***Guard's Keys***: All are seated in a circle or square. Two people in the middle, one with eyes shut. This is the guard. A set of keys is placed near the guard. The other person has her eyes open and must carry the keys out of the circle without the guard pointing to her. The guard gets 3 tries. If the guard points at the person with the keys, the guard 'wins' and another person tries to get the keys. For a team variation, see *Grandmother's Keys*.

Sources Anna Scher (1982) calls this *The Hunter and the Hunted.* Christine Poulter (1987) writes of the variation using keys.

Wink Chair

Victim empathy; self-control; energiser; motivation to change; locus of control
Low focus
Groups of 8 to 20
Time needed: 10 - 25 minutes
Worker participation: one stays out, others optional

Method

Form a large, inward facing, square arrangement of chairs, using a number of chairs equal to approximately 3/4 of group members present. Example: If there are 12 group members, there will be 9 chairs set out in a square.

A group member stands behind each of the chairs, at arm's length from the back of it. These are the captors. The remaining group members sit in any of the chairs in the square. These are the prisoners.

At any time, any captor who does not have someone seated in their chair can secretly catch the eye of a prisoner and wink at him. If people find winking difficult, they can use any non verbal signal. This 'frees' the prisoner, who will now try to move from his chair and cross the circle to sit on the chair in front of the captor who has just signalled him. But this is very difficult to do, because his current captor is standing right behind him, and if the captor detects a move he can tap his prisoner on the shoulder to recapture him. If the prisoner successfully escapes from his chair, he goes and sits on the chair in front of the person who 'freed' him, and the process starts again.

After several minutes of play, swap some captors and prisoners around.

Comments/ concerns Because the 'prisoners' must move so quickly, this can be a very physically intense game. Younger groups tend to find this a very fun game because of the 'cat and mouse' aspects and the secret signalling. Be clear that captors are only allowed to *tap* their prisoners on the back, between the shoulders and waist band. No pushing or grabbing.

General processing *What is it like to be a captor or a prisoner? What are some real life equivalents of these roles, other than the obvious ones of prisoner and prison officer?*

Personal processing: *self-control* *Let's make some connections with self-control: Where did the impulse to move come from? Where did the impulse to stop come from? Who or what controls your impulses and what you do with them? Where does the impulse to offend come from? Name a situation where you find it difficult to control yourself. What do you want to do about that, if anything?*

Variations Vary the rules as appropriate. For example, to highlight the theme of locus of control, you may wish to replay the game with the new rule that the prisoners themselves decide when to 'escape' and they also decide whether or not to abide by the 'shoulder tap' rule keeping them seated. How does this change the game and the power relationship among the players? This could move into a discussion about change and what holds us back from change: *Why is it hard to see new possibilities other than following the same old rules? In a sense, we are all prisoners of our own roles and the limits we set ourselves and have set by others. What happens if we choose to set new limits and develop new roles? Do other possibilities exist? What keeps us in old patterns? How do we identify and modify how we relate to internal and external 'captors?'*

Master/Servant

Victim empathy; power and control; self-control; offending tactics; responsibility
Low focus
Groups of 2 and up
Time needed: 10 - 30 minutes
Worker participation: one stays out, others optional

Method

In pairs, participants label themselves A and B. For one or two minutes, A commands B to do anything within the limits of decency and B's physical capability, and B must do it. As a safety measure, B retains the right to refuse a command if it is distasteful, inappropriate or dangerous.

After several minutes, swap over, so B commands A.

Option: One person volunteers and becomes similarly powerful over the whole group.

General processing *It is very rare that people in the 'master' role command their servants to be their equals. Why is this? What is so attractive about power? Did any of you give up your power? Did anyone abuse it? Did anyone refuse a command? Why? What was the command?*

Personal processing: *power and control* *How did it feel to give and receive orders? What is the connection between this exercise and your relationships with other people? In what other areas of life do you feel either powerful or powerless? Does this relate to your offending?*

Variations

This exercise is closely related to and can be combined with *Tin Soldiers, Into Spoken Self Talk.*

Relationships Ladder

Relationships and sexuality; relationship skills; gender issues; emotional awareness
Low to high focus
Group size: any number
Time needed: 20 minutes or more
Worker participation: no

Method

1. Begin with an opening question: *Can you give an example of a relationship - either based on real life or hypothetical - where both partners are equal? Unequal?* Examples may include: A married couple or couple in a long term relationship; a couple who are dating; brother/ sister; parent/ child.

Ask the group to define: 'What is an adult?' 'What do we mean by describing behaviour as adult?' (Bring in the idea of adults having personal responsibility and other responsibilities extending beyond the self). What defines a child other than simply age? How do their responsibilities differ? Is it easier to be one or the other? Why? Which would you prefer to be, like a child or like an adult?

2. Explore the definition of 'consent.' Help the group reach a definition of 'true consent,' (e.g. that 'consent' is not consent if the person fears negative repercussions for saying no, for example if they are afraid that if they say no they will be hurt, ridiculed or left alone in a strange place, etc.)

3. Explore words associated with power and control, and the ways in which power and control can be abused in relationships.

4. The Relationships Ladder: Draw a picture of a simple step ladder on the flipchart, or create an image of a stepladder on the floor, using string perhaps. Describe the first rung of the ladder as being the very start of a new relationship. Using basic *Group Character Creation* techniques, have group members provide all of the details, e.g. 'Who is meeting?' 'Man and woman?' 'Teenage boy and girl?' 'Two people of same sex?' Steer the options so that the relationship will be representative of a consenting sexual relationship in an age group similar to those in the group. Then ask 'Where do they meet?' 'What do they talk about when they first meet?' 'What physical contact is there between them?' etc.

Continue the process for each rung up the ladder, the top rung representing the two people forming a permanent relationship or lasting commitment, e.g. seeing each other exclusively, moving in together, getting married or engaged, or going through some other form of commitment ritual/ ceremony.

At each rung of the ladder, ask the group to talk about how the move to the next rung is negotiated. Who directs the move? Is it mutual? What would happen if one person tries to force it up the ladder? What are the hallmarks of a healthy relationship?

Variation For adults: Ask the participants to stand on a *Continuum* representing the ladder, on the floor. Ask them to stand where they have been in their closest intimate relationship – as an adult - when it was at its height (ensure that they are discussing a legal relationship). Note: some group members may never have had an intimate relationship, and therefore this variation should only be used with caution and where you are certain that there will be group support for such individuals.

Encourage the group members to talk about how they met that person and how they determined how the relationship progressed. Was there an imbalance? Did they want it to end? Did the other person? How and why do their relationships generally end?

Roles and Responsibility

Responsibility; relapse prevention; motivation to change; self-control
Low to (voluntary) high focus
Groups of any size
Time needed: 30 minutes or more
Worker participation: one stays out, others optional

Method

Discuss with the group all of the roles that exist among them, or have existed among them in the past. Get at least thirty roles on the flipchart, e.g. father, son, brother, worker, boss, consumer, carer, provider, counsellor, driver, prisoner, neighbour, etc. Discuss favourites, least favourites. Discuss ones that are no longer practised, or ones that are sought. Discuss the ways in which roles can come or go, e.g. the role of son can be lost through a parent's death, but still remain in the memory.

Consider a few typical examples of role behaviours, e.g. the role of father: disciplining the children, or teaching the children. Or: the role of fisherman: baiting and casting the line, waiting.

Now draw a circle, representing a pie chart. Using various examples of interpersonal behaviours, ask the group to determine how much responsibility lies with the 'doer' of an action, and how much responsibility lies elsewhere. Example: if a father smacks his son for misbehaving, how much responsibility for the smack lies with the father and how much with the son? Represent the percentage by dividing the pie chart accordingly and writing the percentage.

Encourage the group members to debate the following point: that in all situations where the 'doer' is not under coercion, as long as they are of age and in control of their mental faculties, the responsibility for their actions is fully theirs.

Move on to give examples of the role of 'offender.' Have the group analyse who is responsible in percentage terms in various hypothetical offending examples (e.g. a home burglary; car theft; shoplifting; robbery; drug dealing; driving while intoxicated; domestic violence; sexual abuse; street violence). Encourage the group members to see that taking full responsibility for their own actions and decisions is the surest way to take control of their lives and stop offending – if that is the choice they want to make. Discuss why the hypothetical offenders in these examples might not want to accept full responsibility. *Why might he want to blame others, or the victim?*

Optional: Discuss and list 'the excuses/justifications for offending and avoiding responsibility.'

Comments/concerns This is largely a discussion-based exercise, but at the point of considering hypothetical examples it can be moved into *Frozen Pictures* or *Role Play.*

It is useful to raise the discussion about how a person might feel if he is forced to take on a role which he does not want or is not prepared for, e.g. the role of parent, or caretaker of younger siblings. What behaviour might result?

General note regarding role analysis: It can be extremely beneficial and empowering for the group members to identify their strongest/ healthiest/ most positive roles. They can be encouraged to use this role strength to carry over into other roles (e.g. 'new me' roles). This might be a session of its own, encouraging self-esteem.

Obstacle Course

Goal setting; problem solving; co-operation; offending tactics; concentration; communication
Low to (voluntary) high focus
Groups up to 16
Time needed: 15 - 30 minutes or more
Worker participation: one stays out, others optional

Method

The group members create an obstacle course throughout the room, using chairs, tables, etc. In pairs, one person verbally guides his partner (who has eyes closed) through the course to a designated goal. If the person with his eyes closed touches any obstacles, he can either start again or, optionally, he will lose one of his three 'lives.' Emphasise communication and listening skills. Repeat for other partner. Optional: have multiple pairs doing this all at once, starting from various points of the room to minimise collisions.

(Optional): Offer the pairs a second attempt. This time add the proviso that each participant may change one aspect of the exercise. However, they may not repeat a change made by someone else. Possible changes include: removing one of the obstacles or changing its position, having someone else act as a guide, and having eyes open. All changes should be accepted, as long as they have not already been attempted by someone else. As a further challenge, some participants will enjoy the chance to go through the course with their eyes closed but with no guide at all.

After this initial phase, the obstacle course can be adapted for many uses, such as:

Goal setting: *What is the goal, and what are the obstacles to reaching it? Which obstacles here might symbolise obstacles in real life?*

Offending behaviour: *What were the obstacles – internal and external - you had to get around in order to commit your offence?*

Comments/concerns Because it has so many applications, we use *Obstacle Course* quite a lot. It can be used early in groups, often on the first day, or well into an intensive piece of work.

The name 'obstacle course' might be a little misleading; it is more of a maze, and people are led through it. No one should be expected to climb over anything, although sometimes a group member will lead their partner underneath an obstacle such as a table. If there is any danger of someone hurting themselves, the leader should ensure that there are plenty of people to act as spotters/ referees.

Personal processing: *goal setting* *What does the goal represent for you? Choose something that you would like to achieve six to twelve months from now. Try not to focus on goals that you have little or no control over, for instance, 'I want to win the Lottery.'*

What might the obstacles in this exercise represent for you? Choose three, and set them out in the obstacle course according to their importance and proximity to you now. Name them. (Ask people to stand by the obstacles as they describe what they represent.) *What do you need to do in order to overcome these obstacles? What skills will you need to practise? What obstacles have you already overcome in your life? What does this say about you, that you have managed to overcome obstacles already?*

Invisible Obstacle Course

Motivation to change; relapse prevention; locus of control; responsibility; trust
High focus
Groups of 4 and up
Time needed: 20 - 40 minutes
Worker participation: no

Method

Clear the floor of all obstacles, tables and chairs, and ask the group members to line up at one end of the room, facing the wall with their eyes closed. Move the chairs and tables around the room as if creating an obstacle course in the room. However, do not actually place any obstacles in the central area; the room should be kept in exactly the layout as it was before the participants closed their eyes. They should believe an obstacle course has been created, whereas in reality nothing has changed.

Ask one group member to turn around with her eyes closed. Guide her through the 'obstacle course' using instructions such as 'take two steps forward, one step to the left, turn 90 degrees to the right,' etc. When the group member has completed the course, ask her to open her eyes and to remain silent (a surprised reaction will give the game away!).

Ask that group member to guide the next person through the obstacle course. Each group member, on completing the course, should then guide the next person through.

Comments/ concerns If you have a large group, speed up the exercise by having two or three people being guided at once.

Group members who 'cheat' by opening their eyes will see through the deception. It will be very useful to involve them in the processing, as 'cheating' in this game allows one to take more responsibility. As leaders, this paradox demands from us a confident and generous attitude toward the participants, because part of the message is that there are some instructions that are best not followed. To allow for the creative solutions that arise from 'cheating,' we must not consider the 'cheating' to be defiance, but rather as opportunities for useful processing and signs of independent thinking which are to be praised and encouraged!

General processing *Who assumed that I had created an obstacle course? How does this exercise relate to the theme of trust? How did you feel?*

Optional (where applicable): *Why did everybody guide the next person as if an obstacle course existed?*

Or: *What happened when the instructions changed when some people realised there was no obstacle course? What does this represent? What's the message?*

Personal processing: *Motivation to change* *What 'lessons' might be in the exercise about personal responsibility and overcoming obstacles that are or aren't there? Which obstacles are absolute and which are of our own making? What 'obstacles' do we create to justify our behaviour or to avoid change? How do our thoughts and feelings affect our expectations of a situation? If we expect rejection, failure or danger, how does this affect our behaviour?*

Barriers to Change

Motivation to change; goal setting; locus of control; relapse prevention; responsibility
Low to (voluntary) high focus
Groups of any size
Time needed: 15 - 45 minutes
Worker participation: no

Method

This exercise works best either directly after or soon after the exercise *Cup, Table, Chair.*

Using the cup, table and chair, place the chair behind the table with the table on its side, acting as a barrier between the chair and the group members. Place the cup some distance in front of the table and in line with the chair.

Ask the group members what the chair and table might represent. Often, they will see the table as a barrier and themselves - or someone like them - as sitting in the chair. Ask what the cup might represent. This is often seen as something they are aiming for, like 'freedom' or 'a job.'

Ask, 'If the table is a barrier, what is it made up of? How does it work?'

Ask for a volunteer to sit in the chair to represent 'someone trying to change.' Ask the group members to identify issues or events that might be creating the barrier to change for this hypothetical person. Ask the group members to stand up by the table after they contribute an idea about what the barrier might consist of. In this way, the barrier gradually becomes densely populated.

Now ask the group to identify what the person in the chair needs to do in order to overcome the barrier. At this point it is best to allow the group members to improvise through the rest of this exercise, exploring the responses from the group and seeing where the discussion leads. Nothing should be too fixed. Encourage a dialogue to develop between those who represent the 'barrier' and the person representing the 'person trying to change.' Rotate the roles and use other *processing techniques* as appropriate.

Comments/ concerns It is important that this is a group exercise. Although it is possible to concentrate on one individual's issues, the exercise is best used at the level of *one step removed* in order to allow the roles to be exchanged more freely.

Cycle of Change

Motivation to change; personal disclosure; locus of control
High focus
Groups of any size
Time needed: 20 - 40 minutes or more
Worker participation: no (although personal examples may be useful)

Method
Place seven sheets of paper on the floor, labelled with the various stages of the motivational cycle of change developed by Prochaska and DiClemente (1986). The sequence runs as follows:

Pre-contemplation Not thinking about change (although there may be awareness of the problem).
Contemplation Acknowledging the problem; weighing up the pros and cons of the behaviour; assessing the potential to effect change; seeing the potential first step.
Determination Making the decision to change and preparing for action.
Action Putting the change into practice.
Maintenance Continuing the new form of behaviour indefinitely.
Lapse May occur at any point in the cycle. This may be a mental lapse or a partial retreat to the old behaviour. The message is to be aware of it and expect it, otherwise it may turn into:
Relapse A full retreat to the previous behaviour.

Begin with examples unrelated to offending. Ask the participants to apply one habit they have changed (e.g. smoking, gambling, binge drinking, nail biting) to this cycle of change. Ask them to place themselves on this cycle according to where they were at some time in the past, where they are now, and where they want to be in the future. Ask questions about what prompted the change. What supported the behaviour? How easy or difficult was changing? What might lead to relapse? How many times have they lapsed or relapsed? What other habits are they trying to change? Participants can also discuss the relative success of voluntary versus involuntary changes.

Having discussed non-offending examples, the group members can explore what it is like to change offending behaviour and to be at various points of the cycle. Again, ask the participants to speak from the point of view of themselves at points in the past, where they are now, and desired points in the future, but this time in reference to their offending. They can talk with each other from various places on the cycle of change: 'What's it like over there at maintenance? I'm still just thinking about changing.'

Encourage discussion about the need to combine internal and external change. Example: The violent offender who makes a commitment to non-violence (internal change) but who still goes to the same pub where he has been in numerous fights (no external change).

Variation
A useful variation that uses drama and story-telling: Group members try to keep a hypothetical offender moving forward through the change cycle despite many challenges and potential relapses. The offender can be represented through simple story telling, *Group Character Creation*, *Worker in Role* or other techniques. Group members may speak for the victims or potential victims who will be hurt if the 'offender' lapses.

For a more detailed look at the stage of *contemplation*, you can break it down into seven components (O'Reilly, Morrison *et al.*, 2001): 1. I accept there is a problem; 2. I have some responsibility for the problem; 3. I have some discomfort about the problem and my part in it; 4. I believe things must change; 5. I can see that I can be part of the solution; 6. I can make a choice; 7. I can see the first steps towards change.

Offence Cycle

Offending cycle; motivation; victim empathy; responsibility; relapse prevention
High focus
Groups of up to 10
Time needed: 20 - 60 minutes or more per person
Worker participation: no

Method By understanding his typical pattern of thoughts, feelings and behaviour when offending – his offence cycle – the participant is often better able to modify and control his behaviour. To help the participant identify his cycle of offending, set out four chairs representing (1) the lead-up; (2) just before; (3) during; and (4) after the offence. Ask the participant to speak from each chair in relation to an offence he has committed. In each chair, he speaks about his thoughts, feelings and behaviour at that point in time. These thoughts, feelings and behaviours can be recorded using *Thinking Reports*, described on the following pages. Repeat the process for two or more offences, so a pattern, or typical offence cycle, emerges by comparing thinking reports. This can serve as the basis for modifying attitudes and beliefs and also identifying interpersonal skills and self-control strategies for practice using role play.

It may be useful to draw on models, or templates, for the cycle of offending which is typical of your offender group. For example, some of the typical models for violent offenders and sex offenders are:

Typical violent offence cycle:

Perceived insult
(e.g. Someone looks at me the wrong way or violates my rights).

↘ *intervention?*

Victim stance/ feeling humiliated/ threatened (e.g. He's disrespecting me/ putting me down).

intervention? ↓

Righteousness/ replace powerless feeling with powerful feelings/ anger (e.g. He has no right to look at me that way!).

← *intervention?* ←

Angry/ put-down thoughts; (e.g. He's a wanker and everyone knows it).

↑ *intervention?*

Pumping thoughts
(e.g. I'll show you. I'll make you sorry!).

↑ *intervention?*

***Act of violence, followed by Justification** (e.g. He got what he deserved)

* **Note:** It can also be useful to ask the participant for examples of violence he did NOT commit. This will highlight the skills he already has at intervening in his violence cycle, sometimes also called the *violence wheel.* If you use the analogy of the *wheel*, this has the advantage of being an active metaphor; you can process with the participant how he can 'stop the wheel spinning out of control' (i.e. stopping himself from being violent). Invite the participants to think of their own analogies. Encourage the participant to think of the different options he has for intervening at each stage of the wheel, in order to 'stop the wheel' and avoid violence. Encourage him to 'rewrite the script' of his violence wheel (often, the best place to intervene in the wheel is at the start).

Typical sexual offence cycle:

Motivation (e.g. Attraction to a certain type of person; wanting revenge, or to feel loved, powerful or comforted).

↓

Trigger (e.g. low mood or distressing event. Feeling like a victim. Feeling powerless). Anxiety: need to relieve or reduce anxiety/ need for comfort.

↓ *intervention?*

Fantasy Retreat to abusive fantasy to get revenge, feel more powerful (fuels distorted thoughts about victims).

↓ *intervention?*

Target victim in order to make fantasy a reality. Plan the offence. Overcome internal inhibitions.

↓ *intervention?*

Groom victim and environment around victim. e.g. encourage victim's trust; use threats or intimidation.

↓ *intervention?*

Offend

↓

In some cases:
Transitory guilt/ remorse

↓

Push away guilt using thinking distortions
(e.g. 'She wanted it.'
'I didn't hurt him/ he didn't complain.')

→ (back to Motivation)

(Ref: Wolf, 1988.)

Comments/ concerns This is a high focus, personal exercise. You may wish to introduce it by using a *one step removed* example first.

If you use templates for offending cycles, as given here, be aware that participants will vary in how their pattern 'fits' with a cycle. Allow for these differences when you explain the cycle, and use the cycles only as a general guide.

Variations This can be transformed into a powerful victim empathy exercise. To do this, set up two parallel sets of four chairs. One set represents the offender's point of view at the four different times, (i.e. the lead-up, just before, during, and after the offence). The other set represents the victim's point of view during the same time frame. Ask the group member to speak from each chair in succession, and encourage him to consider how his perspective differs from his victim's. Use the *Thinking Report for Self and Other* to record this sequence (this variation is similar to *Offence Reconstruction).*

Thinking Reports

Offending cycle; motivation to change; victim empathy; options out of offending
High focus
Groups of up to 20
Time needed: 30 - 60 minutes per Thinking Report
Worker participation: no

Method Thinking Reports are an effective tool for helping the participant identify his thoughts, feelings and behaviour during a certain event or period of time (this could be a minute, an hour or a day). The time frame is normally divided into segments: 'the lead-up (to the offence)'; 'just before'; 'during'; and 'after'. Thinking reports are best used in conjunction with either the *Offence Cycle* (see previous exercise) or with *Offence Reconstruction.*

Thinking reports help the participant to identify:

- In what way his thinking and behaviour is cyclical;
- The beliefs, irrational or otherwise, that support his behaviour;
- His 'high-risk' situations and how he deals with them;
- What potential interventions are available to him;
- What skills does he need to learn in order to practise the interventions?
- The effects of his behaviour on others *(Thinking Report for Self and Other)*

A Thinking Report is set out as follows (see templates on p.119):

- **What happened** A brief summary of what happened.
- **Thoughts** A list of all the thoughts that you remember leading up to, during and after the incident.
- **Feelings** A list of all the feelings that you experienced or that can be related to specific thoughts. If one feeling is repeated several times, give each entry a number rating, 1 - 10 (e.g. anger level 2; anger level 7). It is useful to encourage people to expand their typical feelings vocabulary, e.g. what does someone mean when they say they feel 'gutted' or 'pissed off.' Ask, 'Where in the body are those feelings? In the head? The stomach?'
- **Actions** A list of what you actually did, moment by moment.
- **'Old me'** and **'New me'** A summary of how the Thinking Report *then* would be different if the same incident were to occur *now.* This is intended to motivate the participant.

There is an example of a completed Thinking Report in the description of *Offence Reconstruction.* This example shows the usefulness of doing a *Thinking Report for Self and Other,* which emphasises the effect of one's behaviour on other people and encourages victim awareness.

Option: A motivational Thinking Report: One way to encourage a participant to believe in his ability to control his own behaviour is to ask him to complete a Thinking Report about a situation in which he *successfully* intervened in a high risk situation. Using this strategy acts as an affirmation of the skills he already possesses.

Comments/ concerns Thinking Reports must be facilitated in a spirit of mutual exploration with the participants, and not just as a means of extracting information or 'breaking through' denial. We have sometimes seen Thinking Reports used oppressively as way of 'catching out' participants or 'making them see' their distortions. Obviously we do not endorse this approach, and once again encourage you to read the note of caution on p.33 before facilitating personal level Thinking Reports.

(Continued)

(Thinking Reports continued)

Be aware that the Thinking Report is not intended to capture an exhaustive, detailed account of an offence. It is focused on key moments in order to gain essential information.

Thinking Reports move naturally into *Role Plays*. For example, from the Thinking Report we can help the participant role play typical situations where he may offend. Using role play, he can try different approaches and rehearse a better solution.

Thinking Reports have a further advantage in that they can be used very effectively in individual work.

For those participants who have difficulty with reading or writing, audio tape recorders can be provided. Alternatively, a member of staff or another participant could write for them (note: it is important to use the individual's exact words, avoiding paraphrasing).

In general, thoughts and feelings should be reported in the first person, present tense, e.g. 'What's he looking at?' rather than 'I was wondering what he was looking at'.

Variations

In order to gain a good picture of the range of responses a participant uses, ask him to complete Thinking Reports on a range of themes, for example: 'the last time that I felt disrespected,' 'the last time that I wanted to offend,' or 'the most significant incident this week.'

You can teach the concept of the Thinking Report while leading exercises such as *Frozen Picture*, *Three Picture Scene*, or *Narrated Scene*.

A useful variation of the written Thinking Report is the live action Thinking Report, which can be done using the *Frozen Picture* technique in combination with any of the processing techniques. When looking at these pictures and scenes, use the live action Thinking Reports to access the thoughts, feelings and actions of the characters in them. Where appropriate, the facilitator can advance or rewind the scene 'frame by frame' to access the thoughts and feelings of the characters at various moments in time.

Source Dr. John M Bush (1993) first developed Thinking Reports. We use an adapted version.

Thinking Report for Self

Name .... Date ....

WHAT HAPPENED: ....

THOUGHTS	FEELINGS	ACTIONS
Lead up		
Just before		
During		
After		

Underlying beliefs at the time that supported the behaviour ('Old me' thinking and beliefs):

'New me' thinking and beliefs:

Victim Awareness: Thinking Report for Self and Other

Name .... Date ....

WHAT HAPPENED: ....

ME			OTHER PERSON		
THOUGHTS	FEELINGS	ACTIONS	THOUGHTS	FEELINGS	ACTIONS
Lead up			Lead up		
Just before			Just before		
During			During		
Just after			After		

Underlying beliefs at the time that supported the behaviour ('Old me' thinking and beliefs):

'New me' thinking and beliefs:

These templates are repeated in *Appendix A* in a larger format for copying.
There is an example of a completed Thinking Report in the description of *Offence Reconstruction.*

Grandmother's Footsteps

Offending tactics; risk-taking; goal setting; group building
Low to medium focus
Groups of 6 to 20
Time needed: 15 - 30 minutes
Worker participation: one stays out, others optional

Method

This is a well known game from the school playground. A volunteer takes on the role of 'Grandmother' and stands at one end of the room facing the wall. Everyone else starts at the opposite end of the room, which will be their 'base.'

It is your task to creep up to Grandma and touch her on the shoulder without her seeing you. At any point Grandma can turn and look behind herself in your direction. At this point, you must stand absolutely still. If Grandma sees you moving she may send you back to the base, where you may start again. Grandma's decision is final. When someone reaches Grandma and touches her on the shoulder, that person becomes Grandma and we start again.

(Optional): After the group has had several successful attempts, move on to the version called ***Grandmother's Keys.*** In this version, a set of keys is placed at Grandma's heels as she again faces the wall. The difference now is that while the focus in the first version is on individual achievement, this time the exercise concentrates on team work: *It is your task, working as a team, to creep up to Grandma, get the keys, and bring them back to your base. Grandma will again turn round whenever she pleases, and if she sees you moving she will send you back to the beginning. Once the keys have been moved, Grandma has one guess each time she turns around at who has them. If she guesses correctly, then you must replace the keys and all start again. On their journey back, the keys must be passed between at least three different sets of hands and mustn't be thrown or slid along the ground. One last point: if Grandma sends you back for moving and you hold the keys, you must declare them and everyone must go back to base and start again.* (Optional rule: If Grandma guesses incorrectly three times, the team wins).

Groups usually take two or three attempts at *Grandmother's Keys.* It can be useful to encourage the team to take time outs to discuss tactics.

General processing *Did the group work together? How did you feel at each stage of the exercise? What did you do to improve your chances at each stage of the exercise? How did you feel when you got sent back?* Other areas to process: crime and getting caught; risk taking.

Personal processing: risk taking *If we think of Grandma as a symbol, who or what does she represent for you? What do the keys represent? What does getting sent back to the start represent? Was it worth the risk trying to reach Grandma, or to get the keys? Relate this exercise to risk taking and trying to achieve goals. Who or what gets in the way of you achieving your goals? What risks are worth taking to achieve them?*

Point of View Circle

Perspective taking; thinking distortions; victim empathy; handling conflict
Low to (voluntary) high focus
Groups of any size
Time needed: 5 - 20 minutes
Worker participation: yes

Method
This exercise is in two parts:

Part one With group members standing in a circle, ask for a volunteer to stand in the centre. The volunteer should stand neutrally, looking ahead and with his arms at his sides.

Ask each person in the circle to say exactly how many of the volunteer's eyes, ears and arms they can see from where they are standing. For example, 'I can see one arm, one ear and two eyes' or, 'I can see two arms, two ears and no eyes,' etc. The responses will vary as you progress around the circle person by person.

General processing (for part one) After one round, briefly process what has just occurred: *How is it possible that we are all looking at the same thing, in this case our volunteer, and yet we make such different observations? What connections to life outside this group can you make? What if I say to you there, standing across the circle from me and making such a different observation, that YOU ARE WRONG. Do I have a right to say you are wrong? What would you think about me if I made such a remark? If I totally override your point of view, what skills do you think I lack? Or, if I have those skills, why might I choose to conveniently forget them? If I think my point of view is the only correct one, what am I saying about all of you? Is that right that I should do that? How would you deal with this?*

Part two Ask everyone in the circle to change places (the volunteer does not move). Now do another round with each person saying how many of the volunteer's eyes, ears and hands they can see.

General processing (for part two) *What was the difference in the second responses? Was there a right or a wrong point of view during the exercise? How do we tell who or what is 'correct' in a situation like this? Does one person seeing things differently to you mean one of you must be wrong?*

Personal processing: *victim empathy* *What aspects of your own life would you benefit from seeing from a different point of view? Is it possible, for example, that you would be willing to look at your actions from your victim's point of view? Do they see your offence from a very different but equally correct point of view, just as we have different but equally correct points of view here in this circle? If the person in the middle represents your victim, how did (or do) different people around that person view him or her?*

In general, how do people see you? Are you seen quite differently by different people, or do most people see you in the same sort of way?

Comments/ concerns This exercise is an excellent introduction to role reversal and victim empathy. It can also be used to focus on the many different views that society has of victims (e.g. victims of sexual abuse being seen as 'provocative victims' or 'asking for it,' etc). Ask the participants how these different views of victims may work to the advantage of an abuser.

Source Adapted from Macbeth and Fine (1995).

The Way I See It

Perspective taking; victim empathy; thinking distortions
High focus
Groups of any size
Time needed: 20 to 60 minutes
Worker participation: one stays out, others optional

Method

Ask the group to think of a fictional crime that can serve as the basis of this exercise. Alternatively, you can use a news article. Set out three to five chairs, each representing a different person who has some relationship to the crime. For example, if the crime being considered is a street mugging, the chairs may represent the robber, the victim, the police, the witness, and the partner, child or parent of the robber or victim. Each character will have their own version of events and their own particular interest in the events. As the leader, you can strategically swap round the participants, so that several people have an opportunity to play the key roles. The scene is re-told (not enacted) as a series of improvised monologues by each of the characters from their different points of view. Allow and encourage the participants to become animated in the perspective of their various roles and to discover the validity and importance of each perspective.

Comments/ concerns *The Way I See It* is related to *Whole Group Role Play*, with the important distinction that in this exercise the characters speak only in monologues.

It is important to judge carefully the *readiness level* of the group when undertaking such in-depth victim awareness work.

Personal processing: *perspective taking* Ask the participants what insights they have gained about how others are affected by crime. What did they learn about their own attitudes and behaviour, as they were seeing the 'crime' through different points of view? Are they able to make direct connections with their own offences and how others might have seen them?

Variations

- ***Courtroom Scene:*** Do a courtroom scene based on a fictional crime. First, choose a judge, prosecutor and defence lawyer, and have them wait outside. Then choose a plaintiff and a defendant, and improvise a crime where the plaintiff is 'robbed' or 'harmed' (in a controlled, safe way) in some way by the defendant in front of the rest of the group. Improvise the defendant and plaintiff meeting with their lawyers. Get witnesses from the group, then hold the trial. Change roles around and use other *processing techniques* as appropriate (Brandes & Philips, 1990).

A good follow-on from this exercise is the *Victim Ripple Effect*, which focuses directly on the offences of the participants as opposed to focusing on fictional events.

Jacket on an Alien

Perspective taking; empathy; communication; dealing with pressure; any theme
Medium focus
Groups of any size
Time needed: 15 - 20 minutes or more
Worker participation: one stays out, others optional

Method The group members divide into pairs, A and B. During the first round, person A will be the 'alien' and person B will be the 'earthling':

The alien only understands very simple words and will interpret what you say absolutely literally. He makes no assumptions about how we do things here on Earth because he has never been here before. So if you say 'pick up the jacket,' the alien may use his foot to pick up the jacket, or he may make little picking gestures on the jacket, or he may hold it upside down or inside out. All instructions must be clear and detailed. Now, in your pairs, imagine it is a cold day and the alien is shivering. Imagine there is a jacket next to you (a real jacket can be used) *and person B is going to try to help the alien by explaining how to put the jacket on. Person B cannot demonstrate or use physical contact to get the alien into the jacket.*

Allow the exercise to run for several minutes, and then swap over, so the B's get a chance to be the alien. It should be a fun and frustrating challenge for the group members. As the exercise runs, encourage the aliens to be very literal in their interpretations, and encourage the earthlings to use the clearest and simplest language they can.

In some situations it will be better to describe the alien character not as an alien but as 'A person with no memory' or as 'someone who was born yesterday.' If you use one of these terms, you can call the 'Earthling' character simply the 'Helper.'

Comments/ concerns This exercise can be used to help participants to explore well known situations and concepts in a fresh way. One of the key learning points is that we do not always need to do things in the same way just because we have done them that way in the past. The exercise also contains a powerful message about not assuming other people understand the world as we do.

Processing *Have you ever had an experience like this, for instance trying to teach an infant, or trying to communicate with someone who doesn't speak a language you know? What skills did you use? Where else in life do these skills come in useful?*

Let's apply this more directly to offending and high risk situations. What are the rules you need to follow walking down a street in your neighbourhood? If this chair represents a man who is a complete stranger in your neighbourhood, what rules do you need to teach him so that he can survive there (e.g. 'Don't look at anybody.' 'Try to be invisible.' 'Look ONLY straight ahead.' 'Do absolutely nothing to draw attention.'). *Likewise, what are the rules YOU need to follow in order to survive? Can you name some of the rules you have for controlling yourself inside, for example what you do if you are feeling low or feeling attacked? Can you think of a rule you have followed in the past that has had a negative affect in your life, that does you no good anymore because it ends up hurting you or others? What new rules could you adopt that might be useful for the future?*

Variations Try to teach the alien other skills, for example 'how to tell a lie' or 'how to tell the truth.' The metaphor of teaching the alien can be used to access almost any theme related to an offending behaviour programme. Other examples: 'How to show empathy.' 'How to apologise.' 'How to back away from a potential fight and feel OK about it.' When you know the theme you want to address, identify a core skill needed and put it to the 'teaching an alien' challenge with the group.

Saints and Sinners

Handling conflict; perspective taking; self-control; motivational goal-setting
Low focus
Groups of any size
Time needed: 10 - 20 minutes
Worker participation: one stays out, others optional

Method

The group is divided into two equal teams, one at each end of the room. The worker labels one team 'Saints' and the other 'Sinners' and explains the exercise: *I am going to ask both the Saints and the Sinners a question, or make a statement to both. As a group, you then get into a close huddle for no more than 30 seconds to think of the most 'saintly' or 'sinnerly' one line response – really just a few words will do. Saints, you must be as kind, polite and well mannered as possible, really giving me the benefit of the doubt, without sounding sarcastic. And Sinners, you must be as abusive and rude as possible, giving no benefit of the doubt at all. Be as extreme as you like! When you've decided on your response, you must recite it in unison with appropriate gestures. The first statement is 'Excuse me, I think that is my seat.'*

Let the groups work out and rehearse their response and then repeat the question, first to the saints for their response and then to the sinners for theirs. Ask the groups three questions and then have them change sides so that saints become sinners and vice-versa. Suggested questions/statements:

- Could you sit down, please? I can't see.
- You appear to have picked up my coat by accident.
- Would you mind if I went in front of you? I'm not feeling well.
- Could you turn your music down please?
- Excuse me, I think you spilled my pint.
- Are you staring at me?

Comments/ concerns Be aware that you will need to permit bad language in this exercise; being censorious can defeat the object of the exercise because you will lose the stark contrast between the 'saintly' and 'sinnerly' response.

General processing *How did your perceptions of the questions or statements change? Did you prefer being a Saint or a Sinner? Why? What is it like to have to be polite when you may not want to be?*

Personal processing: *interpreting situations* After both teams have responded as Saints and Sinners, ask group members to place themselves on a *Continuum* according to how they think they generally respond to other people, as a 'Saint' or a 'Sinner' or somewhere in between. Do they respond differently in different circumstances or when with certain people? Do this for past, present and future, as a goal setting exercise.

Source This is an adapted version of a cognitive exercise used by psychologist Dr. Neil Frude.

Be Prepared

Relapse prevention; locus of control; motivation
Low focus
Groups of any size
Time needed: 20 minutes or more
Worker participation: yes (focus is on worker)

Method

Group members form a seated circle or semi-circle, focused on group worker:

1. Ask group members to share experiences of a time when they went on a journey, had experience of travel, walking in the mountains, etc. This could take the form of an opening question such as 'A journey I have been on ...'

2. Place a chair, a volunteer or yourself on centre stage as the focal point, with something to represent a rucksack.

3. Ask the group to imagine that the person represented is about to go on a journey through the mountains, an expedition. Prompt suggestions that can be recorded on flip chart around the suggested sequence:

   What situation or dangers might the traveller anticipate meeting on their journey?
   What might be the consequences if the traveller just waits to see what happens?
   What skills does he need in order to deal with these situations and to stay safe?
   How might the traveller get these skills?
   What tools might the traveller pack in his rucksack to keep himself safe?
   What sort of thinking does the traveller need to do to keep himself safe?

4. (Optional): Using *Frozen Pictures* or other techniques, participants represent and explore all of the above questions at the different stages of the traveller's journey.

General and personal level processing: *relapse prevention*

Apply the metaphor to offending behaviour and preventing relapse: Have a group member symbolically walk through the different stages of the metaphorical journey - preparation, planning, start, middle, overcoming obstacles, anticipating and negotiating hazards, adapting to unforeseen conditions, using a map, calling for help, etc. Prompt the group to make associations and direct connections between each stage of the fictional expedition and the position of an offender leaving the structure of a prison or probation programme (for example) and embarking on their own journey with the relevant risks. *What might you/he need to anticipate? What is the value of anticipating in life in general? How long is the journey ahead?*

Staying Balanced

Relapse prevention; dealing with pressure
Low to medium focus
Groups of 2 and up
Time needed: 10 - 20 minutes or more
Worker participation: one stays out, others optional

Method

Group members divide into pairs, A and B. Person A is told to adopt a physical position where they will be most stable and difficult to push over. Person B is the told to try and push Person A off balance without any use of excessive force. They are not allowed to grab, pull or hold on to limbs. They are told that they must only push lightly at first, and only against areas such as the back and shoulders, gradually increasing the amount of pressure until they unsettle Person A. When Person A moves or is otherwise unsettled (e.g. by being forced to move a foot), swap over so Person B tries to find a very stable position.

General and personal processing

What forces in life tip you over? What do you need to do to remain grounded? What forces, behaviours and life strategies might keep you solidly grounded? Is there anyone or anything that is likely to unsettle you in the future? How can you be prepared? How can you take charge of staying grounded and not falling over again?

Comments/ concerns

This exercise goes well before or after *Knee Tag* or its variations, such as *Equilibrium.*

Tin Soldiers, into Spoken Self-talk

Self-control; locus of control; relapse prevention; self-talk; trust; control of thinking
Low focus
Groups of 2 and up
Time needed: 15 - 30 minutes
Worker participation: one stays out, others optional

Method

Part one: *Tin Soldiers*: In pairs, A and B. Person A is a 'tin soldier' who walks straight ahead in a mechanical fashion unless otherwise directed. Person B is the controller. Both partners agree the control mechanisms, for example one touch between shoulders means go, touch right shoulder means turn right, etc. Important: The tin soldiers must have a 'stop' button. (Where touch is inappropriate, use verbal commands.)

When everyone is ready, person B 'winds up' their mechanical soldier and pushes the 'start button.' B must stay in close contact and redirect the tin soldier before they march into any obstructions or other soldiers. After several minutes, swap over, with person B as the tin soldier.

Intermediate processing (For Part One): *self determination/locus of control* *Are you a robot? How do you know? What makes you different from a tin soldier? Do you have free will? Can you control what your hands do and where your feet take you? Can you control what you say and do? What would lessen your control? What might the controller represent? What happens if the controller is taken away?*

Part two: *Spoken Self-talk* Next, still in pairs, person A, who is no longer a tin soldier, makes a series of decisions to do simple actions in the room and does them. B counts the number of decisions. Person A must narrate out loud all of his decisions and actions, for example, 'I've decided to look out of the window, I'm looking out of the window.' 'I've decided to sit on that chair. I am sitting on the chair.' After a few minutes, swap over, so person B makes and narrates a series of decisions while person A counts them.

Tip: You may need to add the rule: All of the actions must be 'within the realms of decency.'

Part three: *Spoken Self-talk* with interventions Still in pairs, person A makes a series of decisions to do simple actions and then makes the decision NOT to do that action. All of these decisions must be narrated, for example, 'I have decided to press the panic button. I have decided NOT to.' 'I have decided to pour that pitcher of water on the floor. I have decided NOT to.' Again, B counts the decisions. Swap over after one or two minutes.

Comments/ concerns Before attempting these exercises, group members should be comfortable doing trust exercises (e.g. *Trust Walking*). Part one should be done in silence unless there is a real emergency, e.g. someone needs to say 'stop' in order to prevent a collision. Halt the exercise if you need to reinforce the rules.

Processing Focus processing on self-talk and self-management, locus of control, personal responsibility, relapse prevention and decision-making: *What connection exists between this exercise and offending? What is it like to take back full responsibility for all your decisions and actions? Do you prefer it this way, or would you like others to make decisions for you? What are the advantages and disadvantages of being a robot, or of being a responsible human being?*

Variation To emphasise the contrast between external and internal locus of control, run the exercise *Master/ Servant* in between parts one and two of this exercise.

Surrounded

Self-control skills; handling conflict; locus of control
High focus
Group size: four and up
Time needed: 10- 20 minutes per participant
Worker participation: no

Method

Surrounded focuses specifically on coping with direct provocation and 'fight or flight' situations. The exercise is particularly relevant for groups addressing anger, violence and aggression. *Surrounded* follows on naturally from *Get Them to the Corner* or the *Two Person Exercise.*

Preparation: Establish a stage area in one part of the room. Ask for a volunteer, who should stand on the stage in a neutral posture, looking ahead with hands by his side.

1. Just as in the *Two Person Exercise*, ask the group to place the scene in a location outside of the home, for example a pub, club, football match, the street, etc.
2. Ask the group to give the character a name in order to create some distance between the volunteer and the character he is presenting. (For this outline we call the character 'Gavin' and imagine he is at a football match) Explain to the group that as the scene begins, there is no problem; Gavin is simply watching the match.
3. Ask for another volunteer. As in the *Two Person Exercise*, this character stands a few feet behind Gavin, staring at the back of his head. Gavin can look around and get eye contact if he wants to. Do some processing here by asking both observers and onstage characters how Gavin might feel at this stage. Ask for another volunteer. They also stand behind Gavin, adding to the pressure. Again, ask for thoughts and feelings for Gavin. Carry on with this process, so that you gradually set up a semi-circle around Gavin. Explore how Gavin may now feel, and, if he feels threatened, at what point he would act (e.g. run or fight).
4. Ask those in the semi-circle gradually to move in. Process Gavin's thoughts and feelings as they come closer. When they are at arm's length from Gavin, get them to gently restrain him by holding his shoulders and arms. Their grip should be reasonably firm but not too aggressive.
5. Optional: Give the group member playing the character Gavin the task of breaking free from the semi-circle. He must be careful not to be too aggressive. The group must restrain Gavin, but also with care. The struggle is meant to be brief and wordless, lasting only 15 - 20 seconds.

Move into processing immediately, focusing first on Gavin's responses.

Note: Stage five is optional, and should only be attempted when you are certain the group is ready and controlled enough to use overt contact and also that the volunteer playing Gavin can handle this sort of physical challenge without becoming violent or otherwise uncontrollable. As a precaution, before giving the signal to start you should ask participants to remove watches, rings and glasses and anything else that could be damaged or potentially dangerous. You should also practise a 'Stop' signal with them in case you need to end the scene suddenly.

(Continued)

(Surrounded: Continued)

Comments/ concerns

The purpose of *Surrounded* is primarily to generate a live and powerful fight or flight response. Even though the situation is very controlled and all of the participants involved should be reminded that there will be no actual violence, the simulation and the actual physical struggle against the restraining participants will in almost all cases generate powerful feelings and a physical adrenaline rush. These feelings and sensations can then be processed in the here and now, with the participant practising real time calming strategies and talking himself down from a potential fight. When handled with good judgement and the right controls, this exercise can be a highly memorable milestone for the participants, particularly those who struggle with the concept of self-control and self-calming techniques. Exercises such as *Surrounded* can help violent offenders to explore the thoughts, feelings and physiological changes that occur when they become highly fearful, and to practise coping strategies for dealing with direct provocations.

The exercise must be processed thoroughly in order to prevent any negative effects. Start with more able group members in the 'Gavin' role, then offer the less able group members a chance to be the central character.

To do this exercise safely, there needs to be a clear level of group cohesion and respect. Groups often have scapegoats, so ensure that the central volunteer is not someone that the group might otherwise pick on.

Also note: *Surrounded* should only be used when you are confident that all of the group members accept responsibility for their own violence. Otherwise there is a danger that the exercise will reinforce the feeling of being a powerless victim of provocation from others.

General processing

If this were a real situation in the outside world, what would Gavin and the rest of the group have done? How does anyone react when they feel watched, judged or stared at? Ask the group to reflect on their own experience of such situations. How might this relate to their own attitudes to fights and to masculine values? Is this a common or rare occurrence for them? What would precipitate such a scene?

Personal processing

Ask the group member who has played 'Gavin' what is happening right now inside his body. How fast is his heart beating? Is he sweating? Can he feel his muscles tense with adrenaline? What thoughts is he having? Now, the most important bit, what can he do RIGHT NOW to calm himself down? Let him suggest his own self-calming techniques and encourage ideas from the group (e.g. walking around the room, stretching, deep breaths, stepping outside the room or the building). Encourage him to use the techniques 'right here and now,' and watch while he returns to normal. Have him 'narrate' his internal state as he calms himself. Finally, process the personal connections with the 'Gavin' character's situation, and de-role the volunteer.

Variation

You may find that the exercise works well with no setting at all, and all you need to do is set up the central person and the surrounding people to raise the fight/flight response.

The Rabbit's Tale

Control of thinking; relapse prevention; self control
Low focus
Groups of any size
Time needed: 10 minutes
Worker participation: no (focus is on the worker)

Method

Group sitting in a semi-circle, facing worker.

Worker: *I am going to tell a story, and as I tell it, I do not want you to listen to me at all or think of the central character, a rabbit called Harry. No, you absolutely must not imagine or picture Harry the rabbit with big floppy ears as he sits in the front seat of a little red Morris Minor and drives out of the Texaco petrol station at 70 miles per hour, sparks flying and ears flapping out of his car window... And furthermore I don't want you to picture or remember Harry the rabbit speeding through a construction site and narrowly missing a workman with a BLUE stop sign* [sic] *directing traffic, then zooming past Viv's Cafe and Gabrielle's Tattoo Parlour ... etc. etc.*

Continue the story for 90 seconds at most, just enough to make the point. It does not matter what the story is, as long as it contains vivid details and lots of action, to make it harder to ignore. Hint: put in lots of small memorable details, such as names, places, numbers or odd details (e.g. a blue stop sign).

General processing *Who remembers any parts of the story? What bits really drew you in? Who managed not to hear any of it? How did you do that? Were you using a particular technique, such as counting numbers or thinking of something else? Did anything stop the technique from being effective?*

Ask the group members to think about the exercise and some of the tactics they used to block out the story. Would these tactics be useful for someone who is trying to control his behaviour? What aspects of these intervention tactics would group members need to develop?

Personal processing: control of thinking; relapse prevention *Relate this to relapse prevention and self-control. How much do you control what you think about? Do you control your mind or does your mind control you? Can you control or determine EVERY thought that enters your mind? Or is it that you control what you then do with that thought? If thinking about offending has in the past led to you offend, what's the message about controlling thinking? How often do you think about offending? How long does a thought have to last to move from being a lapse to a relapse?*

Variations

In a closely related exercise called ***Make Me Laugh***, group members split into pairs and take it in turns to make the other laugh without resorting to touch in any way. The other person's task is to not laugh.

Another variation, called ***Count Down From 100***, has one of the pair counting down from 100 to 0, while the other person tries to make them hesitate or lose the count. Even more difficult: Count down from 100 in increments of 7 (100, 93, 86, etc.) while being distracted.

CHAPTER 6

Interactive Observer: the First Dramatic Involvement

This chapter covers five techniques illustrating the interactive observer approach:

- **Group Character Creation**
- **The Two Person Exercise**
- **Narrated Scenes**
- **Worker in Role: The Enacted Scene**
- **Worker in Role: Hot Seating**

INTRODUCTION

As we outlined in *Chapter 3*, at the most basic level the term *Interactive Observer* simply describes a group member who actively comments on and responds to a dramatic character or situation from the safety of his own seat.

In Geese Theatre's approach, *Interactive Observer* scenes are usually the first time group members engage with dramatic situations and characters. We often use these techniques before *Frozen Pictures* and *Role Play* (see following chapters) because they are generally *low focus* but they still encourage a high degree of involvement from the group members. Where appropriate, *Interactive Observer* scenes can serve as a stepping stone to the higher focus next levels, *Frozen Pictures* and *Role Plays*, where the participants create and improvise their own characters and scenes.

When using *Interactive Observer* techniques, we devise dramatic characters and situations in order to promote challenging debate about relevant themes. These characters and situations are always *one step removed*, and are presented in one of two ways:

- **Participants on stage** In techniques such as *The Two Person Exercise* and *Narrated Scenes*, one or two participants may be asked to represent the onstage role, but they will not be asked to dramatise the role. Only rarely would we ask a participant to speak in role during an *Interactive Observer* scene. In general, group members will be instructed to just stand still or perform a series of simple actions, while the facilitator and the rest of the group generate the dramatic content and debate the pros and cons of the scene.

- **Worker on stage** In the *Worker in Role* techniques, we present the scenes and characters ourselves, inviting the rest of the group to interact with the characters we present. This gives us total control over the action and allows us to shift focus and emphasis as the need arises.

A note about *Degree of Distance*

In this chapter and in *Chapters 7* and *8*, we include the *Degree of Distance* in the quick reference guide at the start of each new technique. This tells you at a glance whether the technique is suitable for work at *One Step Removed*, the *Personal Level*, or both.

Group Character Creation

Aim: To create representative characters who will help focus attention on any relevant theme
Low to high focus
Group size: any number
Time needed: 5-15 minutes to create the character, unlimited time to utilise the character
Worker participation: no
Degree of distance: One Step Removed only

Method

Group Character Creation is a very adaptable technique where you and the participants invent characters to place in particular circumstances to highlight any relevant theme. By working with invented characters, participants can feel at a safe distance to discuss or narrate events that otherwise might be too close, painful or shameful to discuss on the personal level.

To begin, outline the general theme for the session, for example, 'thoughts and feelings before, during and after the offence.' Then ask the participant(s) to help you create 'a typical person who might be in this group, who has committed an offence that would get him sent to this group,' or another relevant description.

Now, ask questions to build up the profile of this archetypal character (you may want to use a flipchart):

- *Is the character male or female?*
- *How old?*
- *In a relationship?*
- *What are his/her living circumstances? Living alone? With parents? On the street?*
- *Does he/she have a job?*
- *Does he/ she have children?*
- *What are his/ her interests?*
- *Who are his/ her friends?*
- *Imagine you meet this person for the first time. What would your impressions be?*
- *What would he/ she be like on a bad day? On a good day?*
- *What's the offence? What were the circumstances surrounding it?*

Any other questions that will help to build up the character.

(Continued)

(Group Character Creation: Continued)

After the character has been established, you can use the processing techniques to further develop the character. You also have the option of asking a participant to take on the role:

- *If this person were sitting in this chair just prior to the offence, what would he/she be feeling?*
- *Thinking? What would he/she NOT be thinking about?*
- *Who can sit in the chair and represent the character?*
- *How should he sit to represent how the character is feeling just before the offence? During it?*
- *What actions does he do during the offence itself? After the offence? What are the feelings? What are the thoughts?*

After establishing one character, you can go on to create others using the same methods. It is often useful, for example, to build up partner—partner, parent—child or friend—friend pairings, in order to gain different perspectives on the events and themes discussed.

If the participants enjoy the character(s) they have created, you can revisit the characters each session to monitor their progress, like an instalment in a television serial: *'It is now week seven and the last time we saw (our character) he'd gone a month without having a fight. How is he feeling about that? Has he had a lapse this week? How did he deal with it? Did he see it coming? Did he ask for help before the lapse? Did he use any of the strategies he's been practising lately? Why or why not?'*

Comments This technique can be used in combination with a wide array of others such as *Thinking Reports, The Offence Cycle, Frozen Pictures, Role Play* and the other *Interactive Observer* techniques.

Variations *Group Character Creation* can evolve organically from general discussion, and can help participants to get involved imaginatively without having to leave their chairs. For example, in a group session a participant says that she usually gets into trouble when she is bored and 'Everything is boring.' As facilitator, you might take a chair, place it in front of the group, and say, *Alright, here's a chair. Boredom is in it. What is it? Is it a person? How are they seated? What's happening in her life? What's NOT happening? What's making her so bored? What are her choices? Who can come and be her for a moment so we can make this more immediate?* etc.

Other possibilities: It is not necessary to use a chair or a participant to represent the character. You can use one or more masks to represent each character, or drawings or photographs, anything that will denote the character and help the group to become interested in their collective creation.

Two Person Exercise

Aims: Raising discussion about themes of aggression, violence, personal space, thinking skills, perspective taking and other relevant themes
Low to high focus
Group size: 4 or more
Time needed: 20 - 45 minutes
Worker participation: no
Degree of distance: One Step Removed only

Method

The *Two Person Exercise* is perhaps the simplest and most effective way to link together concepts such as the *mask* we present to the outside world, how we interpret other people and situations, inner voice concepts such as self-talk and thinking skills, and personal space, among others. It is also useful in highlighting the distinction between thoughts and feelings and how both influence our behaviour.

Ask two participants to stand neutrally, with hands at their sides and looking straight ahead, facing the rest of the group. Person A should stand a significant distance behind and slightly to the side of person B:

A

B

Ask the group to imagine that the scene they are looking at is out of the room, in some other setting 'where there is a potential for violence or offending.' Build up a story for the picture. Allow all responses, but concentrate on one that is real and relevant to the participants, for example, in the pub, at school, in the street, at a bus stop, at a football match, etc. To prompt ideas, it may help to ask the group to view the picture as if it were a progression of 'stills' from a film they are scripting.

Ask questions that build on this established story and reveal the sub-text:

- *Do you think A and B know each other?*
- *What is A thinking right now? What is B thinking?*
- *What are they feeling?*

Ask A to take a few steps forward and continue looking straight ahead. Develop the story:

- *How has the picture changed?*
- *Who has the most power in this situation? Why?*
- *What are their thoughts and feelings now?*

Ask A to take a few steps forward and to look at the back of B's head. Continue developing the story:

- *Who is in the more powerful position now?*
- *Is B aware that A is looking at the back of his head?*
- *If he is aware, what might he be thinking and feeling?*

(Continued)

(Two Person Exercise: Continued)

Bring A level with B and ask him to keep looking at B. Repeat the questions, and ask further,

- *What is going on under their masks (speaking metaphorically)?*
- *What are the masks that these men would be using now?*
- *What three things could person A do right now to radically change the scene? What about person B?*

Now ask B to return A's stare.

Continue to expand the story, linking the group's responses by developing *Thinking Reports* for both characters as the scene develops.

A and B now turn to face each other.

Process the characters' thoughts and feelings and develop the story verbally to its logical conclusion. After the story reaches its conclusion go back to the *Thinking Reports* and ask the group to identify the thinking and feeling process which leads to the outcome of the scene. For example, if the observers develop a story in which a fight breaks out between A and B, they should be able to look back over the Thinking Report and see the places where, for example, B was feeling threatened, or A misinterpreted B's body language, etc.

Comments On pp.213-214, the Two Person Exercise is used as the basis for a sample of dialogue from a groupwork session. The excerpt demonstrates, among other things, the importance of maintaining a clear focus in processing the Two Person Exercise, which can otherwise become so open to interpretation that it loses its meaning.

Additionally, because the Two Person Exercise represents a scene of potentially volatile conflict, we must be careful that the tension does not get out of control. If you sense the scene is becoming too stressful or too confrontational, either finish the scene or use processing techniques such as *Role Rotation* or *Reworking the Scene* (e.g. 'rewind') to modulate the tension.

The Two Person Exercise has strong connections with the previous technique, *Group Character Creation*, and also to the following technique, *Narrated Scenes.* Indeed it is possible to combine the three techniques into a sequence.

Variations A useful variation is ***Personal Space:*** Ask a participant to stand in front of the group in the position of person B. As person A walks one pace at a time toward him, ask him when person A has crossed into his personal space. Alternatively, run this as a whole group exercise in pairs. Develop this into a group discussion about personal space and what it represents, and what happens if theirs is violated or if they violate someone else's.

Narrated Scenes

Aims: To present characters and scenarios used to focus on any relevant theme; cognitive distortions; empathy; attitudes and beliefs
Low to high focus
Group size: 4 and up
Time needed: 15 - 45 minutes per scene
Worker participation: one stays out, others optional
Degree of distance: One Step Removed only

Method

Narrated Scenes are short, simple scenes devised and directed by the group worker in order to highlight a particular theme. They are always *one step removed* scenes. The great advantage of using Narrated Scenes is that they can be designed with specific details in order to prompt debate about any relevant topic. Even the simplest, shortest (e.g. 30 seconds) Narrated Scenes can provide enough material for long and in-depth group exploration.

Narrated Scenes are effective because they are open to interpretation. They invite observers to find meaning and imagine details. Observers will naturally fill in details that are most familiar to them, which makes Narrated Scenes an excellent means of highlighting themes that are important to the participants. It is absolutely essential that, when facilitating Narrated Scenes, we make every effort to keep the content of the scene open, generic and non-culturally specific so that everyone in the group can 'fill in' details according to their own perception. After the scene is played, everyone is allowed to voice their interpretations, and this usually results in an active debate. This is the point of Narrated Scenes.

1 First, ensure that everyone understands what narration is, perhaps by giving examples of narration from film, books or television. For the purposes here, you can define narration as a voiceover describing the action.

2 Ask for one—or in some cases two—volunteer(s). Instruct them to mime everything you say, to 'do no more and no less than I say in the narration.'

3 After you have set the scene for the volunteers and agreed the layout of the stage area, you narrate a simple scene, using the style we suggest in the examples below. The narration is delivered in the present tense, using generic descriptions that do not imply a particular interpretation of the actions. The narration is meant to result in a scene of pure behaviour that the observers are asked to interpret.

With rare exceptions, don't describe or infer thoughts or feelings. Also, be aware of using loaded words such as 'He looks through the fence in a *sinister* way.' Such descriptions limit the range of interpretation and thus demand less investment from the observers.

The characters you describe should also be as generic as possible. As shown in the examples below, in order to make the characters generic, we recommend you refer to them simply as 'the man,' 'the woman,' 'the boy,' 'the girl', 'the child,' 'he,' 'she,' etc. We have found this helps observers to freely interpret the behaviour without being preoccupied with the particulars of the character.

(Note: It is perfectly acceptable to read out the narration from a script. In fact, it may be better to read out the narration in order to ensure that all of the details you want to highlight are included. It may also reassure volunteers to know that you are not just inventing the scene as you go.)

(Continued)

(Narrated Scenes: Continued)

4 After the scene is played out, go back to the start and process the action as illustrated in the following examples. When *processing* the action, it may help to name the character(s) and give them some personal background.

Examples of *Narrated Scenes*

A one person scene: shoplifting
Group worker speaking to a participant in a women's offending behaviour group: *Alright, I'd like you to stand over here until I begin to narrate the scene. When I do the narration, I'd like you to do only what the narration says, no more and no less. Just so we know where we are, we will say that over here is the entrance to the shop, and over there is the counter where the cashier is. Alright, we can start.*

(The volunteer mimes the following actions as the worker verbally narrates them)

The woman enters the shop, stops, and looks around the shop. She looks over in the direction of the cashier. She goes over to a clothes rack and moves the clothes along the clothes rail one at a time, as if she is looking for a particular item. She chooses one and takes it from the clothes rail. She goes to another part of the shop and picks up another item. She turns her back to the cashier and quickly puts the first item inside her jacket. She puts the second item back on the clothes rail. She looks at her watch and then briefly in the direction of the cashier and then leaves the shop.

After the scene is played out, use the *processing techniques* to examine the motives, thoughts and feelings of the fictional woman in the scene. Focusing on the shoplifting, you may wish to focus on such themes as responsibility, consequences, the offending cycle or relapse prevention. For example, if you wanted to focus on the themes of consequences and relapse prevention, you might process as follows:

Let's go back to the moment just before she goes into the shop and hear some thoughts and feelings from the audience. Now she's entered the shop, and she's looking around. What's she looking for? What is she thinking right now? What is she NOT thinking about? ... Now let's go to the moment she is leaving the shop. Again, what's she thinking now? What's the feeling? ... Now what if we go forward in time? What's the next scene? What does she do with the clothes?... Has she been caught? Has she done this before? Was someone else involved? Did she do this willingly or was someone pressuring her? Her friends? Her boyfriend? Does she have children? Does that make a difference? What are the consequences for her and for them if she gets caught? Has she been caught before?

The processing may lead to further scenes, *Frozen Pictures* or *Role Plays.*

A two person scene: sexual harassment at school
Two volunteers (both male group members) stand in the stage area of the room. One is meant to be a 15-year-old boy standing in the corridor with a group of his friends, the other is meant to be a girl the same age.

(Note: Where you are using two people in a scene, explain the limits of any physical contact there will be before starting. In most cases, you would explain that any physical contact will only be broadly indicated by gestures and that no actual contact will take place. You may wish to demonstrate exactly what you mean by having, for example, two group members shake hands while standing ten feet apart from each other. This will establish the theatrical convention that characters can be in contact even though the actors are not in contact.)

(Continued)

(Narrated Scenes: Continued)

The boy is standing with a group of friends. The girl walks past. The boy raises his hand to his mouth as if to shout something, and then turns back to his friends. The girl stops, looks behind her at the boy, and walks on. The boy walks several paces behind her and waves his hand as if to say hello. The girl turns and holds her right hand out with the palm facing the boy. The boy holds both of his hands out to his sides with his palms facing up. He looks back at his friends again.

After the scene is played, use *processing techniques* to focus on themes such as power and control, empathy, personal responsibility, self-control, boys' sexual attitudes, the influence of peers, or any of the themes related to sexual aggression (e.g. distorted beliefs such as 'when a girl says no she means maybe'). It will be particularly useful to focus on the hand gestures, what they mean, what they are intended to say and how they are interpreted by the characters and the observers.

Depending on the group, the scene can be adapted to reflect an older age group or a different type of harassment/ abuse (e.g. the genders could be reversed). Regardless of the specific theme focused on, it will be crucial for the audience to voice what the victim character is thinking and feeling in relation to what the abuser is doing. This is to avoid any possible misinterpretation about the abusive nature of the interaction.

Note: Remember to *de-role* participants.

Further examples of narrated scenes

One person scenes:

Burglary *The man walks slowly to the back fence, stops, and puts on his gloves. He reaches over the gate and unlatches it from the inside. He walks into the back garden and walks to the kitchen window. He looks in. He takes out a tool and begins to lever the window open.*

Violence *The man is standing at the bar, drinking from a pint glass. He looks across the room at another person and nods his head once as if he is acknowledging the other person. He looks away and takes a drink. ... He looks back in the same direction. He looks away and takes another drink. ... He looks back a third time, puts the glass on the bar, and gestures with both hands out to his sides with his palms up. He takes his pint glass and throws whatever is left in the glass onto the floor and walks two steps in the direction of the other person.*

Domestic violence *The man sits and watches television. Somebody walks in the room. He looks at his watch. He looks off to his left at the other person, and his eyes follow the other person as they walk across the room in front of him. He looks back at the television. He looks again in the direction where we imagine the other person is now. Holding the look, he gets up and switches off the television. He takes something off the top of the television. He faces the other person and holds out the object in his hand. He lets it drop to the floor.*

Sexual offending *The man sits at his desk at a computer keyboard. He looks at the screen. He types. He waits. He types some more. He pulls a second chair along side his own. He turns to his right and holds his hand to his mouth as if he is calling out to another person.*

(Continued)

(Narrated Scenes: Continued)

Two person scene:

Car theft/ joyriding *The two young men are in the car, and the driver is turning the wheel in a way that indicates he is driving very fast. Both of them gesture out of the windows as if they are shouting to people they know. The passenger waves his hand forward as if to say 'go faster.' The driver accelerates. The passenger nods his head a few times. The driver points out of the window and looks to his right. As he points the passenger quickly puts his hands in front of his face and they both jerk forward as if the car is braking suddenly. The car has stopped. They both turn and look back through the rear window. They both look forward again and the driver accelerates away.*

Comments

Allow plenty of time for *processing* after Narrated Scenes. Participants who take the roles in the scene often need extra time to process, especially if they have committed offences or been victims of offences similar to those portrayed.

As your confidence grows in using Narrated Scenes, you will see that they provide a very fluid dramatic form that can be adapted to a wide range of group suggestions and needs. Start by using the most basic processing technique, *Opening Up Discussion* ('What do you think is going on?'). Where appropriate, use *Role Rotation* and *Inner Voice from the Audience* to further develop the discussion.

One last point: When processing Narrated Scenes, avoid relying on the volunteers who have portrayed the scene to be arbiters of what the scene is 'really' about or what their character's were 'really' thinking. Remember that the volunteers know the scene no better than the observers; they portrayed the scene simply by following the narration. Therefore it is best to avoid using *Interview in Role* or *Inner Voice from the Characters* when processing Narrated Scenes.

Variation

Narrated Scenes can also be based on news stories, as long as they do not relate directly to anyone in the group.

Worker in Role: The Enacted Scene

Aims: any relevant theme
Low focus
Group size: 4 and up
Time needed: 20 - 60 minutes
Worker participation: yes (the worker is in role). Co-worker required
Degree of distance: One Step Removed only

Method

The Enacted Scene is one of only two techniques in this handbook (the following technique, *Hot Seating*, is the other) requiring a group worker to enter into role. If this is not an option for you, *Group Character Creation*, the *Two Person Exercise* or *Narrated Scenes* or can be just as useful if you want to use an *Interactive Observer* approach.

An Enacted Scene is a short, simple and naturalistic performance, lasting 30 seconds to three minutes, which is performed by one or more of the group workers to mirror the participants' own experiences and dilemmas and to prompt debate about the central themes of the group. The scene is always tailored to the specific offending behaviour group it is presented in, and usually shows an offence which is relevant to the offenders present. The scene presented will always be at *one step removed.*

Enacted Scenes have much in common with *Narrated Scenes.* The key difference is that in the Enacted Scene the worker performs the scene and there is no narration. Enacted Scenes can also use spoken dialogue while *Narrated Scenes* are always silent.

1 Before performing the scene, tell the observers where it is set. Outline for them where the door is, for example, where particular rooms are, where certain important objects are located. On some occasions, you may wish to leave the surroundings ambiguous in order to promote discussion and debate about what happens in the scene. With some groups, particularly those who find it difficult to tolerate ambiguity, you may need to be highly specific about the imagined environment.

2 Next, establish with the group how you will let them know when you are in or out of role. For example, you may use a particular item of clothing such as a jacket when you are in role. When you remove the jacket, this will represent leaving the role. This is an absolutely essential convention if you wish to avoid confusion about the difference between you and the character you will portray.

3 Perform the scene (see example).

4 Replay the scene, allowing the group members to stop the action at any point and imagine the character's thoughts and feelings in that moment. Use any of the *Processing Techniques* to develop the interaction between your character and the observers.

Example: 'Man walks into a pub'

This is an example of an Enacted Scene we have used in hundreds of groups addressing violence and anger. The scene is presented by one worker and is performed silently, using simple mime. Watching in silence allows the observers to fill in the dialogue, imagining what the characters are saying to each other and what tones of voice are used.

(Continued)

(Worker in Role: The Enacted Scene: Continued)

Description of the mimed scene: *The man slams his front door quickly and walks out into the street. He looks up at the sky, pulls his jacket collar up around his neck, and hunches his shoulders up as if it is raining and cold. He is frowning and walks with heavy steps ... He walks for some time ... He walks into the pub, and stops to look around at the people sitting at tables. He walks to the bar. He raises his hand and orders a drink. He stands two feet back from the bar as he waits for his drink. He looks down the bar and nods at another man at the bar. He gets his drink and pays for it, then walks to a seat and sits with his back against the wall. He watches two men playing pool in the opposite corner. He walks over and puts money on the table for a game, nodding to both men. He returns to his seat and carries on drinking. He notices that the two men at the pool table are setting up another game. He walks over to the two men and gestures with his hands as if to say, 'What's going on?' He points his finger at one. He grabs a pool cue (mimed), ready to strike. The scene freezes.*

Go back to the start and process the thoughts and feelings of the main character. As the worker in role returns to the start of the scene, the co-worker can start the processing with questions such as:

What did you see? Let's go through it step by step. (After coming to an agreed version of the 'facts', proceed with): *Why do you think he slammed the door? What was he thinking and feeling as he walked to the pub? Did he know where he was going? What was he doing when he looked around the pub when he walked in? Why did he stand back from the bar? By his behaviour, would you say he has been in fights before? Why did he nod to the other man down the bar from him? Why sit with his back to a wall? Why the fight? What does fighting do for him? How is the fight related to the door slam earlier in the scene? Etc.*

Alright, let's go with the idea that this man has already had previous arrests for this kind of violence. What if he has already been through a programme like this, and he thought he had his violence sorted? What should he be thinking or doing when he leaves his house or even when he walks into the pub? What should he NOT be thinking or doing? Let's have someone try a new idea or thought that the man could have, or ask the man a question, or try out a different option by coming up and being the man for a moment.

Optional further exploration: *What's happened in his life to make him so ready for a fight? What has never happened in his life?*

Comments As this example shows, even when there is more than one character in a scene, it can still be performed by just one worker. The audience imagines the actions of the unseen character(s) based on the behaviour of the observable character. Moreover, as the piece is performed with only one actor, the observers must imagine what the other characters in the scene are saying, thinking and feeling at each point. This is particularly useful for increasing empathy skills.

Don't be afraid to perform these simple scenes. They serve as a good example for the participants. When they see you are willing to portray a character, they will see it is a natural way of working and will be that much more willing to do it themselves. Don't worry about giving a polished performance; the scene simply needs to be understandable and believable.

Variations After the scene is portrayed and run again with audience interaction, one of the group members can be invited to take the role of the victim or other significant person in it.

Other variations: You can combine the Enacted Offence with *Thinking Reports* by asking the observing group members to build up a *Thinking Report* for the observed offence.

When you go back over the scene, it is sometimes useful to verbalise short phrases which will make your character's actions or intent clearer. You can highlight key moments, such as the moment in the above example when the man gestures with his hands as if to say, 'What's going on?' You could then voice what he says next, and debate with the group from role about the way to handle this situation.

Source See *Glossary*.

Worker in Role: Hot Seating

Aims: any theme
Low focus
Group size: 4 and up
Time needed: 20 - 40 minutes
Worker participation: yes (the worker is in role). Co-worker required
Degree of distance: One Step Removed only

Method

Hot Seating is a technique very much akin to the processing technique *Interview in Role*, but differs in that we usually focus on one character, and that character is usually played by the worker. Hot Seating also differs in that it is always done at *one step removed.*

Hot Seating can be usefully done as the continuation of an *Enacted Scene* (see previous exercise). Occasionally it may be used both before and after an *Enacted Scene*.

In Hot Seating, the worker speaks in character and answers questions put to her by the participants/ observers. This provides a good opportunity for the questioners to encounter points of view and attitudes different from their own. When participants confront an onstage character, they are encouraged to challenge their own belief systems. This is very often a key stage before the participant can explicitly address his own personal issues and offending behaviour.

Alternatively, the worker in role may offer information or ask questions of the participants, depending on the nature of the character and the aim of the session.

A useful technique: The participants ask questions of your character as if they are experts in the relevant field (e.g. child abuse experts; police detectives; forensic psychologists).

There are different types of role that a worker may portray, and different functions for the interactions that result:

ROLE	FUNCTION
Offender	Can put the observers in the role of expert questioners, spotting and challenging his distortions, justifications and irresponsible thinking. Can put observers in the position of advice-givers, helping him to 'go straight.' Can talk about the thinking behind his offence, seeking to establish collusion with the participants by saying 'we all know the score.' Invites paradoxical reaction against his pro-offending thinking.
Professional	Can offer professional opinions, e.g. a child care worker speaking about the effects of abuse on children. A useful strategy: The worker is the 'professional' and the observers are the 'supervisors' (e.g. The worker is a child protection officer and the observers are the line manager consulting on a difficult case; or: The worker is a teacher and the observers are the head teacher. The teacher is asking advice about how to deal with a boy who has been taking money and jewellery from other pupils.) By making the group members the 'supervisor', the worker in role can 'withhold expertise' (Heathcote & Bolton, 1995) and encourage the group members to become 'experts' on the issue.
Witness	Can tell the participants what he saw and ask them what they think it was about and what the effects might be, e.g. a next door neighbour who overhears a woman being beaten by her husband night after night.

(Continued)

(Worker in Role: Hot Seating: Continued)

Victim Can put the participants in the position of being responsible, offering concerned advice, e.g. a burglary victim asks for advice. Or: a victim of bullying asks for advice. Note: The victim role can be a particularly difficult role for workers to play, and demands a great deal of skill to be carried out safely and with clear boundaries. In particular, playing a victim role may make it difficult to return to one's own role as facilitator.

Reporter Asks for the expertise of the participants in a co-operative effort to find out what 'really happened' and how people were affected, e.g. (in sexual abuse groups) a reporter investigates why a girl tried to run away the day before her stepfather was released from prison.

Comments

A useful aspect of this technique is that while in role you can reflect back to the group members many of their own distortions and justifications, and then encourage them to argue against their own thinking. If this is done respectfully, the participants will want to engage with your character. For example, if you are in role as an offender, group members may spontaneously identify with certain statements you make, i.e. 'That's what I used to say.'

Another tendency is that group members will often pick up and challenge the onstage offender about certain behaviours they recognise as being close to their own. For example: You have enacted a scene in which you portray a burglar stealing from a house. During Hot Seating, a group member reminds you that you pulled out a (mimed) screwdriver in order to break into the house. He challenges you when you say 'I didn't plan it, I just saw the open window and went in. It's their fault. Anyone would have done the same.'

Group members often become angry at these sorts of distortions and justifications. If they do, so much the better, because in role as the offender you can now challenge them in the same way: 'Well if you're going to challenge me like that, tell me what excuses YOU use.' This is where *Hot Seating* comes into its own as a powerful consciousness-raising technique, as it affords you the unique, privileged position of being both facilitator and 'group member' simultaneously. While in role as an offender, the dramatic convention allows you to enter into dialogue with the participants as if you too are a group member. Your 'expert distance' is temporarily removed. Assuming you are working from a position of rapport and respect for the group members, you can, while in a 'peer' role, challenge distortions and justifications with far more effect than you can from the position of facilitator or 'authority figure.'

Reminder:
Please read *Worker in Role: The Enacted Scene* for guidance about defining when you are in and out of role.

Source See *Glossary*

CHAPTER 7

Frozen Pictures: Creating Static Scenes and Characters

This chapter describes several of the most common and effective types of *Frozen Pictures:*

- **Single Frozen Picture**
- **Monuments**
- **Add to the Picture**
- **Three Picture Scenes**

INTRODUCTION

Frozen Pictures are sometimes called by equivalent terms such as 'still images,' 'sculpts' or 'tableaux.' They are the live equivalent of a photographic snapshot. They are created by the participants, who enter into a dramatic or 'as if' situation and hold, or 'freeze', a moment in time.

We normally use Frozen Pictures to focus directly on offending related themes. The dramatic situation portrayed in Frozen Pictures can be *one step removed* or on the *personal level.* Any of the *processing techniques* can be used to explore the thinking, feeling and behaviour of the characters, and also to develop the scene.

A note about *Degree of Distance*
As in *Chapters 6* and *8*, in this chapter we include the *Degree of Distance* in the italicised quick reference guide at the start of each new *Frozen Picture* technique. This tells you whether the technique is suitable for work at *one step removed,* the *personal level,* or both.

Single Frozen Picture

Aim: any theme
Medium to high individual focus
Minimum of 2 people required
Time needed: 10 - 30 minutes
Worker participation: optional
Degree of distance: One Step Removed or Personal Level

Method

The Single Frozen Picture is probably the simplest and easiest form of dramatic exercise we use. It can be used to address any relevant theme, and can often become the centrepiece for whole sessions.

To create Frozen Pictures, form groups of two to five people and ask each group to create a Frozen Picture. If there are only two participants, have one sculpt himself into a Frozen Picture while the other acts as observer. Likening the picture to a photograph, statue or paused video film may help explain the concept. It may also be useful to demonstrate a Frozen Picture with a co-worker or another member of the group. It is important to stress that it is just a picture and that there is no movement or speech. It may also be useful to stress that because the group only have their bodies and faces to convey what is happening, they need to be as precise as possible (It may be useful to do *Monuments* first in order to teach this).

As an option, you can give the groups a title for their Frozen Picture, for example 'The Argument' or 'The Secret.' More examples are given below. The picture can either be an amalgamation of different group members' experiences or a fictional situation that has some resonance with the group. Where appropriate, the picture could also be of a specific situation that a participant has been involved in.

Encourage the groups to spend only a brief time discussing their ideas and to start creating their picture as soon as possible. Five to ten minutes is usually long enough for groups to create a picture from scratch.

Tip: If a group is having trouble generating a Frozen Picture, you can 'unstick' them by asking them questions such as where it might be set, what the problem is, what day of the week it is, what time of day, etc.

When everyone is ready, ask the group to form an audience. The small groups then take it in turns to show their picture to the rest of the group. It may help if you count down '3-2-1 freeze!' in order to facilitate each scene. Participants must hold their positions while the group discusses their picture, so it is important not to keep the pictures frozen for too long, as some positions may be difficult to hold. When each Frozen Picture is presented, you can lead the discussion using any of the *processing techniques.* Make sure that each group gets a round of applause when they have finished.

One step removed Frozen Picture titles

The Offence; The argument; The secret; The lie; The outsider; Anger; Aggression; Violence; Rock bottom; Craving; Boredom; Greed; Pride; Fear; Breakdown in communication; A visit; Mates/ associates; The victim; The fight; The moment after the offence; What's good or bad about crime, drugs, etc; It wasn't my fault; The police; In court; Life on the street; The family; The football match; The consequence; The trigger.

(Continued)

(Single Frozen Picture: Continued)

Personal level Frozen Picture titles

Frozen Pictures can be extremely useful on the *Personal Level*, with the offender using other group members to take on the image of some aspect of his offending or his offence cycle. He can either be in the image or out of it. Be aware that these titles suggest very personal, high focus scenes, and should only be used subject to the note caution on p.33.

Example titles for the personal level: *The smallest thing that ever got me angry; The last time I was angry; The moment before my offence; The moment after my offence; Me, pushing away the guilt after an offence; Me, giving myself permission to offend; The first moment I would know I was into my offending cycle again; Me in a high risk situation in the future; A problem my family faces while I am in prison; How I see my victim; How my victim sees me; My victim before, during or after the offence; Missing home; My arrest; Me in prison; How I want it to be in (X) years/ How I will get there; Obstacles in the way of my dream; My first friend.*

Comments

Frozen Pictures are an excellent way of starting to look at inner thoughts and feelings and to begin approaching deeper emotional terrain. They are reasonably safe and unthreatening for participants and are much more controllable than improvised role plays. Because they can encapsulate an issue so powerfully and in concentrated form, Frozen Pictures make ideal raw material for development using all of the *processing techniques.*

Variations

You can direct a Frozen Picture yourself by predetermining the image you want and asking for volunteers to form the picture.

There are some cases when it may be advantageous for a facilitator to take on a role. This should only be done if there is another facilitator remaining out of role. Also, for female facilitators in male groups, it is generally more beneficial for women NOT to take the role of women, as this limits the opportunities for male participants to take on the role of females and gain insight into their point of view.

Finally, newspaper articles, particularly those dealing with issues relevant to the group (e.g. accounts of crimes), are a useful resource for ideas for Frozen Pictures. Similarly, Frozen Pictures can be based on news photographs.

Monuments

Aim: To introduce groups to frozen images and working theatrically
Low to medium individual focus
For groups of 3 and up
Time needed: 10 to 20 minutes
Worker participation: optional
Degree of distance: One Step Removed only

Method

This is a great exercise for teaching groups the basics of creating *Frozen Pictures.* In purely creative work, it also serves as a great introduction to creating theatre because it demands the most basic but essential presentational skills. It is meant to be run quickly and with a light touch, as it is mainly a preparatory exercise.

Split the group into smaller groups of between three and six people: *Each group is going to build a monument to a famous event in history. You only have yourselves to build the monument and it must be frozen like a statue. Don't take too long choosing the historical event—concentrate on how you are going to represent it physically. Make sure that you can hold the positions you take up for a reasonable length of time. When we come back together in five minutes, you'll each show your monument to the other groups and we'll see if we can guess what the event is. Your sculpture can be realistic or very symbolic—that's up to you.*

Once the groups have built their monuments, they show them to each other and the observers try to work out what the famous event is. If they cannot work it out, the monument can be changed slightly or clues given using some of the *processing techniques* such as *Inner Voice from the Character.*

General processing *What was it about some of the monuments that made the content clear? What made particular monuments visually exciting or interesting?* (Talk about facial expressions, use of space, etc). *How is this exercise like creating a piece of theatre?*

Variations All of the following variations can be as naturalistic or abstract as the group wishes:

Recent News Event Another good starting point is to ask the groups to base their monument on a recent news event rather than an historical event.

Actual Monument The groups build real monuments or famous buildings, for example Big Ben or the Statue of Liberty.

Everyday Objects They can also form everyday objects such as a washing machine, toaster or car (these can have moving parts). See *Self-supporting Structures* for a similar variation.

Film Freezes The groups make Frozen Pictures of a film they are familiar with. The film freeze can represent either a scene from the film, an overall flavour of the film or the title of the film.

Option: Where appropriate, monuments can have moving parts or sound effects.

Add to the Picture

Aim: any theme
Medium to high individual focus
For groups of 5 and up
Time needed: 5 - 15 minutes
Worker participation: one stays out, others optional
Degree of distance: One Step Removed only

Method
In Add to the Picture, a single picture is built organically, one person at a time, in front of the whole group. This allows the facilitator to make suggestions and ask questions as the image takes shape. The picture created can be a purely creative one, with no particular theme in mind, or you can set the theme specifically to the aims of a particular session.

Preparation: If the group has not yet worked with *Frozen Pictures,* you will need to explain what this entails. It is useful to get the group to form an audience at one end of the room. Ask them to stay standing because their involvement in the exercise will be almost immediate.

This is a group exercise but I need a volunteer to get it started. Thank you, Sandra. Now, think about the work we've been doing around (e.g. dealing with high risk situations). Now I'd like you to go on to the stage and take a position that has something to do with high risk situations. ... Thanks, that's good. Now I would like the rest of the group to look at the image. Without sharing your thoughts with other people, try and think about the following questions. What do you think Sandra's image represents? What kind of atmosphere does the image have? What I would like the rest of the group to do is to add yourselves one by one to the picture, each time creating an element that will add to the story. Try and think about how you relate to the other characters and what your relationship is to them when you join the image. Use the full amount of space available. Is your character more or less powerful than the others? Why? Are you representing another person, or are you representing an object, or even something symbolic like tension or temptation?

General processing Access thoughts and feelings of the different characters in the picture. From this the group can move on and compare their interpretations of what was 'really' going on. *What decisions did you make along the way? Did your interpretation change as the image evolved? What are the power relationships like in the image? Who is more powerful, or less powerful? Why? What role does body language play in your interpretation? Where might this scene take place? What happens next?* After the group considers questions such as these, they may decide they want to spend more time with the image and develop it further. If so, you can use *processing techniques* such as *Interview in Role, Role Rotation* or *Reworking the Scene.*

Processing on a personal level Here are some examples of processing questions based on an image created to focus on power. While the image was created, the group members were asked to make each additional person in the image more powerful than the last: *How can we relate what we discovered from our image to our experiences in life? Have we experienced power dynamics like these in our daily lives? In what types of situations do we experience them? If we wanted to change the power dynamic in our picture so that it was based more on equality, what would we have to do? What would we have to do in real life situations to make the power dynamic more equal? What are the obstacles we would need to negotiate? What skills would we need?*

Comments Add to the Picture can serve as an ideal lead-in to *Forum Role Play* and *Whole Group Role Play,* which are described in the next chapter.

Three Picture Scenes

Aims: To focus on any theme; to develop simple dramatic stories
Medium to high focus
Group size: 4 and up
Time needed: 10 - 30 minutes or more
Worker participation: one stays out, others optional
Degree of distance: One Step Removed or Personal Level

Method
As the name implies, Three Picture Scenes are simple stories told in three frozen pictures. Normally, you would first have the participants form small groups and create *Single Frozen Pictures* in order to learn the procedure. Then you can either use these frozen pictures as the basis for Three Picture Scenes, or you can ask the groups to create entirely new stories.

The basic procedures for creating Three Picture Scenes are the same as those that apply to creating *Single Frozen Pictures,* so we will not repeat that description here. The main difference is that the story is told in three 'snapshots' instead of one, which affords more scope for plot, character development and other dramatic elements. The series of three pictures would usually show some kind of progression, following a story with one or more central characters. The time scale of the story can be from several seconds to many years. The three pictures can be based on structures such as:

- General structure: Beginning, middle and end;
- Offence focused: Before, during and after the offence (also called *antecedents, behaviour and consequences*); and
- Ad-hoc Based on particular thematic issues/ titles (see suggestions below).

After each group presents its Three Picture Scene, you can use any of the *processing techniques* to dissect the scene. The amount of time this takes is variable, depending on whether you wish to further develop the scenes. Because they already portray a story, Three Picture Scenes can readily expand into active *Role Plays*. These *Role Plays* can either be separately rehearsed or developed on the spot, in front of the whole group.

Tips: It is easier and clearer if all three pictures focus on one central character. Other characters may come and go, and participants may even play multiple roles, as long as at least one participant stays consistent in a central role. In many cases, the same characters will appear in all three pictures, which is fine.

If groups need a little extra help to get going, it is sometimes easier to create the middle picture first and then create the before and after images.

Suggested titles As with *Single Frozen Pictures*, it is often useful to give predetermined titles to the groups and ask them to use the title to focus on a relevant theme. It is possible to use any of the titles suggested in the description of *Single Frozen Pictures.* Some other suggestions for both *one step removed* and *personal level* Three Picture Scenes: *The lead up to the offence; Peer pressure; My most likely/ least likely/ most hopeful futures; You would have done the same in my shoes; A victim confronts an offender/ My victim confronts me; A victim/ my victim before, during and after the offence; An advertisement for an alcohol/ drug free lifestyle; An advertisement for offending behaviour/ against offending behaviour; Where I am now/ Where I want to be/ What's standing in between the two.*

Other possible sources for titles or story ideas are newspaper articles, particularly those covering offence-related issues.

Also, the group could do three picture versions of well-known stories, comics, films or rhymes.

CHAPTER 8

Role Play

'To see another person as a full-fledged, conscious human being, capable of thinking and feeling and suffering, is the first step toward true morality.'
Richard Hornby, *The End of Acting* (1992, p. 20)

This chapter covers:

- **Introduction and Definition**
- **Two Points to Bear in Mind About Role Play**
- **The Two Broad Categories of Role Play**
- **Using Role Play Flexibly While Staying Focused**
- **The Variables Within Role Play**
- **Some Practical Tips**
- **Making the Space Safe and Positive**
- **Types of Role Play:**

  1 Whole Group Role Play
  2 Demonstration Role Play
  3 Forum Role Play
  4 Role Play for Empathy, Feedback and Self- talk
  5 Monologues
  6 Offence Reconstruction
  7 Role Modelling
  8 Skills Practice Role Play
  9 Role Tests

INTRODUCTION AND DEFINITION

When using role play, it is important to understand that there are different types of role play used with different aims. In this chapter we divide role play into nine basic types according to their main aim. The chapter also provides a range of practical suggestions to help you run effective role plays.

Decades of research have shown that role play is a crucial component in social learning (Bandura, 1977) and in the most effective offending behaviour groupwork (Antonowicz and Ross, 1994). Among its many benefits, role play helps the participant expand his *role repertoire* through the practising of new behavioural skills and roles. Role play can also help the participant to become more aware of himself and how his behaviour impacts on others. It is the most direct way of simulating life situations in which participants can show their own true-to-life solutions in action. This makes the group session a practical laboratory for safely testing new responses. When conducted with enough safety, clarity and enthusiasm, role play is a highly motivating activity, as it allows participants to get actively involved and gain immediate feedback about their behaviour. In our experience, offenders have often stated at the end of programmes that the role play sessions were among the most useful and memorable.

Role play is used and adapted so widely that there is no universally agreed definition. The term 'role play' is used to describe a wide range of activities including the imaginative play of children, therapeutic enactments in clinical settings, skills practice and large scale simulations, such as when a hospital practises a disaster plan using live 'casualties.' Some authors describe role play as being primarily useful for behavioural practice (e.g. Wolpe, 1969). Others use 'role play' as an all-encompassing term that includes behavioural practice as well as *psychodrama* (Kipper, 1986; Corsini, 1967; Yablonsky, 1976).

As role play is so broadly defined, for the purposes of this book we offer a definition that we find helpful in thinking about our work. By offering this definition and spelling out some of the distinctions between *one step removed role play, personal level role play* and *psychodrama* in *Table 8.1* overleaf, we offer guidance that we hope will help you design safe, effective sessions that stay within clear boundaries. No doubt some readers will disagree with our definition, so we emphasise that ours should not be seen as an attempt at a comprehensive or final definition.

TWO POINTS TO BEAR IN MIND ABOUT ROLE PLAY

Is it acting? Role play is often confused with acting, but there is a crucial difference. Acting is primarily concerned with the entertainment, enrichment and/or education of an audience. By contrast, the main focus of role play is the personal development of the role player(s).

Role play also differs from acting in that it emphasises the role rather the character. Role play asks the participant to play a certain role (self or other) as accurately as possible based on current knowledge and skills, but it does not emphasise taking on character traits such as accents, costume, idiosyncratic walks, etc. to the extent an actor would. It is often useful to explain this distinction to participants, who may at first reject role play, assuming they will be asked to become involved in 'make-believe' acting.

The central importance of 'as if' There is, however, a major feature that both acting and role play share in common, which is the importance of entering into an 'as if' situation requiring a suspension of disbelief on the part of both performer and audience. 'As if' is a key ingredient in both acting and role play, and refers to the quality of behaving 'as if' one is in another situation, another role or a role representing a part of one's self. An actor in role as Hamlet will perform 'as if' he is really Hamlet, just as a role player in the role of 'police officer' behaves 'as if' he really is a police officer. In both cases, those on stage suspend their disbelief in order to perform the scene, and those observing suspend their disbelief in order to follow the action.

THE TWO BROAD CATEGORIES OF ROLE PLAY

Role play can be divided into two main groupings:

1. Role play for exploring, raising awareness and encouraging change The first category contains those types of role play devoted to exploring, learning, increasing awareness and changing attitudes. The role plays in this category allow participants opportunities to both examine and present their lives and their ideas in a live and realistic way, and also to challenge each other's ideas and attitudes. The types of role play in this category are: *Whole Group Role Play; Demonstration Role Play; Forum Role Play; Role Play for Empathy, Feedback and Self-talk, Monologues* and *Offence Reconstruction.*

2. Skills focused role plays The second category of role play is devoted to assessing, modelling, practising and testing new behaviours, roles and skills. These role plays demand a carefully controlled structure and detailed preparation and facilitation. There are three types of role play within this category: *Role Modelling; Skills Practice Role Play;* and *Role Tests.*

USING ROLE PLAY FLEXIBLY WHILE STAYING FOCUSED

It is important to stress that the nine different types of role play described in this chapter overlap and inter-relate. One role play will naturally suggest another, and it is entirely possible that a single role play can be used to achieve multiple aims as it evolves. The crucial factor to bear in mind is that you keep to a main focus. With so many possible aims that can be achieved, it is all the more important to narrow the focus to just one aim and one technique at a time.

For example, a *Demonstration Role Play* devised by two participants to show the peer pressures they face may develop into a one step removed *Forum Role Play* where other group members try out different approaches to dealing with peer pressure in a similar but fictionalised scenario. This role play may in turn lead to further *Role Modelling* and *Skills Practice Role Plays* focusing on building interpersonal skills such as assertiveness or saying no. Other types of role play may be brought in as needed, all resulting from the one original role play.

THE VARIABLES WITHIN ROLE PLAY

We can create an infinite variety of role plays using a few variables relating to four main areas: the roles played by the participants, the situation enacted, the learning aims and logistical factors. We are indebted to van Mentz (1983), whose basic outline we have adapted:

The roles played by the role players

- **Self** The role player plays the role of 'myself.'
- **Real person** The role player plays the role of a real person who is or is not present in the room. This can include real people described, for example, in news articles.
- **Imagined person** The role player plays the role of an imagined person or created character. This could include established fictional characters or even fantastical characters such as cartoon super heroes.

A definition of role play: 'Role play takes place when someone portrays the role of himself or someone else in a given situation in order to express his own ideas or gain insight, experience, empathy, understanding or new skills.'[1]

Table 8.1: **Factors Distinguishing One Step Removed Role Play, Personal Level Role Play and Psychodrama**
(Psychodrama is not covered in this book)

Type	Description	Setting	Focus	Amount of Role Play Experience/ Therapy Training/ Supervision Needed
One Step Removed Role Play	Participant plays self or other(s) in enactments of purely hypothetical or close-to-life (fictionalised) situations or roles. One step removed role play can also be based on news events, or close-to-life situations that are 'fictionalised' (i.e. names and details changed sufficiently to create distance from real events in the life of anyone present).	Any setting, including education, groupwork, professional skills training, community events, etc.	—Personal, social, educational and professional development. —Practising behavioural change. Looking at alternatives. —Expanding role repertoire and range of emotional expression. —Developing empathy and understanding consequences. —Insight. Change in attitudes. —Increased spontaneity and creativity.	Role play experience and training needed. Awareness of basic therapy issues (e.g. need for containment; boundaries; non-oppressive practice) essential.
Personal Level Role Play	Participant plays self or other in role plays which directly recreate personal situations and relationships with no attempt to fictionalise, or distance, the material. This is done only within strict boundaries: Sufficiently experienced workers may help the participant re-enact a non-traumatic event, such as a difficult social interaction, in order to help the participant to practise alternatives and develop greater empathy and self-understanding. Similarly, personal level role plays may be used to prepare for difficult scenarios in the future (e.g. high risk situations, potential consequences or anticipated conversations).	Clinical/ therapeutic, workplace or institutional setting.	All of the above, plus: —Insight and change in attitudes towards specific individuals as well as groups. —Practising new skills relevant to personal needs.	Greater amount of experience and training in role play. Some training in groupwork and basic therapy issues. Adequate supervision required (preferably with a supervisor familiar with role play).

Personal Level Role Play (continued)	The emphasis of such role plays is on improving the social interaction skills of the participant and not on therapeutic 'working through.' Where *processing techniques* are used to help the participant identify his or her thoughts and feelings during the situation, this is done with a focus on developing better coping strategies for dealing with difficult situations as opposed to exploring the psychological roots of his or her behaviour. The category of personal level role play does not include the re-enactment of an individual's offence. In particular, re-staging offences of violence or interpersonal abuse may be counter-productive or destructive to the participant and the other group members. Such re-enactments fall into the category of psychodrama and should be facilitated by trained psychodramatists. See *Offence Reconstruction* later in this chapter for a structured approach to staging offences which can be used by professionals who do not have psychodrama training.	Groupwork, professional supervision, team development, personal development workshops.	—Self-awareness: identifying typical patterns of coping with difficult situations or negative emotions. Practising alternatives. —Increased internal resilience.	
Psychodrama	All of the above, plus: Participant plays self or other in directly personal scenes exploring life concerns, including emotional issues, internal conflicts, problems in relationships, early life issues or unresolved trauma. Particular focus is given to linking the participant's current strategies with his or her early life experiences and patterns of self-protection in order to help him or her work through, gain insight, modify perceptions of other people and events, and learn new strategies. Personal events—including offences and early experiences—may be re-enacted using established procedures. The realism and spontaneity of the scene, leading, for example, to emotional catharsis, is one of the prime healing factors. Behavioural practise for the future is also an essential feature. See Karp *et al* (1998) or Blatner (1997).	All of the above, especially clinical/ therapeutic settings.	All of the above, plus: —Catharsis, insight and change related to resolution of emotional difficulties and internal conflicts. Particular emphasis on working through problems in relationships and how one deals with painful or negative emotions. —Resolution of trauma and loss. Emphasis on learning from the past and moving beyond grief, anger, hatred (of self or others), resentment, etc	Qualified psychodramatists, or qualified psychotherapists with adequate psychodrama training. Supervision required.

[1] This definition is based on the work of van Mentz (1983) and accords with the use of the terms *'Role Play'*, *'Psychodrama'* and *'Psychodramatic Role Play'* by authors such as Kipper (1986) and Yardley-Matwiejczuk (1997). Read Yardley-Matwiejczuk for a detailed discussion of the problem of defining role play, as well as a comprehensive 'redefinition.'

The situation enacted in the role play

- **Re-enactment/ familiar/ similar/ new** The role play can re-enact an actual event in the participant's life. Or the role play can 'fictionalise' an event so that the participant is portraying a situation 'like one I've been in.' Likewise, the role play can take the issue or problem behaviour and put it into a similar or new context.

Learning aims

- **Goal setting/ feedback** The participant will receive feedback from staff and group participants about her functioning in the role play. She will also be encouraged to assess her own functioning in the role play and to set new learning targets for herself.

- **Attitude shift/ self-esteem** Through the role play, the participant will discover new points of view and will be able to challenge and modify his beliefs and attitudes about himself and others.

- **Empathy/ insight** The participant will become more sensitive and aware of his internal thinking and feeling process, the feelings of others and how his behaviour affects them.

- **New skill, behaviour or role** The central participant in the role play practises a new skill, behaviour or role.

Logistical factors

- **Solo/ two person / whole group** The role play can be a monologue, a dialogue or a complex, whole group enactment. There are of course intermediate stages, such as role plays involving three, four or five players.

- **Detailed induction/ short outline/ spontaneous** Prior to the start of a role play, the participants may be given a highly detailed induction, or briefing, regarding the characteristics and motivations of their role. In some situations, it may even be appropriate to provide role players with fully scripted scenes. *Skills Practice Role Plays* will demand detailed induction and preparation. Similarly, *Role Play for Empathy, Feedback and Self-talk* will require fairly detailed induction as the depth of the characters is important.

  Alternatively, the participants may be given only a short outline of the key characteristics (e.g. name, age, gender, relation to other person, motivation in the scene) before starting. *Role Tests*, for example, demand a minimal induction in order to retain the element of surprise.

- **Duration** The types of role play described in this chapter are generally intended to last between 30 seconds and ten minutes. The exception is *Whole Group Role Play*, which may last for most of a session.

- **Setting** The role play may take place in a real or imagined setting.

SOME PRACTICAL TIPS

Introduce dramatic situations early on If the participants become familiar with creating characters, stories and dramatic situations from the earliest phase of the group, they will be more likely to actively engage in role play. To be used for optimal effect, the drama-based work should become part of the fabric of the programme, and not a separate or special event. Because of this, we very often involve participants in *Games and Exercises, Interactive Observer* scenes and also *Frozen Pictures* in their first session together. This sets the stage for role play to follow.

Rules for setting up role plays These four rules can help us set up role plays quickly and effectively:

- **Have clear characters** Examples: landlord/tenant, boss/worker, prisoner/officer, lender/borrower, parent/child. When processing the scene, it is often useful to focus on one character as well as what is going on between the characters.

- **Have a clear tension or problem** In other words, A wants this and B wants that. Without some problem or tension, the role play will lack interest or become pointless.

- **Decide on a clear setting** Examples: kitchen, work place, cell, garage, shop, prison landing, pub, playground.

- **In general, have only two at a time on stage** This keeps the focus clear and avoids the problem of people talking over each other, which can easily happen when three or more characters are in a scene. This rule does not apply to *Whole Group Role Play* or *Monologues*.

  You can make exceptions to this rule where appropriate, but be aware that this demands more skill from the participants as well as from the worker because scenes with more than two people can easily become chaotic. Note especially that when working with young people, it is particularly important to allow time for each participant to speak and have some focus if they have created a character. Otherwise the process can be especially frustrating for them.

Setting up the stage Before starting a role play, it is important to define clearly where the stage is and where the audience/ observers are. Usually, the stage will simply be a designated part of the room.

Using the light If there is natural light coming into the room, arrange the stage so that the light is behind the audience/ observers. This way, they will not have to look into the glare from the outside light.

Stay open Staying open means that the actors, or in this case the participants in the role play, perform in such a way that the audience can clearly see their faces and hear their words. There are certain times when this rule can be broken, and this is almost always for dramatic effect.

Getting involvement from the observers and using processing questions If you sense that the group members may tune out while watching a role play, get them involved by using the *processing techniques*. For example, you can freeze a role play and spend a few moments processing the thoughts and feelings of the characters. Or you can rotate new participants into the various roles. Vary the pace, the process and the participants as necessary in order to preserve interest and involvement.

Another useful tactic to keep observers interested in the action is to give all observers a role or task. Examples: 'You look for any negative body language,' or, 'You look at this as a potential employer, you look at this as if you were his most trusted friend,' etc. This keeps the observers involved and can also be a source of useful feedback.

Tip: You can use the *Role Play Rating Sheet* (*Appendix A*) as the basis for processing role plays.

Props In role play, it is best to keep hand props (e.g. telephone, dishes, t.v., sports equipment) to a minimum. Far from clarifying the action, they can make it far too cluttered, inhibiting the flow of the story. Props can also be a safety hazard.

MAKING THE SPACE SAFE AND POSITIVE

Starting a role play

Worker: *Okay, now we're going to do a role play.*
Participant: *You're joking! I'm not doing any acting.*

In some situations, using the term 'role play' can bring a session to a grinding halt as the anxiety of group members shoots through the roof. This is why we often do not use the term role play until the participants are no longer anxious about participating in scenes. For ideas on how to prevent such anxiety and potential resistance, review the section on working with resistance in *Chapter 2*. In particular, re-read the short description of how to make seamless transitions from discussion into role play. To recap two of the main points:

- **Building a role play using the simplest questions and invitations** Example: Place two chairs in the stage area of the room. Ask, *Where are we? Who is there? What are they like? What does A want? What does B want? Let's have two people up there and see the scene. You don't have to worry about being right or wrong, let's just start to explore the situation.* In a similar way, we can develop role plays seamlessly from *Games and Exercises* or *Frozen Pictures*.

- **Use the group's ideas** The best ideas for role plays often come from the group members. With this in mind, you can start a role play with an open question such as, *What would be a typical example of a situation where you would be likely to do something you regret? Show us a situation like that. Show us how you normally deal with this situation.*

Invent names for the characters In general, it is best to use fictional names for characters in a *one step removed* scene. Let the group members choose the names. Make sure that the names chosen are not names of anyone present. In addition, check to see that no one present has a close friend or relative with the same name as the character, as this can be distracting.

Let participants set their goals As group workers, we can easily fall into the trap of thinking that we know what skills a participant needs to develop, in effect identifying his problem and deciding a solution in one go. If you make this a habit, the participants may lose sight of the point of role play, because they do not understand why they are being asked to perform a certain function or role. To counter this, try wherever possible to get participants involved in their own assessment (see self-assessment form in *Appendix A*). For example, write up paper 'goals on the wall' to refer back to so goals can be assessed and monitored as action proceeds. If the participants identify their own needs, they are far more likely to become actively interested and involved in skills building role plays. Likewise, it is usually best to rely on the group to create the situation and characters in a role play, in order to maintain interest in the characters and the dilemma.

Respect We are pro-active in fostering an atmosphere of respect among group members. The issue of respect is particularly crucial when participants are engaged in role play, because they are especially conscious of 'losing face' when doing such high focus work. Because of this, we emphasise that it takes courage to become involved in a scene, so those who do get involved can take pride in making the effort.

The issue of respect also applies to the characters represented in a role play. For example, if the observers laugh at the character of an elderly person falling to the ground after being hit during a robbery, we will remark about this and perhaps ask about the reasons for the laughter.

We might also ask the participant in role as the elderly person to speak from their point of view about the robbery. Using such strategies, we would seek to underscore the importance of respect for others generally, without resorting to hectoring or moralising.

Stage fright Participants as well as group workers often face enormous performance anxiety when doing role play. You needn't worry about getting a great performance out of the group, just as the participants needn't worry about giving a great performance. Acknowledge their anxiety and reassure them that they don't have to be great actors. Let them know that the important thing is that they show the scene rather than talk about it.

And the role play need not last long. A scene of ten seconds can provide ample discussion material.

Swearing and discriminatory remarks during role plays This can be a tricky problem, so it needs very clear boundaries. The rule we use is that within a role play examining a personal experience or a typical problem situation faced by the participant, the participant is allowed to use his or her authentic language, even if it includes swearing or is discriminatory.

Participants should be encouraged to give a true portrayal of their behaviour in real life. This will give you, the group members and the participant in the role play a great deal of spontaneous behaviour to respond to and challenge through role feedback (from the other person in the role play), *Role Reversal* or any of the other *processing techniques.*

It is worth noting that directly challenging such words and beliefs is almost always futile or indeed counter-productive. Using *processing techniques* such as *Role Reversal* or *Role Rotation* is almost always a more effective strategy, because it allows the participant to challenge his own behaviour while saving face.

By contrast, bad language or discriminatory remarks are generally not allowed in other forms of role play, such as in *Modelling Role Plays* or *Skills Practice Role Plays.*

Finally, outside of role plays, during general group discussions, standard rules of group behaviour and language would apply.

In our experience, as long as these rules are clearly given, participants (even those who swear a great deal) generally find that they can stick to the rules.

A note about *Degree of Distance* As in *Chapters 6* and *7*, in this chapter we include the *Degree of Distance* in the italicised quick reference guide at the start of each new Role Play technique. This tells you whether the Role Play is suitable for work at *one step removed,* the *personal level,* or both.

Whole Group Role Play

To explore a social situation or dilemma; to raise consciousness of broader issues and differing perspectives; motivation to change
High focus
Groups of 4 and up
Time needed: 20 minutes to 2 hours, or more
Worker participation: One stays out, others optional
Degree of distance: One Step Removed only

Method

After beginning discussion on a given theme, invite the group to create a dramatic situation where everyone will have a role. This can be done in phases, so at first you may have only one or two people in role. Eventually, everyone in the group should have a chance to enter and speak from one or more roles (Whole Group Role Play is always done at *one step removed*).

The interaction between the characters may be minimal or prolonged. For example, you may wish to ask only for a series of monologues from the characters. Alternatively, there can be extended dialogue among the characters.

The main purpose of Whole Group Role Play is to encourage group members to experience different roles and different perspectives, most importantly different perspectives related to offending. In thinking and speaking, even arguing, from a variety of roles, the participants will be challenged to expand their awareness about other people and how one person's behaviour impacts on another.

• • •

Example In a probation group for those convicted of burglary and other types of property crime, the focus of the session is on the consequences of crime for both victims and offenders. Each group member is asked to take the role of someone involved in a hypothetical house burglary and its after-effects. Roles include the victims, the burglars, the police, the loss adjuster, the locksmith, etc.

After a brief introduction to the theme, the group members arrange the chairs and other objects in the room to represent the rooms of a house and the personal belongings of the people living there.

As they do this, the group members create a story about the family who live in the house. They decide that it is the home of a woman, a man and their two children, a boy aged ten and a girl aged eight. The group names the family members and gives both parents an occupation. The mother is a part-time teaching assistant and the father is self-employed, running a building contracting business from home.

Four group members take on the roles of the family members. Interviewed by other group members, they talk about their home and family. They give a guided tour of the house and show off their valued possessions such as jewellery, family heirlooms, a computer, a television and, for the children, a stereo and a video game.

Soon, the family are asked to leave the group room and wait outside in the corridor. They are going to visit a sick relative. While they are out of the room, two group members who have volunteered to play the part of burglars enter the home and steal as many items as they can carry. The burglars are excited and laughing. They mime in great detail breaking the window, climbing in and turning over furniture. One burglar even stops to turn over the fish tank which had been carefully placed by the boy in the family. There is a tense mixture of grimacing and laughter from the group as they imagine the fish flopping on the floor and dying.

(Continued)

(Whole Group Role Play: Continued)

The family returns, and are outraged to discover their home ransacked, their possessions gone. The two children find that their toys and video game have been taken, the fish tank is shattered and all the fish are dead. The father angrily rings the police, a role quickly taken up by another group member.

The observing group members ask the family what they'd like to do to the burglars. The family answers furiously, 'Lock them up! Make them suffer, too! They don't care about anyone but themselves.'

Meanwhile, the two 'burglars' watch silently from a corner of the group room.

After being visited by group members in role as the police, a fingerprint technician, the loss adjuster, the window repairer and a Victim Support worker, the two home owners turn spontaneously to the two burglars and tell them that they have caused a huge amount of misery. 'You have no right to do this to us. Why don't you think of anyone but yourself?' The two burglars shrug their shoulders and say they don't care.

The home owners and the burglars now exchange roles, and the two group members who have moments before shrugged their shoulders in apathy now begin shouting at the burglars. The burglars respond, 'What do you care? You're insured.' To which the home owners reply that nothing can replace their sense of security, and the man's business is in jeopardy because they took his tools and all of his records were in the computer. They are now afraid to be in their home and also afraid to leave it in case it gets burgled again. They are furious at the burglars for justifying the crime and denying the damage they have done.

By the end of the hour, each group member has taken the part of a family member, a burglar or one of the supporting roles. In later sessions, they enact similar scenarios of commercial burglary, shoplifting and car crime. Each group member argues from a victim's point of view and experiences first hand what it is like to be on the receiving end of their own offences.

• • •

Variations An often used variation is ***Living Newspaper***, a method dating back centuries, in which events of the day are performed for onlookers. In groupwork, you would follow the same procedure described above, but base the scenario on a relevant news event. Example: In a group for those convicted of stealing cars and 'joy riding,' a news article is read which details an actual incident. For example (based on an actual news article): 'A girl and boy, aged eight and six, have been seriously injured after joyriders crashed into their parents' car in (place). Both children are in intensive care at (hospital). Their parents received head and neck injuries, and were treated and released. One of the joyriders was also admitted to intensive care in critical condition.' After reading the article, the group members are then asked to take the roles of the various people, for example, the parents who were injured, the joyriders, the families of the joyriders, the families of those injured, the police and ambulance attendants, etc.

Or: in a young offender institution, the trainees enact roles based on a news item about bullying between trainees at another institution. Present in the enactment would be the bullies, the victim(s), other trainees, parents, prison officers, teachers, prison visitors, the governor, etc.

Comments *Whole Group Role Play* is closely related to *The Way I See It*, and benefits particularly from processing techniques such as *Inner Voice from the Characters, Interview in Role, Role Rotation, Role Reversal* and *Reworking the Scene. Add to the Picture* is a good preparation exercise for *Whole Group Role Play.*

Demonstration Role Play

To help participants present the difficulties they face and their usual way of handling problems
High focus
Groups of any size
Time needed: 10—30 minutes per role play
Worker participation: One stays out, others optional
Degree of distance: One Step Removed or Personal Level

Method

In this type of role play, the participants demonstrate what they perceive to be a typical problem or situation they face in their everyday lives and how they normally handle it. In practise, we might call this type of role play 'the way it was,' 'the way it is,' or 'the way I deal with things.'

When this type of role play is used on the *personal level*, one group member will usually enact his own role with one or more other group members playing others in 'a typical problem situation.' The role players will normally have a few minutes to rehearse the scene, and will then present the scene to the rest of the group, at which point you can help the central role player identify what he finds difficult about this situation. Other characters in the scene, and the observers, can give reactions and feedback. Based on this exploration, you might suggest moving on to *Forum Role Play, Role Modelling* or *Skills Practice Role Plays* to help the participant learn and practise new ways of dealing with this difficulty.

It is possible to run this type of role play at *one step removed* by finding a difficulty common to most of the group members and creating an archetypal scene.

• • •

Examples of one step removed Demonstration Role Plays

- Janeen, Claire and Sarah present a 'typical day in the life' of any of the three of them. A series of events unfolds which adds one pressure on top of another (e.g. no money, child is ill, bills are overdue, argument with boyfriend), ending in Janeen's character committing a theft.
- Terry and Jamie present a role play demonstrating a typical peer pressure situation involving drugs. Optional: They are given a title to work to, such as: 'Just this once', 'Everyone does it', or 'Go on, it'll be a laugh'.

Examples of personal level Demonstration Role Plays

- Craig and Steven enact a role play demonstrating how Craig recently became verbally abusive toward a social worker who came to visit his family in order to make a child protection assessment. Craig plays himself in the role play, while Steven takes the role of the social worker.
- Darren and Peter present a role play showing how Darren recently reacted when the police stopped and searched him when he was 'just minding my own business.' Darren plays himself in the role play, while Peter takes the role of a police officer.

• • •

Comments/ concerns Please read the word of caution on p.33 if you are considering using role play on the personal level.

Variations Participant role plays a typical event that can trigger his or her offending. Participant demonstrates how he or she handled a recent lapse.

Forum Role Play

Looking at alternatives; problem solving; awareness of self and others
Low to high focus
Number of participants: 5 and up
Time needed: 10 - 60 minutes per scenario
Worker participation: one stays out, others optional
Degree of distance: One Step Removed only

Method

Forum Role Play is an active approach to problem solving. It is a useful tool for exploring alternative strategies, and can be an excellent opportunity for enjoyable debate and creativity. Forum Role Play does not offer easy solutions, but poses the question, 'What can be done about this?'

To create a Forum Role Play, work with the group to establish a contentious issue that concerns them or a real dilemma that any of the group might face, e.g. an aggressive provocation, relationship problems, dealing with authority figures or peer pressure. Ask them to divide into pairs or small groups to create a short scene that ends in a crisis or moment of decision. A Forum Role Play should always be a *one step removed* situation. If it is not appropriate to break into pairs or small groups, the scene can be created on the spot using volunteers and suggestions.

Alternatively, workers can rehearse and present a scene. One worker will need to remain out of the scene to act as facilitator.

Each scene is shown to the whole group. Once it has been played through (it need be only one to five minutes long), it is repeated, with group members now allowed to stop the action at any moment when they think they would have acted differently in that situation. Ask for a volunteer to show their idea about how to deal with such a situation. Where appropriate, you may wish to suggest that particular kinds of solutions be attempted, for example a passive / aggressive / assertive solution. Rather than verbally debating, ask volunteers to *perform* their solution, however far-fetched, as long as it does not involve violence or overtly sexual behaviour. Use any of the *processing techniques* in order to promote the maximum amount of debate and interest in the scene.

It is crucial to emphasise the *real world,* showing that any solution we may try may not always provide the outcome we desire. If an unrealistic solution is offered or accepted by the on stage characters (e.g. 'I just won the lottery, here's a million pounds'), check this out with the group and encourage them to stay with more realistic suggestions.

In most Forum Role Plays, it is useful to focus on only one character in the scene - the one with the problem. This emphasises the point that, in life, we can only change our own behaviour and not the behaviour of others. Being able to change only the behaviour of one character on stage presents us with the same reality, because the other characters in the scene will still be striving for their own aims.

To make suggestions for the central character on stage, group members call 'stop' to the action and then can either tell the performer how to modify her behaviour, or they can come onto the stage and take on the role themselves. This may of course change the scene, depending on the solution being offered. Some solutions will be effective, and others will be overrun or dismissed by the 'opposing' character(s) in the scene. The participant or worker playing the 'opposing' character must still strive to achieve their aim in the scene, but must remain flexible enough to allow for a potential solution. In other words, they must not override every suggestion, but must adapt their response to suit the offered alternative. This is a difficult balance to strike, and not every group member will be able to work with the necessary flexibility.

(Continued)

(Forum Role Play: Continued)

Examples

- John works at a garage and is called into his supervisor's office because a customer's purse has been removed from her car. The supervisor accuses John of taking the purse, and mentions that John is the most likely suspect because of his previous offending record. Several other mechanics and other employees had access to the car while it was in the shop. John did not take the purse, yet his supervisor threatens to fire him and becomes abusive. How should John handle this situation?

- Daryl is a new pupil at school, and on his way to school Paul and Scott steal his books and tease him for speaking with a 'funny' accent. How should Daryl deal with this situation?

- Carl returns home, tired after a long day at work. As he sits down, his partner Sandra tells him that she has been called at short notice to her nursing job at the hospital due to a large-scale accident with many people injured. She tells Carl he will have to look after the children (ages four and six, already asleep in their rooms) and that yesterday's dinner is warming in the oven. Carl grows angry and refuses to let Sandra leave, as he had been looking forward to a night out with his mates. How should Sandra deal with this situation? Alternatively, how should Carl deal with this situation?

- Vicky is a single parent living with her three year old daughter. Her boyfriend comes over with his car full of stolen electronic gear, and he asks her if he can stash the equipment in her flat until he can sell it on. When he comes to the door he is carrying some of the equipment. When she protests, he continues to bring the equipment in, saying it is only for a short time. How should Vicky deal with this situation?

• • •

Important elements in Forum Role Plays What do these examples share in common? There are a number of essential ingredients to include when devising Forum Role Plays. All of these ingredients should be included in the initial scene (adapted from Rohd, 1998):

- First and foremost, the stakes must be high enough to provoke the participants into wanting to find a solution. The scenes end unsatisfactorily, and we must be 'on the edge of our seats' wanting and needing to change the outcome. If we are not gripped by the scene, it needs more work.

- There is a clear conflict between the characters (A wants this and B wants that), and the intentions and aims of the characters are clear.

- There is a clear setting for the scene.

- The scene begins without conflict, and the conflict develops during the course of the scene.

- The 'opposing character' is realistic, has some human depth and has a realistic aim (i.e. he is not a stereotype villain). Similarly, the situation itself must be realistic.

- There is a clear central character, facing a moment of decision, with whom the group members identify. The group must care about what happens to this person.

- The central character faces a difficult decision and fails to achieve his aim in the scene.

- The central character fails to achieve his aim because of the actions or attitudes of the 'opposing' character.

(Continued)

(Forum Role Play: Continued)

- We must have a sense that the central character partly fails to achieve his aim because of his own thoughts, feelings, attitudes and beliefs. (Example: 'John' may have difficulty being assertive with his supervisor because he needs to keep his job, and he has not been in the job long enough to confidently speak with the supervisor).
- There is a clear central question underlying the scene. The examples given above ask central questions such as, 'What can someone do if they are falsely accused?', 'What is bullying, and what can someone do when they are being bullied?', 'What is 'compromise,' and what can someone do when their partner's needs conflict with their own?' and, 'What can someone do when they are pressured into being an accomplice in a crime?'

Variation: *Forum in Reverse*, also called ***A Day in the Life*** This variation turns the idea of problem solving on its head by asking the group members to *create* problems for the central character. A typical scene would involve one of the group members playing a fictional role of a central character getting up to start the day. After brainstorming all the people and pressures this character may have to deal with in the course of a day, group members can one at a time stop the action, enter the scene as a character and introduce

- a problem;
- a complaint;
- a request; or
- a solution.

For example, a group member may knock at the door and, as the landlord, demand the rent. Another may be a neighbour whose pipes have burst and the water is about to come into the flat. Another may suddenly appear and introduce herself as the plumber who is here to fix the leak. Another group member may telephone the central character and, taking the part of an employer, say, 'Don't bother coming in, your whole department has been made redundant!'

One use for this variation is to test the coping abilities of the central role player, while allowing her plenty of opportunities to seek advice and any assistance in order to cope with the pressures. It can offer an ideal opportunity to model or practise passive, assertive and aggressive responses to stressful events. Sometimes, we use *A Day in the Life* simply as an opportunity for group members to laugh—in recognition and affirmation—at the scale and volume of disasters that befall the central character. This can lead into an exploration of some of the stresses and mishaps that the participants typically deal with, and an exploration of alternative solutions to the stresses that can contribute to offending.

Source As far as we know, Dransfield (2001) is the first person to use the specific term *Forum Role Play,* a term which acknowledges the link with Boal's (1979) Forum Theatre. Rohd (1998) describes a variation he calls *activating scenes.*

Note

Add to the Picture is often a useful preparation exercise for *Forum Role Play. Forum in Reverse* is similar to the exercise *Fool Factors* (and its variations).

Role Play for Empathy, Feedback and Self-talk

Empathy; sensitivity; insight; self-talk skills
High focus
Number of participants: any number
Time needed: 10 to 30 minutes per role play
Worker participation: one stays out, others optional
Degree of distance: One Step Removed or Personal Level

Method This category is something of a misnomer, because *Role Plays for Empathy, Feedback* and *Self-talk* are not just types of role play, they are also role play strategies that can be used in conjunction with other types of role play. When used in conjunction with other types of role play, they become, in effect, *processing techniques* to deepen the meaning and significance of role plays.

However, because these three techniques offer such fundamental and wide-ranging potential benefits, they can also stand on their own as the central focus of role plays. This is why we have made them a separate category.

These techniques can be used for scenes based on *one step removed* or *personal material,* remembering the cautions about personal work noted on p.33. The techniques are:

1. **Role play to increase empathy** The main aim of this type of role play is to give participants the experience of 'being in another's shoes'. This includes reversing roles with the other character in the scene, so they can learn first hand what it is like to be on the receiving end of their own behaviour.

   For example, in a *one step removed* role play based on a real event in his own life, inmate Matthew plays the role of fictional inmate 'Tommy'. In the scene, Tommy shouts abuse at a prison officer because he has been made to wait longer than he expected to be let out of his cell. After the scene is played once through, the roles are reversed, so that now Matthew is the officer being shouted at. After this second enactment, Matthew is asked, while still in role as the officer, what his reaction is to Tommy's behaviour and what alternative behaviour would have been more productive. He is also given an opportunity to explain why he took so long to open Tommy's cell. Matthew is then asked to return to his own role and, perhaps, to play the scene differently based on his new perceptions which should now converge more closely with the officer's. This may lead on to *Modelling Role Plays* and *Skills Practice Role Plays.*

   When used as a processing technique with other types of role play, this technique is equivalent to *Role Reversal* and *Role Rotation.*

2. **Role play to provide feedback** The main aim of this type of role play is to give feedback to the participant in the central role on how he coped with the scene. The feedback can come from the other participant in the scene (the other character) or from the observers in the group.

   For example, *a one step removed* role play is enacted it in which 'Daniel' has loaned his personal stereo to his friend 'Joe', but when Joe returns the stereo is broken. Daniel is required to bring up the subject of the damage. After the scene is played, the participant playing the role of Joe gives feedback to the participant playing Daniel about how he came across, whether he was aggressive, friendly, conciliatory, passive, etc. The scene can then be replayed with the participant playing the role of Daniel making adjustments as suggested by the feedback he has received.

3. **Role play to practise self-talk** Continuing with the example above, the participant playing the role of 'Daniel' can also practise active self-talk by stopping the scene periodically and making an 'aside' to the audience, stating his inner thoughts and feelings as the scene progresses. This technique can help role players and observers become accustomed to the practice of active self talk as a method for controlling their thinking and behaviour.

Monologues

Aims: Perspective taking; empathy; cognitive distortions; attitudes; motivation; responsibility; goal setting
High focus
Number of participants: one or more
Time needed: flexible
Worker participation: No
Degree of distance: One Step Removed or Personal Level

Method

As the name implies, this type of scene needs only one participant, who takes on one or more roles during a particular sequence. It is an ideal technique for one to one work, and can be used to good effect in groups as well.

In the Monologue technique, the participant may take on the role of himself in the recent past, present or future, parts of his own internal belief system, such as the parts that are for and against offending, or he may take on the roles of other people. When the participant plays his own role or 'parts of self,' the aim is largely to encourage him to take responsibility for his own actions and to become motivated to change his behaviour. When the participant takes the role of others, the aim is mainly to encourage empathy and perspective taking and also to modify his distorted beliefs about others.

Please see the word of caution regarding personal level work on p.33 before facilitating Monologues on the *personal level.*

• • •

Examples

1. **A positive influence** Set out two chairs. Ask the group, or the particular group member you are focusing on, to think of a particular person in their life with whom they have had a positive relationship. This person might be a friend, mentor, family member or other positive person. You might phrase it as being someone who has 'a stake in your doing well on this programme.' Where participants cannot think of anyone, you might suggest someone from their immediate circumstances (e.g. one of the hostel staff, if they are living at a hostel), someone in the group, or even yourself.

   The participant then speaks from his own chair to his friend/ mentor/ positive figure who he imagines is sitting in the other chair. He might wish to thank the other person, for example, or express his feelings about them, or explain the changes he is trying to make. When he is done, he changes chairs and speaks to himself from the role of the other person. Each participant can be taken through this process, allowing 5 to 20 minutes per participant.

   Note: Be aware that this exercise can evoke a great deal of feeling, particularly if the person chosen is absent from the participant's life through a court order, having moved away, death, etc.

2. **Internal roles** Set out two chairs several feet apart, representing opposing internal roles, or internal drives. Ask the participant to speak from one chair and then the other in order to get in touch with these opposing forces and gain greater control over how he balances them.

   Examples: the part that wants to offend and the part that doesn't; the part that is confident and the part that takes away confidence; the part that wants to be on the programme and the part that doesn't; the part that can take responsibility for his actions and the part that doesn't want to; the part that can make friends and the part that is shy and isolated; the part that wants to be open and honest and the part that puts up a front or 'mask' in order to cope.

(Continued)

(Monologues: Continued)

After the participant has spoken from alternative internal roles, ask him to assess where he is now on a continuum between the two chairs, where he was at some point in the past and where he would like to be at some point in the future. This can be an excellent motivational and goal setting exercise.

3. **Victim Ripple Effect (also called 'Victim Monologues')** This form of multiple monologue can be effective for victim empathy work and challenging cognitive distortions. In the technique, the participant sets out chairs to represent the 'ripple effect' of all the people who have been affected by his offences. One at a time, he takes the role of as many of these people as possible in order to gain an understanding of how they have been affected. The group worker interviews the participant while he is in each role.

When you have reached a point in the session where you feel it is appropriate, ask the offender to take the role of the direct victim. The group workers and, where appropriate, group members, can now ask the victim any questions that might seem appropriate. For instance, the group worker might ask about the victim's thoughts and feelings in relation to the crime, and in particular what they might think about the protagonist and what he has done to them. If the 'victim' responds in a way that you feel is incongruent, and so clearly displays the *offender's* biased interpretation, bring the offender out of role and back into role as himself. If he is sitting, ask him to stand. Clarify that he should speak as the victim and not as himself, in order to give respect to the victim's point of view. In some cases it may be useful to ask the offender to stand back from the role and watch another group member or worker 'play back' his portrayal of the victim. This technique, known as mirroring, may help him to see his distortions more clearly.

Important This type of victim empathy technique can be the most powerful tool in the dramatic arsenal, especially if the offender is asked to explore the experience of his offence from the point of view of his victim. However, one must choose the right time, and be reasonably confident that the participant will willingly take on this role, playing his victim truthfully. When attempted too early or too forcefully, victim empathy work can be destructive as it can cause the participant to become defensive and blame the victim even more. As a rule, don't attempt victim empathy work unless the participant fully admits his offence and takes responsibility for his actions. Otherwise, it could make the situation worse.

Tip: Where the participant takes on the role of a victim who was a child at the time of the offence, it is often advisable to 'age' the victim so that they are an adult looking back in time. This is a safer option, because it prevents the participant having to play the role of a child victim, which may correspond too closely with his own experience of childhood. It also gets around the distraction of the participant trying to portray a child.

Variation This technique is also very effective on the level of *one step removed.* Use *Group Character Creation* to establish the characters first. The exercise *The Way I See It* is closely related to the one step removed version of *Monologues.*

Another useful variation is the ***Victim Apology***, where the participant apologises to his victim, imagined in the opposite chair. The participant then takes the other chair and responds in role as the victim.

You can broaden the use of this technique beyond the dichotomy of victim and offender. For example, a participant may consider how his dependency on alcohol has affected his family, friends, etc. by speaking from the roles of these people.

(Continued)

(Monologues: Continued)

4. **Past, present, future** The participant takes on the role of himself at some point in the recent past, in the present, and/ or at some point in the future. The facilitator and group members interview him regarding the influences on his thinking, feeling and behaviour, his attitudes toward himself and others, his behaviour, etc. In role as himself in the future, the participant can be asked questions about the choices he has made and what his life is like now. Various options can be played out, for example a non-offending future vs. an offending future (e.g. the interview takes place in a prison cell).

Note: If the participant goes into role as himself in the past, it is important to agree the purpose of the exercise and the boundaries about what sort of questions will be asked. For obvious reasons, going into role as one's self in the past can quickly access highly troubling and traumatic events in a very immediate way. It is important, therefore, to agree before hand that the questions will only relate, for example, to the participant's prior offences, to positive relationships and perhaps to attitudes, beliefs and behaviours at the time. Beware that even with all 'safeties' in place, going into the past can trigger very powerful feelings. As a further precaution, you may place a limit on how far back in the past you ask the participant to go. Six months in the past is often adequate for the purposes of addressing offending behaviour and offending patterns and the influences on offending and other life choices.

• • •

Comments The *Monologue* technique has the obvious advantage that it can be used in one-to-one work. It is also a useful technique for groupwork, although it can become tedious for observing group members. See some of the tips included at the start of the chapter for ideas about how to keep the observers involved.

When interviewing a participant in role as another person, start with factual questions in order to give the participant an opportunity to feel comfortable in the role and to give him confidence that he can answer questions and make observations from another person's point of view. Later, you can move on to questions that demand more use of imagination and emotional sensitivity.

Be aware that the insights may only be incremental. There may not be any great 'Eureka!' moment.

When using two or more chairs to represent the participant and other people, ask the participant which chair he wants for himself and which chair will represent the other person(s). This helps the participant to 'own' his role in the role play. Begin and end with the participant in his own chair.

Monologues is closely akin to *Interview in Role*, one of the *processing techniques.*

Offence Reconstruction

Aims: Disclosure; insight; empathy; eliciting offence cycle; looking at alternatives; motivation to change; other aims described below
Very high focus
Number of participants: 1—15
Time needed: 30—60 minutes per offence
Worker participation: no
Degree of distance: normally on the Personal Level, but can also be done at One Step Removed (see Variation)

Method

The Offence Reconstruction is a technique increasingly used in offending behaviour work to help participants better understand their offending behaviour and the options they have to choose their future behaviour. It is also used to promote victim empathy, personal responsibility and the motivation to change.

In the technique, the participant is asked to reconstruct the events leading up to, during and following his offence in a series of freeze-frames, or pauses in time. Each pause allows the opportunity to examine the thoughts, feelings and behaviour of the key people in the scene at a given moment in time. As workers, we facilitate reconstructions very closely in order to ensure that the aim remains clear and that the boundaries are respected.

Of all the techniques in this book, the Offence Reconstruction undoubtedly counts as the most advanced and needs the most skilled and sensitive leadership, as there are many ways in which it can be damaging to the group and counter-productive for the participant. This is because Offence Reconstruction, when done on the personal level, focuses directly on what are often the participant's most highly volatile, vulnerable or shameful actions. Nevertheless, when properly facilitated, Offence Reconstruction can be highly beneficial for participants, which is why it is increasingly used and why we include it here.

***Important* Please read the note of caution on p.33 regarding personally focused work before you consider using this technique, and also the comments and concerns below.**

To begin, ask the participant briefly to describe an offence he has committed. For young people at risk, this may not be a criminal offence, but may be some other anti-social or destructive act. Once he has given a broad outline of the offence, ask him to 'show us how it was.'

In order to aid the participant's recall and help the group to understand the events, it will help to have the participant arrange chairs and other furniture in the room to represent the setting.

Where appropriate, use other group members to represent other people who were present during the scene. Otherwise, use only the offender to represent all of the people present. Bear in mind that in the reconstruction the others in the scene are simply representing the position of the other person and are not asked to speak in role or otherwise perform the role. To do this would move the scene into a re-enactment of a real-life scene and this is NOT the aim of offence reconstruction.

The reconstruction will include numerous pauses, at which point you and the group can help the participant to recall his thinking, feeling and behaviour at each moment during the lead-up to the offence. See *Thinking Reports* and *Offence Cycles* for ideas about how to record the information gathered during the reconstruction. Depending on the *readiness levels*, you may wish to use some of the *processing techniques* to encourage the participant to see his offending from other points of view and to challenge his own perceptions and beliefs.

(Continued)

Table 8.2: Victim Awareness: Thinking Report for Self and Other (From a sample session dialogue)

Name: *Jim* **What happened:** *I came home from the pub. I'd had six pints. Chrissie had a go at me and I hit her. She had to go to the hospital. I was arrested.*

ME (Jim as self)			**OTHER PERSON** (Jim speaking as Chrissie)		
THOUGHTS	**FEELINGS**	**BEHAVIOUR**	**THOUGHTS**	**FEELINGS**	**BEHAVIOUR**
Here it comes. She's going to give me grief again. It's always arguments these days. She's always having a go at me.	*I'm angry at her.* *Depressed about what's happening and not happening in my life.* *A little drunk.*	*I shout from the street because she's left the slide bolt latched inside the front door.*	*Here it comes. He's pissed again.*	*I'm angry, because I told him not to go out on the piss tonight with his mates. I'm not well and the kids need looking after. I'm frightened, too. I know what he's like when he's pissed.*	*I hear Jim say, 'Open the door, you f****** bitch.'*
Bloody stupid woman. I've told her how angry it makes me when she locks me out. Now I have to wake up the kids and the neighbours.	*Really angry.*	*Shouting for her to open front door. She opens the door and says I'm drunk.*	*I want it to stop. I'm not putting up with him anymore.*	*At my wit's end with him. Really angry.*	*I unbolt the lock.*

I think 'so what?' I've had a good night out.	*Losing it completely.*	*I walk in and all hell breaks loose. She shouts at me and says she's moving out and taking the kids to her parents. The fight starts.*	[Violence] *Don't hurt me, and don't hurt my kids.*	[Violence] *Afraid.* *It hurts like hell.*	*We're both shouting, and my eldest boy comes downstairs. Jim has a go at him. I tell Jim to leave him alone, and he hits me. He punches me in the mouth and splits my lip. I fall against the wall.*

Underlying beliefs at the time that supported the behaviour ('Old me' thinking and beliefs):
When I don't get my own way and I'm feeling misunderstood or 'got at,' I have the right to take out my anger on Chrissie and the kids, use violence against her and make her do what I want her to do. I don't care what effect it has on the kids, but I apologise later because I feel guilty. I believe I'm entitled to what I want when I want it.

'New me' thinking and beliefs:
I've made a lot of mistakes and I can see how my behaviour hurt my wife and children. I never have the right to use violence in the home, and I do not have the right to take out my anger on other people. I need to think first about the consequences of my actions and think about what's going on inside, then talk to other people without shouting or getting abusive.

(Offence Reconstruction: Continued)

Some aims of offence reconstruction In order to do the Offence Reconstruction effectively, it is important to know what the aim is. The technique can be used with the following aims:

- To record thoughts, feelings, attitudes and beliefs before, during and after the offence in order to elicit the individual's *offence cycle;*
- To encourage disclosure about the offence. In a conducive setting, the realism of the scene often helps offenders to think themselves back into the moment of the offence.
- To examine behaviour and underline the offender's responsibility for his own actions at each moment;
- To examine cognitive distortions and justifications;
- To encourage victim awareness and empathy;
- To detect patterns of thinking and behaviour (e.g. by looking at several similar offences);
- Motivation and goal setting. Use the *Offence Reconstruction* as a motivator to avoid offending next time, and to lead into role plays giving concrete examples of how this could be done;
- To help the participant identify what skills he lacked at the time of the offence that he can practise on the programme.

Comments/concerns It is important to stress that when working on the personal level with offences of violence, including sexual offences, the moments of the offending should only be referred to and must never be demonstrated, even in a stylised or 'stop-start' manner. Demonstrating these types of offences may cause extreme distress among the observers and co-participants, and it also runs the risk of traumatising the offender. Even more worryingly, we may inadvertently reinforce the offending behaviour by allowing the offender an opportunity to re-experience the positive 'buzz' (e.g. power, control, drug-induced euphoria, sexual thrill) of his offending. In short, this technique can easily become abusive or counter-productive.

To avoid this pitfall, use a before and after approach. For example, in the reconstruction of a violent offence in the home, it is possible that the scene explores the moments leading up to and following the offence. In most cases, analysing the lead up to the offence, and then the after-effects, is sufficient to accomplish the aim. By focusing on the violence itself, we can easily lose track of the meaning of the violence and the reasons for it. The following dialogue from a sample session explains this in more detail:

• • •

Sample dialogue from an offence reconstruction:

In an offending behaviour group for men convicted of battering women, the session is focused on personal responsibility and the motivation to change. Jim (J) has offered to reconstruct an offence against his wife. He has set out several chairs to represent the sitting room of their home (he is no longer living there). In this reconstruction, for reasons of safety the group worker (G) decides to use only Jim on stage, and not a group member in role as Jim's wife.

Note: This illustration represents an abridged version of what would normally be a session lasting 30 to 90 minutes.

G: *Where have you just come from?*
J: *I've been down at the pub.*
G: *How long?*
J: *A few hours. I've had about six pints. It's just past ten at night.*

Group worker decides to use a *Thinking Report for Self and Other* to help Jim track his thoughts, feelings and actions as the situation develops. This version of the *Thinking Report* also reports on the reactions of the victim, in this case Jim's wife, Chrissie. During this sequence, another worker, or group member, records the thoughts, feelings and actions (See sample *Thinking Report,* Fig. 8.2).

(Continued)

(Offence Reconstruction: Continued)

G: *When you come to the door, what are you thinking?*
J: *I'm thinking, 'Here it comes, she's going to give me grief again.'*
G : *And the feeling?*
J : *I'm angry at her, because it's all arguments these days. She's always having a go at me.*
G: *And how do you come in?*
J : *I shout from the street. She's forgot to leave the slide bolt undone, so I have to shout.*
G: *And the thought?*
J : *Bloody stupid woman!*
G: *And the feeling?*
J: *Really angry, because I've told her how angry it makes me when she locks me out. Now I have to wake up the kids and the neighbours.*
G: *And what happens next?*
J: *She opens the door. I walk in and all hell breaks loose. She shouts at me and says she's moving out and taking the kids to her parents in the morning, and that's when I just lost it completely. That's when the fight started.*
G: *Be specific. What happened first?*
J: *She said I was drunk.*
G: *And your thought when she said that?*
J: *So what? I've had a good night out.*

The reconstruction continues for several minutes, with a more detailed picture developing of Jim's thoughts, feelings and actions during this attack on his wife. The group worker decides to interview Jim in role as his wife in order to hear her thinking report for the same period of time. The focus of the following section is on victim awareness, working toward the more general aim of Jim taking responsibility for his violence:

G: *Alright, I'll ask you to stand on this side of the door now and be Chrissie, your wife. Chrissie, when you hear Jim shout in the street, what do you hear him say?*
Jim as Chrissie (J/C): *You really want me to say it?*
G: *Yes, we need the exact words.*
J/C: *'Open the door, you effing bitch.'*
G: *And what was your thought when he shouted that?*
J: *How do I know what she was thinking?*
G: *Stay in role as Chrissie. What's your best guess? What is your sense of what you thought, Chrissie, when you heard Jim shout those words from the street?*

(NB: Jim is taking on the role of his *perception* of Chrissie, not Chrissie herself. This gets us past the difficulty of 'not knowing what she was thinking,' as Jim protests here. It is acceptable not to know; what is important is that Jim tries to gain a *sense* of how Chrissie thinks and feels in relation to his behaviour toward her.)

J/C: *Here it comes. He's pissed again.*
G: *And the feeling?*
J/C: *Angry, because I asked him not to go out on the piss tonight with his mates. I'm not feeling well and the kids need looking after.*
G: *Other feelings?*
J/C: *(long silence) I suppose frightened as well. I know what he's like when he's pissed.*
G: *And when you unbolt the lock, what's the thought?*
J/C: *I want it to stop. I'm not putting up with him anymore.*
G: *And the feeling?*
J/C: *At my wit's end with him. Really angry.*

(Continued)

(Offence Reconstruction: Continued)

The interview continues for several minutes, at which point the group worker decides to jump forward in time, continuing to interview Jim in role as Chrissie, but *after the violence.* The rest of the participants (P) are encouraged to ask 'Chrissie' questions.

G: *Let's go forward in time to after Jim hit you. As Chrissie, can you describe what happens?*
J/C: *We are both shouting, and my oldest boy comes down the stairs. When I tell him to go back upstairs Jim has a go at him. When I tell Jim to leave him alone, that's when he hits me.*
P: *Where does he hit you?*
J/C: *He punches me in the mouth. I fall back against the wall.*
P: *What do you think at that point?*
J/C: *Don't hurt me, and don't hurt my kids.*
G: *And the feeling?*
J/C: *Afraid. I'm in pain. It hurts like hell. He also split my lip.*

Group worker asks Jim to leave the role of Chrissie and to look back over the two *Thinking Reports*, one for him and one for Chrissie. Jim is encouraged to draw distinctions between 'old me' and 'new me' thinking, feeling, attitudes and behaviour.

G: *Looking at these two thinking reports, what are some of your thoughts about the incident? Let's focus on 'old me' versus 'new me' thoughts, feelings, attitudes and behaviour. Looking to the future, what is it you want to work on that was too difficult here?*

Note: This reconstruction involved only Jim on stage and did not require him to re-enact the situation. This is an important distinction. To have have gone into action would have been to cross into re-enactment, which is outside the boundary of our normal practice and should only be facilitated by those with extensive experience and training in such methods. Finally, note that this reconstruction did not re-create the physical violence, but instead focused on the lead up to the attack, and Jim's thoughts about it now.

• • •

Variations For variations of the *Offence Reconstruction* that are simpler to facilitate but which can still be highly effective, we would suggest you use ***Story Boarding*** (as in story boarding a film) or a format such as *Frozen Pictures* or *Three Picture Scenes.* Alternatively, for groups where it is not appropriate to directly address offences of the participants, you can conduct an *Offence Reconstruction* using a fictional character created by the group members. The fictional character should be an offender broadly reflecting their own experiences. See *Group Character Creation* for guidance on generating characters and scenes.

Role Modelling

Aim: To model a behavioural skill for participants
High focus for role models
Number of participants: any number
Time needed: 5—10 minutes per demonstration
Worker participation: optional
Degree of distance: normally One Step Removed, but can also be done on the Personal Level

Method

In this type of role play, the group worker can model suggested skills and behaviours for the participants. The modelling role play may involve two group workers in a prepared scene, or it may involve a group worker and a group member. Where appropriate and feasible, it is often an advantage if the participants themselves act as 'role models,' and demonstrate suggested skills for each other. This is explained below.

Role modelling is based on the natural, instinctive manner in which most of us learn from the earliest age. Think of a parent modelling a new skill such as tying shoes to a child, or an instructor teaching a swimming stroke. The skill is demonstrated, then broken into steps, with each step practised separately, then combined into a sequence. The skill is then repeatedly practised with occasional input from the parent/ instructor. Finally, the learner performs the skill on her own. The same pattern applies to all learned behaviours, although the degree of instruction will of course vary; many skills are never explicitly taught, but are learned through observation and replication.

According to social learning theorist Albert Bandura (1977), and other authors such as McGuire and Priestley (1981 and 1987) and Goldstein (1999), modelling and skills acquisition are most effectively accomplished under the following conditions:

- **Instruction** When there is clear *instruction* about the steps to be followed when performing the skill.
- **Modelling** When the model is *similar to the trainee* (for example in age, in regional background or in life experience) and is seen as being 'not too expert' or is portrayed as such within the characterisation. For this reason, it is often an advantage to have more able participants demonstrate suggested behaviours for less able participants, rather than relying on group workers to demonstrate the behaviours. By using other participants to demonstrate the skills, the observers are reassured that the skill being suggested and demonstrated is attainable and realistic for 'someone like me.' Some programmes use former 'graduates' as models for just this reason; their modelling is perhaps more credible because they have been through the same struggle as the others in the group, yet they have managed to get through the programme and have become a role model for others to follow. Techniques such as *Worker in Role* allow group workers to enter into a role which is closely akin to the participants, and thus help the group worker to bridge the gap by temporarily taking on a persona more similar to the participants.
- **Skills labelled** When there is a clear *verbal narrative* labelling the model's behaviour. It is not sufficient to simply play out a suggested behaviour. The behaviour itself must be clearly described, with each component or 'micro-skill' being labelled. It is often useful to give behavioural skills simple phrase labels, for example 'stop and think'; 'listen and repeat'; 'think before you speak'; 'be polite but firm'; 'see it from their point of view'.
- **Multiple models** When a number of different models are used. This allows for immediate feedback and adjustment, and also allows for multiple examples of the same skill.

(Continued)

(Role Modelling: Continued)

- **Favourable consequences** When the suggested behaviour is seen to lead to favourable consequences (a useful strategy is to show an undesirable behaviour and outcome first, and then a desirable behaviour and consequence).
- **Multiple practice** When the participant is given multiple opportunities to practise the skill in a safe supportive context, with gradually increasing levels of difficulty in order to 'harden' the skill. See *Skills Practice Role Play.*
- **Real life practice** When the participant is given *opportunities for 'real life' practice* of the new skill within a short time of learning.

This sequence provides the rationale for the sequence in which we present skills-oriented role plays in this chapter: *Modelling, Practice* and *Testing.*

• • •

Example

Skill to be modelled *Telling someone how you feel about their actions.*

Scene A fictional (one step removed) scene is created where two inmates, 'Tony' and 'Bob' are standing on a prison landing. They have been friends up until now, but Tony now questions whether they are still friends because he thinks that Bob has repeated something he told him in confidence. Tony wants to tell Bob that he thinks Bob has betrayed his trust and that he is feeling angry and rejected as a result.

The first step is to provide instruction about the steps, or 'micro-skills,' involved in *telling someone how you feel about their actions.* The group worker instructs the group that the following steps are involved in the skill:

- Decide what you want to say to the other person.
- Decide what body language you will use to convey your point.
- Choose the right time and ask to speak with him. Get his undivided attention.
- Explain to him how you feel in a clear and calm manner.
- Listen to his response.
- Decide how you would like to respond. Take time to think. Make sure you understand what he is saying.
- Respond in a clear and calm manner.

All behavioural skills can be broken down into a number of distinct micro-skills, as illustrated here. For a comprehensive listing of skills and their micro-skills, as well as hundreds of suggestions for Modelling Role Plays, see Goldstein (1999).

The next step is to model the behaviour, providing a narrative that points out the various micro-skills.

Group worker as 'Tony' (G/T) (to audience): *I've decided that I want to tell Bob that I'm angry at him because he told other people something about me and my wife that I told him and asked him to keep private between me and him. I'm going to be honest with him and I'm going to use peaceful body language like not raising my voice or making threatening gestures. We're on general association now, so we should both have some time to talk.* (To Group worker in role as 'Bob'): *Bob, can I speak with you a minute?*

(Continued)

(Role Modelling: Continued)

Group worker in role as 'Bob' (G/B): *Yeah, okay.*
G/T (to audience): *I know I've got his attention now and there aren't any distractions. We've come to a part of the landing where no one walks by at this time of day.* (To Bob) *I want to check something out with you. Remember when I told you about the letter I got from my wife and how upset I'd been?*
G/B: *Yeah, I remember.*
G/T: *Well I'm angry about telling you now because I didn't tell anyone else but some other guys have told me that they know about the situation. A couple guys have made some really out of order remarks, you know what I mean? I trusted you not to tell anyone, and I asked you as a friend. Did you tell anyone?*
G/B: *No, I didn't tell anyone, I wouldn't do that to you. But when you told me, we were by the pool table, and someone could have heard you telling me. Remember? Or maybe it got about some other way, but it definitely wasn't me.*
G/T: (to audience): *So I explained how I was feeling and why, and now he's told me that. I wasn't expecting that answer, but I s'pose someone else could have heard. I decide to apologise and say we're still mates, but I'll be a lot more careful next time about who and where I tell anything that personal again.* (to Bob) *I'm sorry I accused you, but I didn't see how else people would know.*
G/B: *Yeah, no problem. I'm sorry the word got out, too. I know you wanted to keep it quiet.*
(They shake hands)

This modelling role play provides a favourable outcome, and leads directly on to *Skills Practice Role Play*, where the participants themselves practise the skill. In particular, those participants who have identified this particular skill as a difficult one for them would be encouraged to practise it.

• • •

Variations Another option would have been to show a bad outcome first, with the group worker in role as Tony showing aggressive behaviour and the two men ending up in conflict.

Furthermore, it may be useful to offer several different role models, for example several group workers or more able participants who are confident in this skill. Where appropriate, you can use a 'round-robin' approach to modelling, with group members each having an opportunity to model a suggested 'solution' or behaviour. Suggested behaviours should be judged by how realistic they are and what the likely consequence would be. This variation shares much in common with *Forum Role Play*.

Comments It is worth noting that if group workers demonstrate the suggested behaviour, this is effectively an *Interactive Observer* activity. For newer or less confident groups, there can be a distinct advantage in having the group workers demonstrate the skills first, only later moving into active role play work with the participants taking on roles.

Skills Practice Role Play

Aims: Learning and practising new behaviours and interpersonal skills
High focus
Number of participants: any number
Time needed: 20—60 minutes per person for each skill
Worker participation: Optional
Degree of distance: One Step Removed or Personal Level

Method

This is the type of role play people are generally most familiar with. The point of this type of role play is to build up the participant's repertoire of skills, in effect to act as a rehearsal for life. Practising interpersonal skills through role play is useful for the same reason that it is useful to practise the piano or take driving lessons—the advance practice helps us to prepare and rehearse how we will deal with the real event in the heat of the moment. Behavioural rehearsal gives us a better chance to succeed 'in real life' using a wider range of strategies and skills.

In a Skills Practice Role Play, a situation is presented and the participant is asked to use a particular skill to handle the situation. If the scene is *one step removed,* the participant can play the role himself or he can play someone else (e.g. 'someone like me').

The participant is not simply thrown into the situation, but receives a thorough preparation before-hand. The skill is often best presented instructionally and then through *modelling* (see *Role Modelling*). After the skill has been described and modelled, the participant is then asked to describe the skill in his own words, by breaking the skill down into the various micro-skills. Only then is the participant asked to perform the skill in a live role play.

Important An often overlooked but nevertheless key point regarding skills practice is that the participant *must succeed* in practising the skill during this type of role play. Otherwise the role play could be counter-productive and reinforce his sense of failure. To avoid this, the skill must be practised with incremental increases in difficulty. During the first practice, the other role player should make an easy adversary. As the central role player becomes more confident with his new skill, the other role player can be asked to 'raise the stakes' in order to help the participant over-learn the skill.

• • •

Example Continuing on from the example used to explain *Role Modelling*, we can see how modelling leads directly on to skills practice. The scene between 'Tony' and 'Bob' has been considered at length, and the various micro-skills within the skill of *telling someone how you feel about their actions* have also been modelled.

A participant or staff member is inducted into the role of Bob. Before the role play begins, the participant taking the role of Tony is taken through the various micro skills (listed in *Role Modelling*) and is asked to describe his strategy for each one. When it is clear that the participant has sufficient understanding, the role play can begin.

The scene should be repeated a minimum of three times in order to assist memorisation. In the early runs of the scene, the role player taking the part of Bob is asked to play Bob as being very good natured. In later runs, as the participant playing Tony becomes more confident and able, the Bob character can be directed to be increasingly defensive. One way to put this might be to ask the role player to play Bob 'as if he is having a really bad day.' This will provide increasing levels of difficulty for the role player in the role of Tony.

(Continued)

(Skills Practice Role Play: Continued)

Other skills commonly practised:

- handling criticism
- dealing with a put-down
- listening to a friend's problem
- applying for a job/ talking positively about one's self
- saying no
- showing empathy
- dealing with anxiety
- handling jealous feelings
- taking responsibility
- being clear about what you want to do
- recognising triggers and coping with it by verbalisation and self-talk
- dealing with provocation
- apologising
- dealing with boredom
- dealing with rejection/ failure/ disappointment
- communicating with your partner about a difficulty
- telling someone about your offence
- dealing with a police visit/ police stop and search
- asking for help
- joining a conversation
- respecting someone else's personal space
- parenting skills

Note that each skill interconnects with others, though it is possible to practise just one in isolation. See the *Skills Rating Sheet* in *Appendix A* for more examples of typical skills that can be practised using role play.

Breaking skills down into micro-skills As we mentioned in *Role Modelling*, behavioural skills can be broken down into a clear and simple series of micro-skills. Start with the overall skill and the motivation behind it: what is the main participant trying to achieve with the skill (e.g. staying out of a fight, meeting people, getting help, etc.)? The micro-skills should be a series of three to seven steps that will help the person achieve the overall aim. We often generate the micro-skills with the participants during the session. This is often a better strategy than having pre-prepared micro-skills because it invites the participants to get involved in the 'nuts and bolts' of the skill:

Skill: Dealing with a provocation

Micro-skills:

1 Listen to what the other person is saying to you.
2 Stop and think before reacting. Consider your options, and think of the consequences of your actions.
3 Decide how you will respond.
4 State or make your response in a firm but polite manner.
5 If the other person persists in provoking you, state or make your response again in a firm but polite manner, and leave the situation if possible.
6 Give yourself praise for handling the situation without becoming aggressive or violent.

(Continued)

(Skills Practice Role Play: Continued)

Sample role plays focusing on this skill:

- In a pub, a drunk person comes to your table and makes inappropriate remarks to you and your friends.
- At school, another pupil challenges you to a fight.
- While walking down the street, a group of youths pass by and one insults you as they pass. They laugh.

Skill: Starting a conversation

Micro-skills:
1 Decide if it would be appropriate to start a conversation with this person.
2 Decide what you will say first.
3 Say it in a clear and friendly manner, in a way that invites the other person to respond.
4 Listen to (and observe) their response, and decide how to respond.
5 Continue speaking and listening, showing friendly interest in what the other person says.
6 Be aware of getting the balance right between being over friendly and too distant.
7 Give yourself credit for having started a conversation.

Sample role plays focusing on this skill:
- In a staff canteen, a new employee starts a conversation with another employee.
- In a classroom at the start of a new course, one student strikes up a conversation with another.
- At a party for a mutual friend, one person starts a conversation with another party-goer.

Skill: Handling jealous feelings about your partner

Micro-skills:

1 Recognise that you are feeling jealous and be aware of your thoughts about your partner.
2 Try to genuinely see the situation from his/ her point of view.
3 Decide if there are valid grounds for your feelings of jealousy, or whether you are winding yourself up over something trivial or non-existent.
4 If you think your reasons for feeling jealous are valid and serious, share your concerns with your partner in a polite and respectful way.
5 Listen to their response.
6 Think about your response, then respond and try to make an agreement with your partner that will help prevent future jealous feelings. Remind yourself that healthy relationships are built on trust, compromise and honest caring for the well-being and fulfilment of both people.
7 Give yourself praise for handling your jealous feelings well.

Sample role plays focusing on this skill:

- One partner becomes jealous when the other has been out late without ringing to explain why.
- One partner becomes jealous when they see their partner talking with someone else in what they see as a flirtatious manner.
- One partner becomes jealous when the other receives a phone message from a former partner/ boyfriend/ girlfriend.

(Continued)

(Skills Practice Role Play: Continued)

Comments The participant must practise each skill a minimum of three times, and it will often be necessary to have many repetitions to help ensure the new skill 'takes' and transfers to real life situations. Outside the session, new skills must be practised several hundred or even several thousand times in order to become fully integrated to the point of being automatic. The need for prolonged repetition demands a great deal of patience and persistence, which is one reason why skills practise is so often left out of programmes, despite its being one of the most essential aspects of learning for many offenders and young people at risk.

When working at one step removed using role play, there will be times when it becomes clear that there is no need to continue working at such distance. If it seems appropriate, and if the participant is willing, you can drop the fictional pretence and address the participant by his or her own name in the role play.

Another concern: Often, participants who have made a commitment to change have difficulty explaining to their families and friends the changes they are trying to make. Many months of positive groupwork can be undermined with off-hand remarks and dismissive jibes. So it may be useful for the participant to role play telling his family and friends about the changes he is trying to make and asking for support. Where work is done with family members, the participant may directly explain the changes he is trying to make and the family can be helped to adjust appropriately.

Variation With some participants, it may be useful to ask them to play the scene badly first, so that they can obviously play it better the second time. In the first run of the scene, they can be asked to play the scene, for example, 'the opposite of how it should be done,' or, 'as if you are having a bad day,' or 'in a way guaranteed not to get you what you want.' This often leads to an obviously ill-fated and humorous role play, which can then free up the participants to try out the suggested behaviour.

Role Tests

Aims: To assess skills needs and test the integration of new skills
High focus
Number of participants: any number
Time needed: 10 - 30 minutes per role play
Worker participation: one stays out, others optional
Degree of distance: One Step Removed or Personal Level

Method

This type of role play is intended to assess or test the participant's ability to provide an adequate and non-abusive response to a spontaneous situation. It is also known as a 'spontaneous role test' (Haskell, 1975) or 'spontaneity test' (Moreno and Moreno, 1975; Moreno, 1993).

To conduct this type of role play, the facilitators prepare a custom-tailored scene which will test a specific skill that the offender has been practising on the programme. Equally, the scene may be used early in the programme to assess the participant's abilities and skills needs. The facilitators play the 'antagonist' roles in the role test, and pitch the level of difficulty such that the challenge is hard but just achievable.

At the start of the Role Test, the participant enters the stage area with no information about the situation he is about to face. He cannot rehearse his response, nor will he be allowed to repeat this specific scene again in order to practise. Just before the scene begins, the participant is told just enough information to allow him to begin the scene, and is asked to deal with the situation as he would in real life, 'to the best of your abilities.' If the Role Test is being conducted to test the acquisition of a new skill, the participant would be asked to 'use the skills you have practised in this programme in order to deal with the situation that is about to occur.'

Example (This example could be used as an assessment role play at the start of a programme, or as a skills test near the end of a programme.) After the stage has been set up, the participant enters the room. The group worker gives the following instructions: 'You are alone and driving your own car on a dual carriageway. The car is insured and taxed, legal for use on the roads, and you have a valid driving license. After a few moments, something will happen. Use (your best ability/ the skills you have practised in the programme) to deal with the situation.'

After the participant has been 'driving' for a few moments, a police car sounds its siren (vocal sound effect) and the driver is waved over to the side of the road. The police officer, played by a worker, gets out of the police car and walks to the driver's car. The officer gives the driver a long lecture for driving over the speed limit (Note: it should only be a little over the speed limit). If the driver of the car provokes the situation, the staff member in role as the officer may, for example, give a speeding ticket, insist on giving a breath test, arrest him, etc. By contrast, if the driver co-operates, the officer may let him off with a stern warning but no ticket.

Feedback and follow-up After the Role Test, the group members and facilitators give feedback, and the participant gives himself feedback as well. The feedback can be assisted by the use of *Rating Sheet for Role Plays* (*Appendix A*).

Be careful to make the feedback supportive but realistic. Never allow the feedback to be demeaning or otherwise negative. The feedback should be in the form of statements and observations about the actual behaviour shown in the scene (e.g. 'I noticed that you used aggressive hand gestures as soon as you spoke to the officer'). The feedback should not speculate about other contingencies, or ask the protagonist (the one being tested) questions (e.g. 'What would you have done if it was a female officer?').

Also remember to set up a non-violence rule before the Role Tests begin.

(Continued)

(Role Tests: Continued)

Variation A useful option is to make the Role Test in two parts, with a role reversal in the middle. So, to use the example above, in the Role Test with police officer and driver, after the first part is completed, the worker and participant change places and the participant plays the same scene from the start, but this time in role as the officer. The worker plays the role of driver.

Role Tests can be scripted in advance, leaving gaps for the participant's responses. One advantage of having a script is that the Role Test can be delivered in a consistent way to all of the participants in a group, or to an individual as a pre-test and post-test. If you use a script, be sure to make the dialogue loose enough to allow for a range of possible responses from the person being tested.

For more on these variations, see Haskell (1975).

Examples of role test situations:

- Participant is in a cafe. An aggressive person approaches him and asks for money.
- Participant comes to pick up his car from the mechanic, and finds that there is damage that was not there before.
- Participant is playing a game with other residents in a hostel. Another player accuses him of cheating.
- Participant is in a pub with his girlfriend. A drunk man approaches and becomes 'over-friendly' with his girlfriend.
- Participant is alone in his flat. A neighbour comes to complain about the loud music coming from his flat.
- Participant is standing in a queue in the post office when someone comes and stands in front of him.
- Participant needs to make an urgent phone call from a phone box, but someone else is using the phone.
- Participant is at the hairdresser's. The hairdresser finishes and says that the haircut is 'totally different from what you asked for, but I think it looks better this way.'
- Participant is in the pub. Another man stares at him, and then verbally insults him.
- Participant is on the prison landing. Another inmate calls him a demeaning name and directly provokes him.
- Participant is on the prison landing and passes a group of three inmates. As he passes, the three laugh (at him?).
- Same as above, but this time the participant is passing three officers.

Comments Role Tests can be powerful and memorable experiences for participants. They often act as milestones or even rites of passage, affirming that a new stage of change has been entered. Geese Theatre has evolved a highly structured form of role test termed the *Corrida,* and which forms the third part of the *Violent Illusion Trilogy*, described in *Chapter 9*.

CHAPTER 9

Geese Theatre in Performance: 'Lift Your Mask!'

No account of Geese Theatre's work would be complete without a look at our performance approach. After all, we started as a performance company and we continue to perform in a wide variety of criminal justice and related settings. The other half of our work—the workshop and groupwork approach described in *Chapters 1* to *8*—grew out of our issue-based, interactive style of theatre.

The improvisational approach In our improvised performances, we devise the action together with the audience, on the spot. We perform in half-masks, presenting simple and direct scenes that mirror issues crucial to the audience. The performance style is most similar to the *Commedia dell' Arte*[1] as it relies on structured improvisation, instantly recognisable characters and audience interaction. Our performance style also owes much to the satiric-comic improv approach developed in the 1950s and 60s in theatre companies such as the Compass Players and Second City in Chicago. These companies made improvisation and audience suggestions central to their approach. They were part of the international wave of innovation in audience-interactive, socially oriented, educational/ therapeutic, experimental and political theatre occurring from the 1920s through the 1980s (Barker, 1988; Fox, 1986; Casson, 1997; Moreno, 1983). Interactive and nonscripted approaches such as the widely influential Living Theatre, Forum Theatre (Boal; 1979; Schutzman and Cohen-Cruz, 1994), Playback Theatre (Fox, 1986), Environmental Theatre and Theatrical Freestyle (Wirth, 1994) are all part of this wave of innovation in which Geese Theatre has developed, taken inspiration and developed its distinct performance approach.

In our improvised performances, we provoke the audience into lively debate around issues most crucial to their lives, such as family, work, friendship, self-image, survival and finding a way out of offending. When they're going well, the shows are rowdy; there is a heated atmosphere where the audience grows ever more invested in the central characters and their potential success. The drama takes place between the characters on stage, but even more crucially, between the characters and the audience. A character will often need help or advice when facing a desperate situation. He or she turns to speak with the audience: 'What can I do next?' Now the character and the audience are directly linked; the character serves as the conduit for the audience's ideas, fears, frustrations and, often, their disbelief that there is a way out of the cycle of offending. Through this dialogue, the actor extracts the collective knowledge of the audience about a particular issue and filters the ideas through the character. When the audience offers a suggestion, the character may try it out and either succeed or fail. If he does fail, audiences will often become extremely involved and agitated with him, particularly if he keeps making the same mistakes. At times, audience members join us onstage in order to show a character facing a difficult situation 'how it's done.'

Our plays also make use of strong images and metaphors which are later picked up and developed in workshops. Examples include our use of the mask as a visual metaphor (see below), the character of 'Deathbird', symbolising the impulse to re-offend (Deathbird lives in the prison cage and wants to drag you back in), and the Fool, an amoral trickster/ chameleon/ teacher/ master of ceremonies who symbolises, among other things, the 'game' of offending, the abusive part of the self, and the random events of life that can trip us up.

A typical improv scene In a typical situation in one of our improvisational prison shows, an inmate character in *The Plague Game*[2] enters the prison visits room and tells us he is about to receive a visit from his wife and ten year old son. He tells us he's feeling nervous and angry because she is late for the visit and missed the last one. His wife enters with their son, who has been having nightmares and is getting into fights at school. She wants her husband to talk with his son and give him some guidance. The inmate character becomes preoccupied that his wife's hair looks different and she is wearing a new dress. He feels jealous, angry and powerless, and accuses her of having sex with another man. He completely overlooks his son who is trying to get his attention. When an argument develops between the inmate and his wife, the inmate turns to the prisoners in the audience, lifts his mask and complains about her. He blames her for 'winding me up' and not showing enough concern for him. The audience members shout out advice:

- *'Tell her you're sorry!'*
- *You've got to learn to trust her!'*

[1] The form of popular theatre which began in France and Italy during the Renaissance.

[2] A structured improvisational play originally devised in 1982 by John Bergman and Geese Theatre USA.

- *'Slap her and get off the visit! She's winding you up!'*
- *Lift your mask and be real. Listen to what's going on with your son!'*
- *You've got to be a father to your son. Get your priorities right or he'll end up like you!'*

When we have heard from the audience, we play out one or more of the suggestions, at times relying on audience members to come onstage and demonstrate their solution. Where we play out suggestions for destructive behaviour, we also play out the consequences (e.g. his son never wants to visit him again). When a positive suggestion 'succeeds' (e.g. wife and son agree to come to another visit), we play forward until the next dilemma or crisis. The message is always that it doesn't take just one positive choice, but one after the other, day after day. The emphasis is on realistic strategies, not magical solutions.

'Lift your mask!' When we return to work at a prison and ask the inmates who have seen us before what they remember, they most often reply, 'The masks—the way you lift the mask.'

The idea of having to 'wear a mask' to survive came from an inmate in the state prison in Joliet, Illinois, in 1982, when Geese Theatre USA was developing *The Plague Game*. During a discussion about the problems inmates face when they are on a visit with their wife or girlfriend, one inmate broke through the discussion and explained, 'She's got to bring you money so you wear a mask to keep her coming back. The mask gets you what you need.' For John Bergman and the original USA company, this insight inspired what has become Geese Theatre's most powerful and lasting performance metaphor—'lifting the mask.'

To 'lift the mask', we literally raise our character masks on top of our heads and speak directly to the audience or to other characters onstage. When a character lifts his mask, he is trying to 'be real.' It doesn't necessarily mean that he was lying or manipulating before (although he might have been); rather, lifting the mask suggests there may be a deeper truth. When we lift the mask, we highlight the hidden vulnerability, the concealed thoughts and feelings of the characters. Time and again, this metaphor has been an effective way to directly address the most important—often life or death—issues facing our audience, as it allows us to hold up an interactive mirror to their internal as well as their external world.

See pp.20, 43 and the rest of this chapter for more about masks.

'Lifting the Mask' Photo: iD.8 Photography

FRAGMENT MASKS

We have become particularly known for a set of eight specific masks we call *Fragment Masks*. We call them fragment masks because each symbolises a prominent strategy—or fragment of behaviour—used in threatening or stressful situations, or just to 'con' others. In particular, *Fragment Masks* represent key self-protective strategies such as blaming others, denying, using charm, acting out aggressively or playing the victim role. Think of the masks as coping masks, aiding self-protection. When participants understand the situations that provoke their 'fragment mask' strategy, they can also decide whether or not they want to use a different strategy. The focus is not so much on the mask as the function of the behaviour it represents. The eight basic fragment masks we use are:

***The Fist**: 'Don't mess with me!' (push away threat/deny vulnerability)

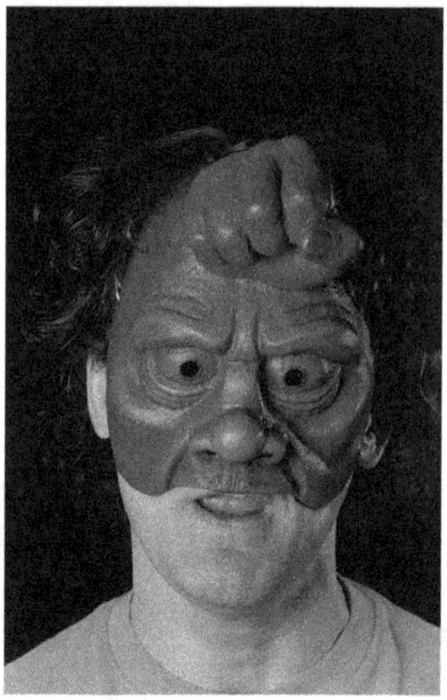

***Mr Cool:** 'Everything is sweet as a nut. I've got no problems – Have you?'

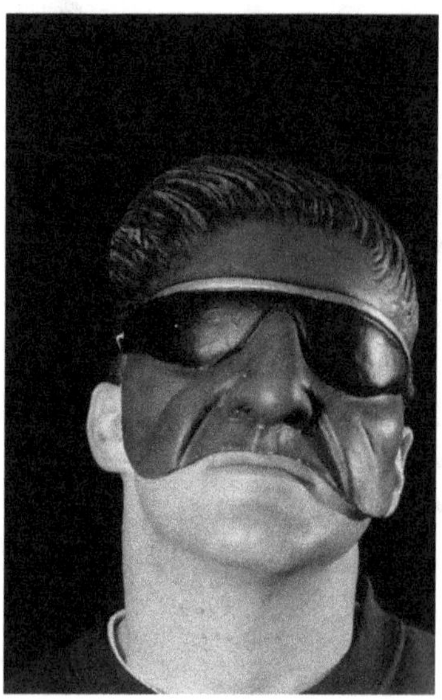

All photos: iD.8 Photography

***The Brick Wall:** 'I didn't do anything. I don't remember. When's the tea break?'

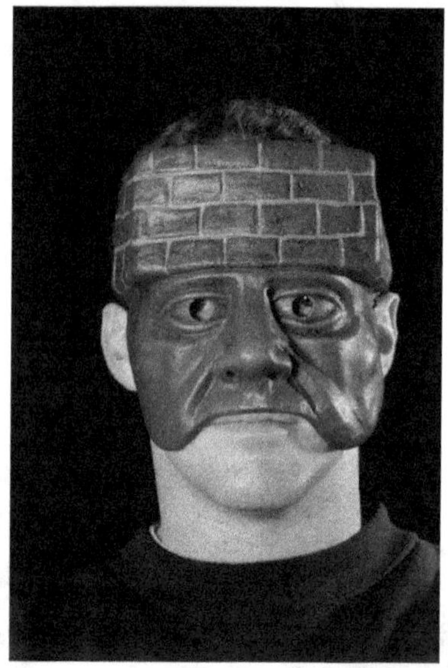

****Good Guy:**'All I'm doing is defending my family. I never hurt anyone who doesn't deserve it.'

****The Mouth** 'I think you'd improve the course if you used more Freud and you could expand our minds and take in a new dimension. Now me, I'm a rage-aholic; I'm addicted to anger. But now I've changed and if I could just explain, when I was a child … etc. (irrelevant digression; functions to keep the problem irresolvable).

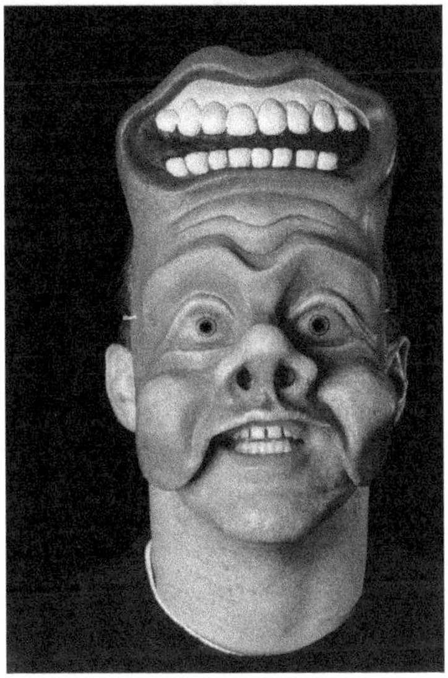

****The Joker:** 'Have you heard the one about..?'

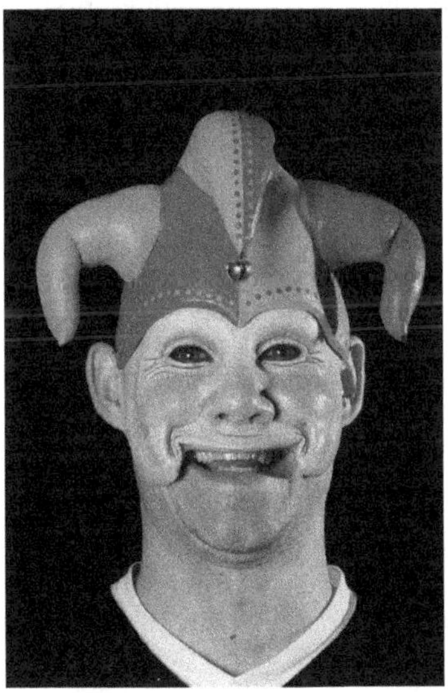

****Poor Me:** 'You don't understand what it's like. I didn't have a choice, the system's against me. That's why I did it.' 'I have the sort of face people like to hit.'

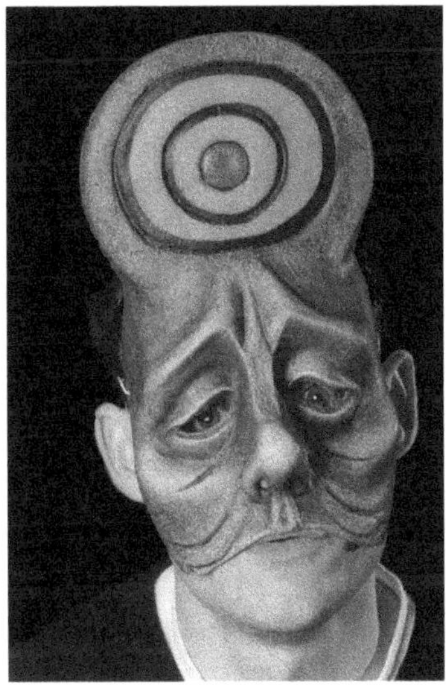

****Rescuer:** 'I don't blame you, mate. I'd have done the same. He deserved a good kicking.'

THE PLAYS

Lifting the Weight

An improvisational play about the first year after release from prison[1]

(Originally created and directed by John Bergman for Geese Theatre USA.)

Lifting the Weight is a structured improvisational play presenting a stark picture of the problems facing men or women prisoners in their first year after release from prison. It shows both how to fail and how to succeed. Two central characters try to win the 'game' by earning tokens representing high risk areas related to issues of survival, family, work, authority and free time. Living in a cage on stage is 'Deathbird', who represents the potential to re-offend, the impulse *not* to think. Deathbird wants to drag the two central characters back to his cage (i.e. prison). The players try to win as many tokens as possible in order to 'build a wall against Deathbird'. On their way, they must make use of whatever support is available in order to survive. They also face hard internal struggles as they try to overcome their own sense of failure, their anger at the social stigma of being an 'ex-con', and their typical impulsive or angry response to high risk situations. Whether they make it to the end of the game or not is largely determined by the suggestions from the audience. If the characters do make it to the end of the game, they face the ultimate challenge: coming to terms with the idea of living a 'straight' life.

Prisoner review from HM Prison Highpoint, Norfolk

> On the 4th of October, Geese Theatre presented a lively performance of their play 'Lifting the Weight' to a cross section of the prison community. The play is a satirical comment on prison and post-prison life. It parodies both the many problems the prisoner encounters while inside and the overwhelming odds and temptations he is forced to face as an ex-convict. It looks at interpersonal and inter-group conflicts that make it mandatory for him to camouflage his true nature and wear a mask.
>
> The play identifies the thorny problems of need, greed, temptation, crime and punishment as a vicious circle from which the ex-convict must extricate himself in order to be permanently free.
>
> As the play unfolds, a vital question continues to re-surface: 'Should we, in the face of grave adversities and stark poverty, revert to crime?' For the inmates who made up 96 per cent of the audience, this is a fundamental question. The play, in an attempt to discuss it, depicts the vastly overpowering dilemmas of the ex-convict as he struggles with the choice of bracing himself against the odds or running the risk of going back to prison. The symbolism of these dilemmas is presented through two major characters: Steven and Henry.
>
> Happy to regain their lost freedom, the two men leave the prison gates with some quiet but firm resolutions never to be back again. They go to their separate homes, one to a frustrated and resentful wife, the other to an invalid mother.
>
> Of course a lot of things have changed, least of which is the furniture. Apart from the intractability of Steve's marriage, which has become shaken and battered by incessant convictions and the attendant long separations, and apart from Henry's financially unviable prospect of carrying the burden of his bedridden mother, the men are also confronted with the difficulty of erasing that indelible stigma of 'ex-convict' with which they have been stamped.

[1] A BAFTA Award-winning Cd-rom version of *Lifting the Weight* is available for use in pre-release programmes. For details, contact Geese Theatre at the address given on p. viii.

Their euphoria at being released is therefore short lived. As they move from one agency to another (probation, employment, the dole, etc), the central themes of the play come into focus. We see them subjected to the whiplash of societal bias, suspicion and rejection. We see their puzzlement grow into resentment, then anger, frustration and finally despair. As their frustration grows, they break their chain of resistance and plunge headlong into a pit of deceit, marital irresponsibility, drunkenness—and crime.

The whole performance is drama at its simplest, devoid of complex themes and plots so as to reach the audience and guarantee our involvement in the presentation. The scenes are improvised. As they unfold, the audience—a mixed-bag of serious, doubtful, suspicious and jeering faces—are invited to participate, to throw in a word or sentence that would either keep the play on its course or change its direction. This of course is another brilliant dramatic ploy designed not only to arouse and maintain the audience's interest, but also to evoke some inward reflections so that we are forced to re-examine our thoughts and opinions about the issues being enacted.

True enough, as the play continues towards its climax, the doubts begin to disappear, the suspicions and the jeers begin to evaporate and are replaced by introspective countenances.

But not for long. Soon the inmates are reeling with laughter as the performers, in the true spirit of dramatic satire, constantly mix subtle criticisms with comical humour. It is as serious as it is hilarious. We frown, we squirm, but we laugh.

Thus, by using satire as its form of presentation, Geese Theatre succeeds in pursuing its goal while still providing entertainment. While recognising the vulnerability of the 'ex-convict' at moments of conflict, the play emphasises the need to take a moral and sensible stand in overcoming such conflicts. The focus is on one point: that conflicts, whether between individual and individual, between individual and family or between individual and society—will always be there. We must expect such conflicts and be prepared to resist the temptation of using unlawful means of resolving them.

This is the play's message. And given the unusually quiet and sober faces of the inmates who filed out that night, I would say the play had succeeded in touching some hidden chords in the hearts of most. The parting shot of the verbose and ubiquitous leader of the cast as the show finishes further drove this message home—'I hope we don't see any of your faces back here again.'

Prisoner review of 'Lifting the Weight' from HM Prison Barlinnie, Glasgow

Under the direction of the 'Fool', in a mask and a red tail coat, it was audience participation with a vengeance as we were exhorted by this Mephistophelean twister to applaud or boo, then accused afterward—with sometimes excruciating clarity—for our moral dishonesty or fickleness.

The play concerned two cons and their lives immediately upon release—with the temptations of booze and easy money and drugs. Also their fair-weather friends and violent reactions to the official sanctions and red tape of bureaucratic nit-picking and harassment.

The hope that it's possible to survive—with courage and dignity and no crying in your beer—was revealed, despite the portrayal of the sometimes hilarious absurdity of a prisoner's Return To Society. But for bringing out the truth about our position after 'Lib', the play was happily unsentimental and struck chords where our personal involvement was made real. It wasn't all fun and games, as at times we were put in a position where we had no choice but to look at our true feelings and venture from behind the mask—in other words, to drop the image that we usually project and look at how we really are.

Lifting the Weight

Photo courtesy of the *Northern Echo*

The Plague Game

An improvisational play about prisoners and their families

(Originally created and directed by John Bergman for Geese Theatre USA)

The Plague Game explores strategies to keep families and friendships from dissolving under the pressure of imprisonment. The play was devised in response to the stark fact that ex-prisoners are four to seven times more likely to re-offend if they do not return to some form of family support after release.

The 'plague' of the title is offending, and the 'game' focuses on the problems encountered by two families when a family member is imprisoned. The play starts at the point of arrest and moves through a series of 'visit levels' through to release. One of the families may learn to communicate effectively, the other may fall apart. The fate of each is largely determined by suggestions from the audience. The play also explores how family members deal not only with the pressure of visits, but with problems facing them in day to day life—housing, debt, finding work, raising children and coping with being a single parent.

Prisoner review from HM Prison The Verne, Dorset

On Thursday, 27th June it sounded as though a riot was in progress here at the Verne. Not to worry, though, it was only a performance by the Geese Theatre performing their play, '*The Plague Game*.' It was a lively occasion lasting two hours, and it was enjoyed by fifty four inmates. The play differs from conventional plays in as much as the script was contrived as the plot progressed. Anything could happen. If a member of the audience disagreed with anything said or done by a member of the cast, the play was stopped and the disagreement was discussed.

It was a very emotional theme, a story of two couples having to cope with situations from arrest, going to court, sentencing and imprisonment, to eventual release. The trials and tribulations of the inmates and their partners, how their partners, how their relationships changed throughout their ordeals. Personally, the play made me realise that my wife and family are not having it easy but suffering just as much as we are in here.

Prisoner review from HM Prison Gloucester

The Geese Theatre Company, a group which specialises in performing plays in prisons, visited in February. Their performance took the form of an improvised 'game' covering the cycle of street-court-prison-street. They were particularly concerned with visits made to the inmates, such as those of family, friends and probation officers, and visits made by family members to solicitors, welfare services and schools, as they coped 'outside.' They portrayed prison visits from the point of view of both the inmate and the visitor.

Prisoner review from HM Prison Wayland, Norfolk

The moral dilemmas posed in the play were incredibly realistic and the use of us in the audience to form and shape the outcome of the play was a wonderful experience to take part in. The suggestions that were played out were acted with brilliant realism and it left me feeling that the company knew the attitudes of inmates intimately, even though they have never been 'inside' themselves. This is one of the good memories of prison that I will take with me when I am released.

The Plague Game

Photo: Rod Morris

'Stay'

A play about domestic violence

(Co-created by Geese Theatre UK with John Bergman, Geese Theatre USA)

'Stay' is a semi-improvised play about domestic abuse, mainly performed as part of programmes addressing domestic abuse. It focuses on the relationship of one man and woman, plotting the man's abuse of power and control and the escalation of his physical and emotional abuse. The play also examines the effects of the man's violence and emotional abuse on the couple's young son. During a series of interactions with the audience, the man attempts to draw the audience into collusive agreement with his denial and justifications. The tension between his distortions and what the audience directly witnesses (including the woman's asides to the audience), exposes his version of 'how it is'.

Stay

Photo: Kate Green

So Far

A play about sexual aggression

(Co-devised by Geese Theatre UK under the direction of James Neale-Kennerly)

So Far is our first play created primarily for sex offender treatment settings. The semi-improvised play examines the experiences of a series of men who commit a range of sexual offences. It addresses themes such as the offence cycle, denial, cognitive distortions, the role of fantasy in offending and the effect of abuse on victims and their families. The action of the play mirrors the process of groupwork, as well as the process of change, by focusing on a central character who is gradually confronted with the reality of his offences. Through debate with this character, audience members are encouraged to make their own links with the material and to share their own suggestions about how the process of change works for them.

A character 'lifts her mask' and speaks to the audience

Photo: iD.8 Photography

Gutted

A play about a man and his beliefs

(Co-devised by Geese Theatre UK under the direction of Tony McBride)

Gutted is the story of one man—the story of how he learns about the world and his role in it. The play plots his development through childhood, adolescence, adulthood and fatherhood. Along the way, he struggles to come to terms with conflicting rules about what it means to be a man. He learns rules about relationships and offending that lead him down dangerous, destructive paths. Ultimately, he learns that his rules are failing to work for him; they hurt him, his partner and his children. The feelings he tries to lock away can no longer be ignored.

Perhaps most significantly, this is a play about feelings. It provides a metaphor for the ways men learn to bottle up or lock away vulnerable feelings, conforming to the 'rules' about being a man. In the end, *Gutted* challenges the audience to offer credible alternatives—a positive, non-abusive vision of what it means to be a man.

Gutted

Photo: iD.8 Photography

The Violent Illusion Trilogy

Addressing violence and the difficult process of change

(Violent Illusion Part One was created and directed by John Bergman for Geese Theatre USA. Parts Two and Three were co-created by Geese Theatre UK with John Bergman, Geese Theatre USA.)

The Violent Illusion Trilogy consists of two plays, a series of workshops and a final 'challenge', all taking place over five days. The work is intended for use in prisons and special hospitals, with men and women who have committed serious and persistent violence. The work is always done in close co-operation with prison staff.

Parts One and Two explore the issue of violence, and the intervening workshops focus on the processes leading to violence. As the week progresses, participants identify and practise new skills for intervening in their own cycle of violence. Part Three is when the participants take centre stage in order to take an important challenge we call 'the Corrida'.

Violent Illusion Part One

Violent Illusion Part One is the story of a child growing up in a violent home. The actors perform in full masks, allowing the audience to 'fill in' the dialogue. The play encourages audience members to identify with all of the characters, victims and perpetrators alike, and to consider the effects of abuse on victims.

Violent Illusion Part One

Photo: Gordon Rainsford

Violent Illusion Part Two

Violent Illusion Part Two is a counterpoint to Part One, as it shows 'a possible way out'. The story focuses on a man with a history of violence returning home from prison to his partner and children. In prison he has made a pledge to be non-violent, but he soon realises that this is not as easy as he thought. The play explores some of the cognitive skills and interventions that men can use to avoid violence and to begin the process of change.

Violent Illusion Part Two

Photo: Gordon Rainsford

Violent Illusion Part Three: *The Corrida*

The final part of the Violent Illusion trilogy is called *The Corrida*—from the Spanish for bullring. The Corrida is an opportunity for up to five of the participants to test out new skills and understanding in a real-time, individually designed challenge. The process has much in common with *Role Tests* (p. 180-181) but differs in its emphasis on formality and a heightened sense of occasion. The Corrida is meant to be a milestone in the participant's life, a rite of passage. It is an emotionally charged experience both for those taking part and those observing.

The set is a complete circle, resembling a bullring. At one end of the circle sit the 'judges': a theatre company member, a member of the prison staff and two peer participants. The other participants in the week's work watch through windows cut into the sides of the set. A Master of Ceremonies directs the start and conclusion of each corrida.

In the Corrida, violence is not an option. The participant enters determined to deal with what ever the 'test' might be. He first gives a 'declaration of intent'—his reason for taking the challenge and what he wants to leave behind in his life. The test itself could be focused on high risk situations such as *dealing with provocation.* Or it could be more personal, such as when the participant is challenged to watch a 'playback' of his work during the week, after which he is asked to lay out a detailed map of his next steps toward change. The challenge is tailored to each participant, with Geese Theatre members taking the other roles. No 'Corrida' has ever been repeated. Spontaneity by all participants is the key.

A full explanation of *Violent Illusion* and *The Corrida* can be found in Bergman and Hewish (1996).

Geese Theatre in Performance

Photo: Gerard Farrell

Performance for Crime Concern

Photo: Len Cross

Hooked on Empty

A play about addiction and recovery

(Co-devised by Geese Theatre UK under the direction of John Bergman, Geese Theatre USA)

No longer performed, *Hooked on Empty* focused on drug and alcohol addiction. The performance followed the stories of a range of characters all struggling with addiction and trying to control the nightmare for at least a short moment. It focused on the cunning of craving, strategies for 'coming down,' and the relationship between using and the fear of feeling empty inside. Ultimately, the play offered a vision of hope that recovery is possible, despite the powerful external and internal forces that can lead to relapse. Although we no longer perform *Hooked on Empty*, we offer workshops based on the production for drug and alcohol programmes.

Prisoner letter, HM Prison Norwich, after seeing *Hooked on Empty*

> Before I went in to watch your play, I said to myself, 'Yeah, yeah, here we go again, people that don't know what they're talking about.' How wrong I was. In every aspect you got it down to a 'T'. Giro day, cooking up, can't score, clucking, being sick. I had been there so many times I think it hurt me to see what I had been through and what I had been putting up with. There was one part of the play that really hit me hard, when you said, 'Waiting, you're always waiting…' You were so right there. The play most definitely put a lot of things in perspective for me. Before I stepped into the room yesterday, I had an 'I don't give a fuck' attitude towards drugs. As soon as I get out I would score again and start jacking up. Back to my old lifestyle. But I swear if I've got anything to do with it, my life is not going to go on like my past.
>
> I came off heroin four weeks ago. Now I don't need it and I don't want it. Step one was coming off. Step two I got past yesterday when I saw the play. Step three I made today with the help of a prison probation officer. I'm now seeking outside help to carry on after I get released. But believe me I would not have made step three today if I had not seen the play yesterday.
>
> I've still got a long road to travel. It all don't stop over night. I've still got some symptoms, but mostly I've got to sort out my life with my family.

Hooked on Empty: 'Buzz'

Photo: Richard Tomlinson

APPENDIX A
Assessment and Evaluation Forms

You can use the forms in this appendix to tailor your programme to the needs of the participants. The forms allow for self-assessment as well as assessment by other group members and group workers. If you are doing pre- and post- testing in order to evaluate effectiveness, the first three forms in particular can be used to quantify changes. We have devised these forms based on earlier work by such authors as McGuire and Priestley (1987), Goldstein (1999), Jones (1996) and Haskell (1975).

Note: Participants who cannot read will need assistance with these forms.

The forms

- The ***Skills Rating Sheet*** is for self-assessment by the participants. It can be used to tailor the sessions to meet prominent themes and skills needs. It can also be used as a post-test for comparison purposes, to see if the participants consider themselves more competent in the stated areas by the end of the programme.

- The ***Rating Sheet for Role Plays*** is a scoring sheet which is used to provide structured feedback for the participants about their performance in *Role Tests*. The sheet should be completed by all present, including observers, workers, the person being rated and the other person(s) in the role play. It is crucial that the person being rated by others also rates himself in order to encourage him to take charge of his own progress. You will probably need to teach the participants how to fill in the sheet by doing a demonstration. The rating sheet can be used continually during a programme, or toward the start and finish in order to provide a comparison. Although using the rating sheet can be time intensive, when pooled together, ratings can offer a useful cumulative view of an individual's change over time. Participants often prefer to use these sheets because the feedback is quite structured. The fact that the feedback is written down also makes it easier to 'know where I stand and what I have to work on.'

- The ***Evaluation of Behaviour in the Group*** is a form allowing workers and participants to assess (or self-assess) the participants' behaviour in the group, session by session, according to different criteria. The form is intended to provide an indication of change over time, and also to encourage participants to practise self-assessment and self-management skills. It can also help workers to plan sessions in order to address individual needs.

- ***Thinking Reports*** can be used for a range of self-assessment, motivational, empathy development and relapse prevention aims as explained in the description of *Thinking Reports* on pp. 117-119. See also Offence Reconstruction, pp. 167-172.

Skills Rating Sheet (for self-assessment) (For participants)

Name ....
Date ....

In general, how good am I at doing the following?

(Circle the number which shows how confident you feel.)

1 means I am **never** good at this
2 means I am **almost never** good at this
3 means I am **sometimes** good at this and sometimes bad at this
4 means I am **almost always** good at this
5 means I am **always** good at this

Social / friendship skills

Starting a conversation with a stranger	1 2 3 4 5
Keeping a conversation going	1 2 3 4 5
Asking someone to do me a favour	1 2 3 4 5
Apologising if I've done something wrong	1 2 3 4 5
Giving a compliment	1 2 3 4 5
Receiving a compliment	1 2 3 4 5

Occupational skills

Interviewing for a job	1 2 3 4 5
Asking questions to clarify what I am being told	1 2 3 4 5
Co-operating with others	1 2 3 4 5
Setting goals and keeping to them	1 2 3 4 5
Asking for feedback about my work performance	1 2 3 4 5
Concentrating on a task	1 2 3 4 5
Handling a complaint about my actions	1 2 3 4 5

Family/ intimacy skills

Communicating with my partner	1 2 3 4 5
Being open and honest with my partner about difficulties I am facing	1 2 3 4 5
Saying 'no'	1 2 3 4 5
Expressing concern for another person	1 2 3 4 5
Talking to people of the opposite sex	1 2 3 4 5
Breaking off/ ending a relationship	1 2 3 4 5
Negotiating and compromising with others	1 2 3 4 5
Handling jealous feelings	1 2 3 4 5
Handling criticism from my parent(s)	1 2 3 4 5
Being open and honest with my parent(s) about difficulties I am facing	1 2 3 4 5
Where relevant:	
Communicating with my child(ren)	1 2 3 4 5
Disciplining/setting limits with my child(ren)	1 2 3 4 5

Dealing with authority

Talking to people in positions of authority	1 2 3 4 5
Making a complaint	1 2 3 4 5
Accepting 'no' from someone in authority	1 2 3 4 5
Dealing with requests/ demands made by someone in authority	1 2 3 4 5
Dealing with a police stop and search	1 2 3 4 5

Alternatives to aggression or offending

Telling someone I am angry with him/ her	1 2 3 4 5
Dealing with my own anger	1 2 3 4 5
Dealing with someone else's anger / aggression	1 2 3 4 5
Responding to someone who is staring at me	1 2 3 4 5
Responding to someone who is provoking/ insulting me	1 2 3 4 5
Dealing with pressure to do something I don't want to do (e.g. offend)	1 2 3 4 5
Dealing with wanting something that is not mine	1 2 3 4 5
Stopping my offending cycle early on	1 2 3 4 5
Dealing with disappointment	1 2 3 4 5

Self-management / self-control

Knowing what my feelings are	1 2 3 4 5
Relaxing when I am stressed	1 2 3 4 5
Using alcohol (or other intoxicants) safely	1 2 3 4 5
Dealing with boredom/ staying positive	1 2 3 4 5

Rating Sheet for Role Plays

Adapted from Haskell (1975 and 1961)

(To be completed by observers, by the participants in the role play and by group leaders)

Date .... **Name of person being rated** ....

Name of rater (if different) ....

Aim of the role play/ skill being tested (examples: 'To assess/ test ability to respond to an aggressive complaint from a customer when in role as a sales assistant'; or: 'To assess/ test ability to respond to a false accusation from a person in authority when in role as self.')

1. Each of the items below reflects a possible trouble spot or skill needing development as shown during the role play. Please score the person being rated (or yourself, if you are rating your own performance in the role play) on each item. Please use the table below for scoring by using the area labelled 'tick here' to place a tick mark each time you observe the behaviour during the role play. Please put down only one tick for each behaviour, even though there are some behaviours that will apply to more than one category:

Possible trouble spot, or skill needing development	**Tick here** each time the behaviour is observed
Failure to listen or respond to the other person	
Lacking confidence/ Too passive	
Hostile/ Aggressive response	
Anti-social/ Self-defeating/ Incorrect response	
Displays 'don't care' attitude	
Displays lack of feeling / Lack of empathy for other person	
Falling out of role/ Breaks out of character	
Other (specify)	
TOTAL SCORE (Number of tick marks) *Lower scores will indicate better performance and a more adequate response to the situation.*	

2. Based on this role play, how would you rate your/ the person's chances of dealing successfully with this situation 'in real life?' (Circle the figure nearest to your personal estimate):

10% 20% 30% 40% 50% 60% 70% 80% 90% 100%

Comments:

Evaluation of Behaviour in the Group

Name of person being evaluated ....
Date ....
Name of evaluator (if different) ....

This evaluation sheet can be used by group leaders or by group participants (for self-assessment)

For group leaders: *How does the group member engage in the group process and activities?*
For individual group members: *How do I engage in the group process and activities?*

A = Always **B** = Usually **C** = Sometimes **D** = Rarely **E** = Never **F** = Negative/ Anti-social behaviour in this category

Does the group member ... / Do I ... (Give a letter score for each session)

Session number:	1	2	3	4	5	6	7
Date of session:							
Engage positively in group discussion without prompting?							
Show consideration and respect for others, including group leaders?							
Express ideas well?							
Maintain concentration?							
Consider and reflect upon *own* responses and feelings?							
Consider and reflect upon *others'* responses and feelings?							
Show willingness to consider other points of view?							
Show willingness to practise new behaviours and social skills?							
Show willingness to do personally focused work?							
Show evidence of positive change outside the group?							

Session number:	8	9	10	11	12	13	14
Date of session:							
Engage positively in group discussion without prompting?							
Show consideration and respect for others, including group leaders?							
Express ideas well?							
Maintain concentration?							
Consider and reflect upon *own* responses and feelings?							
Consider and reflect upon *others'* responses and feelings?							
Show willingness to consider other points of view?							
Show willingness to practise new behaviours and social skills?							
Show willingness to do personally focused work?							
Show evidence of positive change outside the group?							

Thinking Report for Self

Name .... Date ....

WHAT HAPPENED:..
....
....

THOUGHTS	FEELINGS	BEHAVIOUR

Underlying beliefs at the time that supported the behaviour ('Old me' thinking and beliefs):

'New me' thinking and beliefs:

Thinking Reports are explained on pp.117-119 and 167-172. There is an example of a completed Thinking Report on pp.168-169. **Source:** Dr. J M Bush (1993) first developed *Thinking Reports*. Geese Theatre uses an adapted version.

Thinking Report for Self and Other

Name .... Date ....

WHAT HAPPENED:

....

....

....

ME			**OTHER PERSON**		
THOUGHTS	FEELINGS	BEHAVIOUR	THOUGHTS	FEELINGS	BEHAVIOUR

Underlying beliefs at the time that supported the behaviour ('Old me' thinking and beliefs):

'New me' thinking and beliefs:

Thinking Reports are explained on pp.117-119 and 167-172. There is an example of a completed Thinking Report on pp.168-169. **Source:** Dr. John M Bush (1993) first developed *Thinking Reports.* Geese Theatre uses an adapted version.

APPENDIX B
Guidelines for Structuring Offending Behaviour Programmes which Use Drama-based Methods

We can use the four guidelines discussed in *Chapter 3* to inform the design of an entire offending behaviour programme (summarised in *Fig. AB*). The structure we offer here would apply to an offending behaviour programme lasting only two or three days to one lasting many months. Regardless of programme length, the structure itself would remain the same.

In the following outline, a **men's domestic violence group** is used as the basis for examples.

1. **Forming** the group and introducing themes

This stage of the group will generally use *games and exercises* and *interactive observer* scenes.

Areas of involvement used:

Games and Exercises The group begins with introductions, goal setting and setting the group contract, all standard group procedures. Moving into more active involvement, the group members become involved, for example, in the *Continuum* exercise, based on questions and statements related to anger, power and control, personal responsibility and motivation to change. This exercise is *processed* and the participants are encouraged to deepen their level of communication and trust in each other. Increasing amounts of disclosure are encouraged regarding offences and beliefs.

Interactive Observer Where appropriate, the participants may watch simple scenes or characters presented by the facilitators, or directed by the facilitators using group members to represent characters. These scenes and characters reflect themes directly related to domestic violence (e.g. attitudes to women), and the group members are encouraged to interact with the characters. This work is largely done at *one step removed*, relying on fictional scenarios and general discussion. Later, the scenes and the discussion will focus more on individuals in the group.

2. **Exploring** offending behaviour and the thoughts, feelings, attitudes and beliefs supporting offending behaviour

This stage of the group uses all areas of involvement, from active exercises through to role play. At this stage, participants are exploring the themes of the programme and are beginning to understand other points of view. They are revealing their own and each other's attitudes and beliefs, and are seeing more accurately their own typical patterns of thoughts and feelings in the lead up to violence against their partner.

Areas of involvement used:

Games and Exercises The group members participate in an *offending-focused exercise* examining unequal power and control. The exercise encourages the men to discuss pro-offending attitudes (e.g. 'I should have most of the power in a relationship') and encourage debate around the theme of power and control. At this stage, the processing will still focus on general discussion and will not focus on the pro-offending attitudes of a particular group member.

Interactive Observer Still working largely at *one step removed*, and using the technique *Group Character Creation,* the participants identify the distortions and pro-offending beliefs held by an abusive man in a fictional couple. They consider his victim's point of view in great detail. The group members then take the fictional abuser through his own *Motivational Cycle* and consider in detail his process of change.

Frozen Pictures The participants create simple images and characters based on realistic domestic violence scenarios, but at *one step removed.* They may create, for example, a *Frozen Picture* of an argument in the home between a man and woman. All of the *processing techniques* are used to generate relevance and involvement. Group members take on the point of view of both the man and the woman in the picture. The processing encourages the group members to listen sensitively to the characters, and to develop a more thoughtful approach to the complex motivations of the characters and the damaging effects occurring in the scene.

Role Play Moving on to *personal level* work, group members take part in role plays demonstrating typical strategies they use in their relationships. In the role plays, they demonstrate how they typically handle conflicts and how they intentionally or inadvertently abuse their power and control. The role plays may also reveal their 'victim stance' (i.e. the belief that 'I am the victim') and how they use this stance to justify their violence.

On an individual basis, each participant will be helped to identify his typical patterns of thinking, feeling and behaviour in the lead-up to their violence.

Figure AB: **Geese Theatre: A General Structure for Offending Behaviour Programmes Which Use Drama-Based Methods**

Tools:

- **Areas of involvement:**
  —Games and exercises
  —Interactive observer scenes
  —Frozen pictures
  —Role play
- **Processing techniques:**
  —Opening up discussion
  —Inner voice from audience
  —Inner voice from characters
  —Lifting the mask
  —Interview in role
  —Role rotation/ reversal
  —Reworking the scene
- **Social learning sequence**
  —Assess skills needs
  —Instruction
  —Modelling
  —Multiple practices with increasing intensity
  — 'Real life' practice/ feedback and reinforcement

Forming

Forming the group and introducing themes using theatre and drama (games, exercises and interactive observer scenes)

↓

Exploring

Explore offending behaviour and thoughts, feelings, attitudes and beliefs using drama (all areas of involvement)

↓

Reviewing

Identify high risk factors and skills needs. Review/ modify attitudes, beliefs, patterns of thoughts, feelings and behaviour. (all areas of involvement)

Themes Addressed:

- Motivation to change
- Getting past denial
- Power and control
- Peer pressure
- Victim empathy and awareness
- Taking responsibility for one's own actions
- Locus of control/Self-determination
- Cycle of offending/Offending behaviour
- The role of fantasy and planning in offending/ Controlling fantasy and thinking
- Goal setting and planning skills
- Gender attitudes, roles and beliefs
- Assertiveness and communication skills;
- Relationship skills; self-esteem
- Pro-offending attitudes and beliefs
- Racism, sexism and other prejudice
- Attitudes and beliefs about self and others
- Early learning (where appropriate)
- Thinking skills and creative problem-solving
- Self-instruction and self-control skills

Variables:

- Degree of distance: One step removed or Personal level
- Low, medium or high focus
- Readiness levels of all concerned
- Time limitations (this structure applies to programmes lasting from several days to many months)

Key Concepts:

- The metaphor of 'the mask'
- Expanding the role repertoire
- Challenge comes through the role

↓

Practising

Practise cognitive and behavioural skills using drama (Role Play)

↓

Testing

Test new behaviours and coping strategies using drama (Role Play)

- Anger management and reducing hostile aggression
- Perspective taking
- Conflict resolution
- Human sexuality and gender issues
- Substance misuse
- Relaxation skills
- Relapse prevention: coping with high risk situations and maintaining a positive lifestyle; options out of offending

... and other relevant themes.

Note: The contents of the boxes on the left and right apply to all five stages

3. **Reviewing** attitudes, beliefs and patterns of thoughts, feelings and behaviour related to offending

As during the *Exploring* phase of the group, during the *Reviewing* phase you can use any of the areas of involvement. This phase of the programme is intended to help participants identify the ways in which they can take control, review and modify their thinking, feeling and behaviour in order to continue their process of change.

As part of this process, you can ask the participants to assess their high risk situations and identify the skills they need to develop. These self-assessments can be combined with other assessments carried out by staff to create an individually tailored package of skills training role plays.

Areas of involvement used:

Games and Exercises Working almost entirely on the *personal level* now, participants take part in the *Obstacle Course* and set themselves positive goals (e.g. a violence-free lifestyle). They also set plans to overcome obstacles—both internal and external—that stand in the way of their goals.

Interactive Observer Participants interact in short encounters with fictional characters—as presented by the facilitator or by other group members—in order to address the issue of personal change, responsibility, victim empathy or other themes.

Frozen Pictures Working on the *personal level*, participants create *Frozen Pictures* based on real events (not offences). They may find it useful and challenging to reverse roles and see the event from the perspective of another person involved. As facilitator, you can use such a strategy to encourage a participant to become motivated to change his behaviour and make the cognitive shift necessary to move to the next phase, practising change.

Role play Where appropriate, each participant does the *Offence Reconstruction*. Alternatively, they may present fictional role plays based on close-to-life scenarios. Within the *Offence Reconstruction*, they will be asked to take the point of view of their victim or some other person who was affected by the offence. In the domestic violence group, this may be, for example, a son or daughter, or the neighbour who overhears the beatings.

4. **Practising** cognitive and behavioural skills

This phase of the group is largely devoted to the use of role play to help participants practise the skills of 'going straight.' By this phase, participants and staff will be clear about the skills which need practise and which are highest priority. Workers take an active part in providing instructions for carrying out the skills, and, where appropriate, modelling the skills for participants.

Area of involvement used:

Role play Each participant in turn takes on the role of himself or 'someone like me' in role plays which either directly reflect his life events or closely parallel them. In the role plays, each participant is given the opportunity to practise skills for dealing with problem situations.

5. **Testing** new skills, new roles and new coping strategies

The fifth and last phase of the programme uses role play to test the degree to which the participant has assimilated the new skills he has been practising. This phase also considers any opportunities for 'real life' practice that the participant has had.

Area of involvement used:

Role play After several sessions of preparation, each participant is given the opportunity to experience a spontaneous *Role Test*.

For example, in the sample domestic violence group, a participant may, after being given the minimum essential information, be faced with a role play in which his wife asks him to stay home with the children even though it is his 'night out with my mates.'

It is also important in this phase of the programme to consider and process any opportunities the participant has had recently to practise his new skill. For example, in the domestic violence group, a participant may wish to share with the group an episode during the previous week where he was successful or unsuccessful in practising communication skills or self-calming skills. Depending on his success or otherwise, he can be given positive reinforcement or, where needed, further opportunity to practise the skill.

APPENDIX C
Sample Sessions

This appendix gives sample running lists for sessions. These are meant only as general suggestions to get you started, and from which to develop your own session plans. In the following outlines, 'stage of group' refers to the stages described in *Appendix B*.

FIRST SESSION OF AN OFFENDING BEHAVIOUR GROUP - can be adapted for most themes/ types of group

Stage of Group: Forming
Duration: Three hours
Aims: To build group cohesion, encourage disclosure and establish group contract/ norms; Focus the group on the themes to be addressed; Motivation and Goal setting.

- Introduction to session/ programme aims and objectives, emphasising active participation, confidentiality and other important issues.
- *Opening Question*, e.g. 'Something you want to gain from the session(s).'
- *Continuums* and *Map on the Floor*, focusing on motivation and goal setting.
- *Name Game Progression.*
- Warm-up: high-energy games such as *Touch Backs* and *Anyone Who.*
- Problem solving, e.g. *The Knot.*
- Concentration: exercises in pairs such as *Hand/ Face* or *Trust Pairs.*
- Introduction to theatre as a means of exploring real situations. A good exercise to use here is *The Two Person Exercise.* It is simple, unthreatening, and clear.
- *Frozen Pictures.* Split the group into smaller groups. Give each group a title to create from, e.g. 'The Lie,' 'The Secret,' 'The Argument.' When the groups present their *Frozen Pictures,* use any of the *processing techniques.* Develop it into a walking/talking scene by giving an instruction along the lines of - *'When I clap my hands the picture will come alive...'* Ask for only five or ten seconds of action.
- If time: *Obstacle Course* with goal setting.
- *Closure*: One goal for the coming week.

MIDDLE SESSION OF AN OFFENDING BEHAVIOUR GROUP

Stage of group Reviewing
Duration Three hours
Aims To encourage debate and challenge thinking around the issues of personal responsibility and choice; Identifying skills needs.

- Issues arising for participants during the previous week (10-15 minutes max.).
- Workers set theme for the session (e.g. 'making choices and being responsible for our actions').
- *Opening Question.*
- Warm-up: *The Knot, Paper not Floor* or *Tin Soldiers.*
- *Whole Group Role Plays, Forum Role Plays* or (Optional) *Worker in Role: The Enacted Scene.*
- (Optional) *Offence Reconstruction* on personal level, using *Thinking Reports.* Focus on one person. Identify 'New me' thinking, skills needs.
- Feedback on last week's goal, and set new goals.

LATER SESSION OF AN OFFENDING BEHAVIOUR GROUP

Stage of group Practising
Duration Three hours
Aims To practise new skills related to high risk situations and relapse prevention

- Issues arising for participants during the previous week (10-15 minutes max.).
- Dangerous Places, leading into discussion of high risk situations.

- *Modelling Role Plays* and *Skills Practise Role Plays* focused on identified skills needs and high risk situations. Use *one step removed* or *personal level* as appropriate.
- Feedback on last week's goal, and set new goal.

In later sessions, after participants have practised important skills, move on to *Role Tests*, feedback and further goal setting.

A SESSION FOCUSING ON DOMESTIC VIOLENCE

Stage of group Exploring/ Reviewing
Duration Three hours
Aims Participants will examine how they create rules for themselves and their partner.

- Issues arising for participants during the previous week (10-15 minutes maximum).
- *Opening Question.*
- *Paper Not Floor.* Encourage links to issues such as: changing the rules of a situation. Ask how the process of the exercise links to their partners' experience—e.g. narrower and narrower options out.
- *The Knot.* Focus on the difficulty of the exercise, and how they managed to cope with the exercise despite the difficulty. Encourage participants to make links with the difficult process of changing abusive behaviour.
- *Obstacle Course* or *Barriers to Change.* Focusing on 'old me' rules that hinder change and 'new me' rules that will assist change and help reaching positive life/ relationship goals. Optional: where appropriate, the participant takes the role of his partner and speaks about what 'new me' rules she would like to live by and have her partner live by. Note: This exercise can be done at *one step removed* (using *Group Character Creation*) or on the *personal level.*
- Optional: Ask *Continuum* questions with participants in role as their partner, e.g. 'My partner (name) believes I am an equal partner in this relationship(agree/ disagree).' Or: 'My partner (name) shows that he thinks I deserve to be just as free to have friends and a good social life as he does (agree/disagree).' Similarly, ask participants in role as their partner, 'What are the things (material as well as abstract) and who are the people that are important to you, and why? Are there any obstacles keeping you from having things or having these people near you? What are they?'
- Closure. Process feelings, ask what people have learnt. Discussion should not be around which rules are 'good' or 'bad', but around which ones are helpful or unhelpful given their 'new me' aims. Finally, ask each participant for an unhelpful 'old me' rule and a helpful 'new me' rule they'll use in its place.

A PRE-RELEASE SESSION FOR PRISONERS

Stage of group Exploring/ Reviewing
Duration Three hours
Aim To explore potentially high risk situations in the future and develop strategies to deal with them.

- *Warm-up: Anyone Who, How Many Walking, Wink Chair* or others.
- *Dangerous Places* and/ or *Map on the Floor.* Process focusing on high risk situations.
- *Zip Zap Bop.* Connect to how the 'zip', 'zap' and 'bop' might represent real-life equivalents, e.g. high risk thoughts or situations.
- *Grandmother's Footsteps.* Process around: problem solving, and goals that participants may have. Also: the knock-backs that people may receive and how their thoughts and feelings during the exercise may relate to 'dealing with frustration.'
- *Film Freezes.* An introduction to static scene creation which leads directly into...
- *Frozen Pictures* based on an issue which may have emerged during the workshop, e.g. having no money/ facing pressure to offend.
- *Demonstration Role Plays*, leading into *Forum Role Plays.* Focusing on real life problems and solutions.

A SESSION FOR YOUNG OFFENDERS/ YOUNG PEOPLE AT RISK OF OFFENDING

Stage of group Exploring/ Reviewing (This can also be used as a one-off session)
Duration Three hours
Aims To explore issues which may influence offending behaviour, such as peer pressure, boredom, low self-esteem and the desire for immediate gratification. To modify attitudes about these issues.

- *Throwing Names*
- *Same Journey.* This exercise often appeals to young people because it can be very energetic and has a strong element of challenge, although individuals are not in direct competition with each other.
- *Zip Zap Bop.* Use for focus and concentration. Process around theme of communication.
- *Self—Supporting Structures.* Again, this exercise can appeal to younger groups as it is very physical. The problem–solving element provides a challenge and sense of achievement. It can be processed in terms of team work and team roles. It also gives the group the experience of working in a small group to achieve an aim, which links with the next exercise. Be aware that this exercise involves physical contact.
- *Film Freezes.* Small groups produce a *Frozen Picture* of a well known film. The rest of the group try to guess the film. This is a useful way into a more theatrical way of working and gives the participants the experience of presenting to the whole group without feeling too vulnerable.
- *Frozen Pictures.* Small groups produce *one step removed Frozen Pictures* based one or more of the following titles: 'Mates', 'Free time', 'Home' and 'Night Out'. Process using any or all of the *processing techniques.* This often brings up beliefs and attitudes around peer pressure, boredom, excitement etc.
- *Demonstration* and *Forum Role Plays.* The same small groups prepare a short *Demonstration Role Play,* still based on *one step removed* material. This can either be an extension of the *Frozen Picture* they have just produced or it can be based on another stimulus title relevant to the group, e.g. 'Just this once', 'Everyone does it', 'This is boring' or 'Go on, it'll be a buzz'. There may be a particular phrase or word that arises from processing the *Frozen Pictures* which you may want to use as a title e.g. 'They'll think I'm stupid if I don't'. If you want to explore a particular behaviour or move to the *personal level,* you could use a title like 'A time when I did something I regretted.' These scenes can then be processed in terms of thoughts, feelings and consequences for the characters. Possible next step: use *Forum Role Play* to try out various ways to deal with these situations.

A SESSION ADDRESSING: 'DEALING WITH AUTHORITY'

Stage of group	Reviewing/Practising
Duration	Three hours
Aims	Distinguishing passive, aggressive and assertive behaviour. Challenging attitudes to authority.

- *Paper not Floor.* Use processing to focus on real life problems such as 'how we deal with challenging situations or people.' Participants may consider how previous experiences of dealing with a person in authority affected how they approached those in authority later on. Focus on the feelings, attitudes and beliefs (about self and those in authority) resulting from these interactions.
- (Optional) *Master/ Servant.* Processing is similar to *Paper not Floor.*
- *Demonstration Role Plays.* Role play focusing on passive, assertive and aggressive behaviour. In pairs, group members act out a brief scene between a hypothetical employer and employee. They should both take the opportunity to play both characters. These role plays are presented to the whole group. During *processing,* the group identify which solutions are passive, aggressive or assertive. The participants identify which skills are associated with assertiveness and what aims the character has when trying to be assertive.
- *Role Play for Empathy, Feedback and Self-Talk.* At this stage in the workshop, if appropriate, the group could move on to Role Plays concerning their own experiences of authority figures. It is useful when working on personal material for the group member whose experience you are focusing on to *Role Reverse* with the authority figure and to gain an understanding of this person's point of view (e.g. 'just doing my job'; 'I'm going to wind him up'; 'He's a likely suspect'). Another important issue is to get the group member to identify his own beliefs about the situation (e.g. 'the police always stop me', 'it doesn't matter what I do', etc) and look at how these feelings affect his decisions and actions. It may be useful to identify whether these feelings lead on to passive, aggressive or assertive solutions. Finally, it would be useful to explore whether any of the assertiveness skills the group identified in the previous role play involving the employer could be transferred to this situation.

A SESSION FOR PEOPLE CONVICTED OF MOTOR OFFENCES (E.G. CAR THEFT/ JOYRIDING)

Stage of group	Exploring/ Reviewing
Duration	One-and-a-half hours
Aim	Victim Empathy

- *Throwing Names.* Focus on: 'awareness of and consideration of others'.
- *The Way I See It.* Create a car crime scenario. Consider thoughts and feelings of all those affected by the crime. Option: have a 'reporter' speak to the 'owner' of the car or the parent of the child knocked down during the police chase. Where appropriate, have participants speak from role as the various people affected by the crime.
- *Closure.* Ask each person to tell the group about one connection between the work done in the session and their own offence.
- Other option: Small groups devise *Frozen Pictures* based on titles such as: 'How I Feel Behind The Wheel', 'Life Without Wheels' or 'Me and My Car.' This option would be suitable for use early in this session, or in another session focusing on factors leading to offending.

A SESSION FOR A GROUP ADDRESSING DRUG AND ALCOHOL ISSUES

Stage of group Exploring/ Reviewing

Duration Two to six hours

Aim Motivation to change and goal setting

- *Opening Question: 'Where do you want to be in 6 months / two years time?'*
- *Continuum: 'I am in control of the direction my life is heading.' 'I am in control of my use of drugs/ alcohol.'* (0-100 per cent)
- *Bombs and Shields.* Processing: Relate the 'bomb' to drugs/ alcohol. How often does the 'bomb' explode? / What is the fuse made of? / How easy is it to control the bomb? Also, what are your 'shields' (internal and external strengths) that will help you to maintain your goal?
- *Frozen Pictures.* In groups of four, each person to sculpt the others into a Frozen Picture with the title: 'My Addiction', 'My Craving' or 'Rock Bottom'. Encourage the groups to work quickly. Look at each of the pictures briefly but don't go too deeply into processing. Encourage the group to respect each others pictures as they are working at the personal level. Option: Keep the work at *one step removed* and give the groups titles such as: 'Just this once'; 'Rattling'; 'Buzz'; 'The Party'; 'I thought you were my friend'; 'I can handle it'; 'The dare.'
- *Obstacle Course.* Identify the beginning of the obstacle course as the place of 'My Addiction', 'My Craving', or 'Rock Bottom.' It would be useful to elicit this from the group. Move on to identify what the end of the obstacle course would be for each participant. Encourage *realistic* goal-setting and establish a time-frame for that goal. Ask each participant to identify where exactly they see themselves on the obstacle course and what each of the obstacles represent for them (again try to make these realistic obstacles that the group member has some degree of control over.) It is now possible to create work around each of these obstacles, although one piece of work per group member might be advisable depending upon time limitations. Either create Frozen Pictures or scenes of the obstacle and explore possible strategies for overcoming within the group.
- *Closure.* Each group member to feedback on the skills that they already possess that will enable them to reach their realistic goal / aim.

A SESSION ADDRESSING SEXUALLY INAPPROPRIATE/ AGGRESSIVE BEHAVIOUR

Stage of group Exploring/ Reviewing

Duration Three to five hours

Aims Motivation to change; Responsibility; Victim awareness

- *Continuum. How responsible am I for my own behaviour? How much control do I have over my behaviour towards others?* (0-100 per cent)
- *Point of View Circle.* Focus on the rightness of other points of view, e.g. the victim's.
- *Tin Soldiers.* Focus on personal responsibility for decisions. Option: *Roles and Responsibility* for same aim.
- *Relationships Ladder.* Focus on awareness of other person, and rights of others.
- *The Way I See It.* Explore a hypothetical scenario, and all of the people affected by an incident, e.g. abuse/ harassment.
- *Monologues.* Focus on *Internal Roles:* The part of me that wants/ wanted to abuse ('Old me') / The part of me that never wants to abuse again ('New me'). Option: *Victim Apology* (see *Monologues*).
- *Offence Reconstruction.* Where appropriate, focusing on victim's experience of the incident. Use on *personal level* or *one step removed* as appropriate.

APPENDIX D
Sample Session Demonstrating Work at One Step Removed and the Personal Level

The following example demonstrates how a *one step removed* exercise can evolve into *personal level* work (in this example, *Offence Reconstruction*) in carefully negotiated stages.

The Session: The group is discussing the *Two Person Exercise* (pp.134-135). The discussion starts off at the level of *one step removed*, and the facilitator makes a series of judgements about the direction of the session based on the four *readiness levels*. The group contract is to address offending behaviour, and the programme is one for men convicted of violent offending.

Two participants are standing in the 'stage' area of the group room.

Groupworker (G): *What might be going on between these two characters?*
Participant (P): *The one on the left is looking for a fight.*
G: *How can you tell? What are you picking up?*
P1: *He's staring at him.*
G: *How's the one on the right feeling? What's going on inside his head?*
P2: *He's getting ready. He's under threat.*
G: *Speak as if you're inside his head and it's happening to you right now.*
P2: *'What's he looking at? If he moves I'll nut him.'*
G: *What's happening physically, inside him?*
P3: *He's got butterflies, his heart's beating FAST! He's tense. I know the feeling; I've been there.*

Group worker accepts the offer, moves to more *personal level* processing:

G: *You know this situation?*
P3: *Yeah, it's like every time I leave my house.*

Group worker decides that, based on the *readiness levels* and the *contract* with the group, it is appropriate to focus further on the *personal level* with this participant.

G: *What would be a typical situation?*
P3: *Last week. This idiot comes up to me saying I hit one of his mates.*
G: *How did you deal with it?*
P3: *Not very well.*
G: *Were the police involved?*
P3: *Yeah. They arrested me.*
G: *Could you have done anything differently?*
P3: *I don't think so, and anyway I didn't know anything about his mate. He just came up to me too fast.*

One Step Removed Option: Maintaining Distance
At this point, the group worker decides, on the basis of the *readiness levels* of all concerned and the contract with the group, to stay at the level of *one step removed.*

The worker sets up a *Forum Role Play* closely paralleling the incident described by P3, but with the setting and character names altered in order to fictionalise the scene. The aim of the *Forum Role Play* will be to invite a range of solutions to the problem of staying out of fights.

G: *Were the police involved?*
P3: *Yeah. They arrested me.*
G: *Could you have done anything differently?*
P3: *I don't think so, and anyway I didn't know anything about his mate. He just came up to me too fast.*
G: *That's a good example, and we can use it as the basis for setting up a scene and trying out some different approaches that you or anyone in your situation might use. Let's think of a situation like that, but we'll change the details so it is not your scene we are looking at, but a general example. First of all, where could we be if there's going to be a situation where a fight might break out?*
P2: *It could be anywhere.*
P4: *At my local.*
G: *So, In a pub?*

P4: *Yeah.*
G: *Alright, so we set the scene in a pub, not your local but any pub, and a fight might be about to start. Now if we say the pub is over here in this part of the room, where is the bar?*
P5: *Over there.*

Group worker and group set the scene.

G: *Now we have the setting, and what is the situation? Darren gave us an example from his own experience where someone made a false allegation. Let's have an example of another type of provocation.*
P6 *It's time. You always get someone who wants a fight when it's time.*
G: *So who is there?*
P2 : *Three mates who are drinking together, and the barman.*

Group worker confidently asks for volunteers.

G: *Let's quickly have some people up in the scene. How about the four of you? We'll chop and change roles as we go, so it doesn't particularly matter who starts the scene and which roles they have. Great, now because there are four people in the scene, let's try to keep it focused by having only two people speak at once. Let's say the main conversation is between one of the group of mates and the barman. Who is going to be trying to stay out of the fight? One of the group of men or the barman?*
P1: *The barman. One of the blokes is giving him grief.*

The scene continues as a *Forum Role Play*, with a number of re-takes which offer different solutions to the problem of staying out of fights when provoked. After a number of re-takes, it would also be possible to change the situation so that it is the barman who is provoking the fight rather than the patron. Offering both possibilities reinforces the notion that both sides feel justified in their actions, and that it is not as simple as saying that one side is always at fault. It would also be useful to do a *Thinking Report* for the two main characters in this scene. It is often useful to do *Thinking Reports* at *one step removed* before trying them on the *personal level.*

Personal Level Option: The Offence Reconstruction and Beyond
The group worker decides to reconstruct the scene described by participant three, making the work high focus and highly personal. The scene moves from the level of *one step removed* into *personal level work:*

G: *Were the police involved?*
P3: *Yeah. They arrested me.*
G: *Could you have done anything differently?*
P3: *I don't think so, and anyway I didn't know anything about his mate. He just came up to me too fast.*
G: *So can we leave this two person scene and look directly at your situation? Do you feel that would be helpful to you?*
P3: *Yeah, okay. It took me by surprise. I don't know what I could have done.*
G: *Let's have a look at it in 3-d. We'll do a moment by moment reconstruction to look at your thoughts and feelings and your options, but we won't replay the scene in action. When you entered the pub, when did you first become aware of the other man and where were you? Show us.*

Participant stands, begins describing the build-up to the offence.

P3: *I was standing here, and he was over there.*

This example shows the start of an *Offence Reconstruction*. As described on pp.167-172 in *Offence Reconstructions* participants do not re-enact the situation; it is more like a series of freeze-frames in which the participant takes his own role, then perhaps that of the other person in the incident.

Moving into more overtly therapeutic terrain, the following example demonstrates where *personal level* work crosses the boundary into *psychodrama,* which is outside the scope of this handbook:

G: *We have explored the incident in which you attacked the other man who you felt had provoked you, and now I'd like to ask, where else has this happened to you? What other situations does this remind you of, where you felt you had to strike out in order to protect yourself, with no possibility of talking it through or reasoning with the other person? Let's look at that in action.*

GLOSSARY

Applied Theatre and Drama Theatre and drama applied with a particular aim—usually *issue-based*—for specified audiences such as schools, prisons, probation hostels, hospitals, professional groups, etc.

Areas of Involvement In this book, the four categories of drama-based activities: Games and Exercises; Interactive Observer; Frozen Pictures; and Role Play.

Challenge Comes Through the Role One of the key concepts underlying the effectiveness of the drama-based approach. Participants are encouraged to challenge their own attitudes and beliefs when they play roles representing other points of view (e.g. a victim, a witness to a crime, a relative of a victim, the police, self at a different point in time). Rather than the challenge coming from facilitators or other group members, the best challenges often come through the first-person portrayal of another role.

Degree of Distance See *One Step Removed* and *Personal Level.*

Drama in Education Participatory drama within an educational setting. Can be applied across the curriculum to promote learning and personal development. Many of the games, exercises and drama structures we use share much in common with drama-in-education (e.g. *Worker in Role* and *Whole Group Role Play*). Drama-in-education draws heavily on the innovative approach of Dorothy Heathcote described in Heathcote and Bolton, 1995; Johnson and O'Neil, 1984; and Wagner, 1976.

Dramatherapy Therapy applying all aspects of drama, including scripted plays, improvisation, theatre games, ensemble play creation, mask, ritual, metaphor and dramatic movement in order to promote creativity, imagination, insight, growth and healing (Jones, 1997). Dramatherapy differs from psychodrama in that it normally works through dramatic distance, analogy and metaphor (see *one step removed*), whereas psychodrama usually addresses personal material directly.

Doubling In psychodrama, the process whereby one person acts as an extension of another by copying their movements and speaking their inner thoughts and feelings. In this book, we use an adapted form of doubling (see *Inner Voice From the Audience).*

Experiential Therapy Any form of therapy that places primary emphasis on the importance of live, real-time experience as the basis of the therapeutic process. Examples include dramatherapy, psychodrama, adventure therapy (outdoor adventure), dance/ movement therapy, art therapy, play therapy and music therapy.

Focus/ Levels of Focus At a given time, the degree of focus placed on any member of the group: Low, medium, high or passing.

Fool Factors A Geese Theatre term, derived from the character of the Fool in some of our improvised shows. 'Fool Factor' is a metaphor for anything that can go wrong that is outside of our control (e.g. your old co-defendant moves in next door). Particularly useful in relapse prevention role plays.

Forum Theatre A theatrical structure devised by Augusto Boal (1979) in which a problematic scenario is presented and then replayed, with audience members encouraged to enter the action and attempt to change the outcome. Forum Theatre is now a widely used approach.

Frozen Pictures Static scenes, also known as sculpts, presented by the group members to explore any theme.

Games and Exercises One of the four *Areas of Involvement.* Structured activities with a pre-designated focus on generic themes ('general') or offending behaviour themes ('offending-focused'). Games and exercises can be used as warm-ups or as the basis for complete sessions.

Hot Seating See *Worker in Role.*

Inner Voice from the Characters The characters speak their inner thoughts and feelings directly to audience. One of the *processing techniques.*

Inner Voice from the Audience A processing technique where one person speaks the thoughts and feelings of another and helps that person to speak for themselves. Can be used at *one step removed* or on the *personal level.* A technique akin to *Doubling*, one of the central techniques in psychodrama and sociodrama (Moreno, 1985, Blatner, 1997; Sternberg and Garcia, 1989).

Interactive Observer Scenes provoking interaction and debate between stage and audience, or, amongst the audience members in relation to the scene. One of the four *Areas of Involvement.*

Interview in Role Facilitator and audience interview a group member in a given role (including own role). One of the *processing techniques.*

Issue-based Drama / Theatre Performances or drama-based workshops focused on specific social themes of particular relevance to a selected audience. Typical issues: Peer pressure; Bullying; Staying away from crime; Addiction; Surviving on the streets; Sexual health; Goals; Change; Conflict resolution.

Lifting the Mask See *Mask.*

Locus of Control Where one places responsibility for control of one's actions, i.e. internally (self) or externally (outside forces).

Mask In this book, a metaphor for the 'front' we present to others, with our private thoughts and feelings underneath. Leading to the well-known Geese Theatre phrase, 'lifting the mask,' used to describe attempts at deeper personal disclosure and communication.

Monologues One of the techniques related to *Role Play*, in which one person plays all of the roles in a scene or, where no scene is set, speaks from the role of differing perspectives. Also used in *Offence Reconstruction.*

One Step Removed Scenarios and discussion based on fictional events or actual events not directly involving anyone present (e.g. events in the news).

Opening up Discussion ('What do you think is going on?') One of the *processing techniques*, used to gather initial impressions of a scene.

Personal Level Scenarios and discussion focused directly on the personal life experiences of someone present.

Perspective Taking The process of 'stepping outside one's self' in order to see things from another point of view. An essential step in the development of empathy and moral reasoning.

Processing Techniques Processing means drawing out the responses of the participants, enabling them to deepen their thinking and helping to make the work more relevant. The main techniques are*: Opening up Discussion; Inner Voice from the Audience; Inner Voice from the Characters; Lifting the Mask; Interview in Role; Role Rotation and Role Reversal; Re-working the Scene.*

Psychodrama The presentation of one's personal life and subjective perceptions on the stage for the purposes of enhancing personal strength and spontaneity, working through troubling emotional issues and practising behavioural change. Originally developed by J L Moreno, psychodrama gave rise to a range of widely-adapted techniques including role reversal, doubling, the empty chair and role play (Blatner, 1997).

Readiness Levels At a given time, the readiness of an individual, the group, the facilitator, co-workers and the agency as a whole to engage in a particular piece of work.

Relapse Prevention A common feature of cognitive-behavioural, offence-focused programmes, concentrating on the long term skills, strategies and support an individual needs in order to avoid further offending. Also focuses on positive life goals and the skills needed to approach them.

Re-working the Scene Advancing, rewinding, exchanging roles, adding or subtracting characters, adding plot twists, or any of a wide range of other directorial moves made in order to increase the relevance and usefulness of a given scene. One of the *processing techniques.*

Role In the theatre, a dramatic persona assumed by the actor. Also a term used to describe and analyse one's identity and functioning. In this context, *role* describes a set of behaviours that in a given cultural context represent an identifiable form, or set. Roles are often reciprocal (e.g. the roles of employee—boss, parent—son/ daughter, customer—shop assistant, teacher—student). In this book, *role* is used as a way of understanding the importance of helping participants to *expand their role repertoire.*

Role Play Scenarios enacted for skills practice, problem solving, personal/ empathic development and other uses. See further definitions and discussions in *Chapter 8.*

Role Repertoire The range of life skills, strategies and roles that an individual practises in everyday life.

Role Reversal Technique whereby two people change places and experience the other's role and point of view. One of the central techniques in psychodrama and sociodrama (Karp *et al*, 1998).

Role Rotation One of the *processing techniques*, where onstage roles are re-distributed among the group members. Related to *Role Reversal.*

Skills Training The use of role play for the specific purpose of helping someone to learn and practise a skill, strategy or new role. For example, practising the skill of *staying out of fights* or practising a strategy for dealing with boredom.

Social Learning Theory (Bandura, 1977). Theory explaining the means by which much of our learning takes place through interaction, modelling and repetition, among other methods. In structured programmes, social learning is divided into stages (see pp.173-174):

Sociodrama The enactment of society and social issues, often in the form of dramatic exploration of major role relationships such as: Prisoners and Prison Officers; Offenders and Victims; Pupils and Teachers; Parents and Children; Police and Criminals; Dealers and Drug Users; Workers and Bosses; Oppressors and Oppressed; Conservatives and Liberals; etc. (Moreno, 1993). In this book we use several techniques that are related to sociodrama, for example *The Way I See It, Whole Group Role Play* and *Forum Role Play.*

Teaching in Role See *Worker in Role.*

Theatre in Education Related to drama-in-education, but differing in its emphasis on performance. Very often takes the form of theatrical performance by visiting artists, followed by participatory workshops.

Thinking Distortions Attitudes, beliefs and thoughts that are highly distorted and used to justify behaviour or minimise culpability, e.g. 'It was the drink that did it.' Also known as cognitive distortions. In the context of offending, the concept is typically applied to distorted thinking about victims (e.g. 'It was her fault; she should have let go of the handbag so I wouldn't have had to hit her.' 'I only burgle houses where the people are insured, and they always claim for more than I take anyway.' 'If a girl wears clothes like that she's asking for it.').

Worker in Role The worker interacts with group members while in a role that will be useful to the group (e.g. the role of an offender, a witness to a crime, a journalist reporting an event, a child protection officer). The *Worker in Role* techniques are related to the 'teaching-in-role' and 'mantle of the expert' techniques developed by drama-in-education innovator Dorothy Heathcote (Heathcote and Bolton, 1995; Johnson and O'Neill, 1984; Wagner, 1976).

REFERENCES

Antonowicz, D. and Ross, R. (1994) 'Essential Components of Successful Rehabilitation Programs for Offenders', *International Journal of Offender Therapy and Comparative Criminology* 38(2).

Bandura, A.(1977) *Social Learning Theory.* Englewood Cliffs, NJ: Prentice-Hall

Barker, C. (1988) *Theatre Games.* London: Methuen.

Beck, A. T. (1976) *Cognitive Therapy and the Emotional Disorders.* New York: International Universities Press.

Beck, A. and Freeman, A. (1990) *Cognitive Therapy of Personality Disorders.* London: Guilford Press.

Bergman, J. and Hewish, S. (1996) 'Violent Illusion: Dramatherapy and the Dangerous Voyage to the Heart of Change.' In Liebmann, M. (ed.) *Arts Approaches to Conflict.* London: Jessica Kingsley Publishers.

Boal, A. (1979) *Theatre of the Oppressed.* London: Pluto Press.

Boal, A. (1992) *Games for Actors and Non-Actors.* London: Routledge.

Blatner, A. (1997) *Acting-In: Practical Applications of Psychodramatic Methods* (3rd edition). London: Free Association Books, or (1996) New York: Springer Publishing Company.

Blatner, A. with Blatner, A. (1988) *Foundations of Psychodrama: History, Theory and Practice* (3rd edition). New York: Springer Publishing Company.

Brandes, D. and Philips, H. (1990) *Gamesters' Handbook: 140 Games for Teachers and Group Leaders.* Cheltenham: Stanley Thornes Publishers.

Bush, J. (1993) Workshop presented at *What Works* conference on effective practice, Salford, England.

Casson, J. (1997) 'Dramatherapy History in Headlines: Who did What, When, Where?', *The Journal of the British Association for Dramatherapists,* 19 (2) 10-14. (Mentions formation of Geese Theatre USA and Geese Theatre UK)

Cattanach, A. (1996) *Drama for People with Special Needs* (2nd ed.). London: A C Black.

Chapman, T. and Hough, M. (1998) *Evidence Based Practice: A Guide to Effective Practice.* London: HM Inspectorate of Probation.

Chesner, A. (1995) *Dramatherapy for People with Learning Disabilities.* London: Jessica Kingsley.

Chesner, A. (1998) *Groupwork with Learning Disabilities: Creative Drama.* Bicester: Winslow.

Cleveland, W. (2000) *Art in Other Places.* Amherst, MA.: University of Massachusetts Arts Extension Service Press.

Corsini, R.J.(1967) *Role Playing in Psychotherapy.* Chicago: Aldine.

Dransfield, B. (2001) 'Forum Role Play: An Exploration of a Professional Encounter', *The British Journal of Psychodrama and Sociodrama,* 16(1) 29-36.

Dryden, W. (ed) (1999) *Rational Emotive Behavior Therapy: A Training Manual.* New York: Springer Publishing Co.

Ellis, A. and Grieger, R. (eds.) (1986) *Handbook of Rational-emotive Therapy.* Vol. II. New York: Springer Publishing Co.

Fox, J. (1986) *Acts of Service: Spontaneity, Commitment, Tradition in the Nonscripted Theatre.* New Paltz, NY: Tusitala Publishing.

Gergen, K.J. (1972) 'Multiple Identity: The Happy Healthy Human Being Wears Many Masks'. *Psychology Today,* 5(12) 31-35.

Goldstein, A. P. (1999) *The Prepare Curriculum: Teaching Prosocial Competencies.* Champaign, Illinois: Research Press.

Harris, G. and Watkins, D. (1987) *Counselling the Involuntary and Resistant Client.* College Park, Maryland: The American Correctional Association.

Haskell, M. (1961) 'An Alternative to More and Larger Prisons: A Role Training Program for Social Reconnection', *Group Psychotherapy* 14 (1-2) 30-38.

Haskell, M. (1975) *Socioanalysis: Self Direction via Sociodrama and Psychodrama.* California: Role Training Associates of California.

Heathcote, D. and Bolton, G. (1995) *Drama for Learning: Dorothy Heathcote's Mantle of the Expert Approach to Education.* Portsmouth, New Hampshire: Heinemann.

Hornby, R. (1992) *The End of Acting.* New York: Applause.

Jefferies, J. (1991) 'What We are Doing Here is Defusing Bombs.' In P. Holmes and M. Karp (eds) *Psychodrama: Inspiration and Technique.* London: Tavistock/ Routledge.

Jennings, S. (1978) *Remedial Drama.* London: A C Black.

Jennings, S. (1986) *Creative Drama in Groupwork.* Bicester: Winslow Press.

Jennings, S. (1987) *Dramatherapy: Theory and Practice for Teachers and Clinicians.* London: Croom Helm.

Johnson, L. and O'Neill, C. (eds) (1984) *Dorothy Heathcote: Collected Writings on Education and Drama.* London: Hutchinson.

Jones, P. (1996) *Drama as Therapy, Theatre as Living.* London: Routledge.

Karp, M., Holmes, P. and Bradshaw Tauvon, K. (eds) (1998) *The Handbook of Psychodrama.* London: Tavistock/ Routledge.

Kipper, D.A. (1986) *Psychotherapy Through Clinical Role Playing.* New York: Brunner/ Mazel.

Lee, H. (1960) *To Kill a Mockingbird.* Philadelphia: J B Lipincott.

Macbeth, F. and Fine, N. (1995) *Playing with Fire: Creative Conflict Resolution for Young Adults*: New Society Publishing.

Matarosso, F. (1997) *Use or Ornament? the Social Impact of Participation in the Arts.* Stroud: Comedia.

McGuire, J. (2000) *Cognitive-Behavioural Approaches: An Introduction to Theory and Research.* London: HM Inspectorate of Probation.

McGuire, J. and Priestley, P. (1981) *Life After School: A Social Skills Curriculum.* Oxford: Pergamon.

McGuire, J. and Priestley, P. (1987) *Offending Behaviour: Skills and stratagems for going straight.* London: Batsford.

Melnick, M. (1984). 'Skills Through Drama: The Use of Professional Theatre Techniques in the Treatment and Education of Prison and Ex-Offender Populations'. *Journal of Group Psychotherapy, Psychodrama and Sociodrama* 36 (3) 104-116.

Moreno, J.L. (1983) *The Theatre of Spontaneity.* Pennsylvania: Beacon House, Inc. Originally published in Germany, 1923.

Moreno, J.L. (1985) *Psychodrama: Volume One.* New York: Beacon House. Originally published 1946.

Moreno, J.L. (1993) *Who Shall Survive? Foundations of Sociometry, Group Psychotherapy and Sociodrama.* McLean, Virginia: American Society of Group Psychotherapy and Psychodrama. Published through: Roanoke, Virginia: Royal Publishing Company. Student edition.

Moreno, Z. T., Blomkvist, L. and Rutzel, T. (2000) *Psychodrama, Surplus Reality and the Art of Healing.* London: Routledge.

Moreno, J.L. and Moreno, Z. T. (1975) *Psychodrama: Volume Three.* Beacon, NY: Beacon House, Inc.

Mountford, A. and Farrall, M. (1998) 'The House of Four Rooms: Theatre with Violent Offenders.' In Thompson, J. (ed.) *Prison Theatre.* London: Jessica Kingsley Publishers.

O'Reilly, G., Morrison, T., Sheerin, D., and Carr,A. (2001). A Group-based Module for Adolescents to Improve Motivation to Change Sexually Abusive Behaviour. *Child Abuse Review* 10, 150-169.
Peaker, A. and Pratt, B. (1990) *Arts in Prisons: Towards a Sense of Achievement.* Loughborough University: The Centre for Research in Social Policy, Unit for Arts and Offenders.
Peaker, A. and Pratt, B. (1996) *Arts in Prisons.* Loughborough University: The Centre for Research in Social Policy, Unit for Arts and Offenders.
Phillips, L. (1997) *In the Public Interest: Making Art that Makes a Difference in the United States.* Stroud: Comedia.
Poulter, C. (1987) *Playing the Game.* Basingstoke, Hampshire: Macmillan.
Prochaska, J. and Di Clemente, C. (1986) Towards a Comprehensive Model of Change. In Miller, W. and Heather, N. (eds.) *Treating Addictive Behaviors.* New York: Plenum.
Rawlins, G. and Rich, J. (1992) *Look, Listen and Trust: A Framework for Learning Through Drama.* Surrey: T Nelson and Sons.
Reiss, D., Quayle, M., Brett, T., and Meux, C. (1998) 'Dramatherapy for Mentally Disordered Offenders: Changes in Levels of Anger', *Criminal Behaviour and Mental Health* 8, 139-153.
Ringer, M. and Gillis, H.L. (1995) 'Managing Psychological Depth in Adventure Programming', *The Journal of Experiential Education* 19 (1).
Rohd, M. (1998) *Theatre for Community, Conflict and Dialogue: The Hope Is Vital Training Manual.* Portsmouth, New Hampshire: Heinemann/ Reed Elsevier Inc.
Scher, A. and Verrall, C. (1982) *100+ Ideas for Drama.* London: Heinemann Educational Books.
Schutzman, M. and Cohen-Cruz, J. (eds) (1994) *Playing Boal: Theatre, Therapy, Activism.* London and New York: Routledge.
Sternberg, P. and Garcia, A. (1989) *Sociodrama: Who's in Your Shoes?* New York: Praeger.
Thomas, D. (1975) *Under Milkwood.* London: J M Dent & Sons Ltd.
Van Mentz, M. (1983) *The Effective Use of Role play.* London: Kogan Page.
Vennard, J., Hedderman, C., & Sugg, D. (1997) *Changing Offenders Attitudes and Behaviour: What Works*? Home Office Research Study 171. London: Home Office Research and Statistics Directorate.
Wagner, B. J. (1976) *Dorothy Heathcote: Drama as a Learning Medium.* Washington, D.C.: National Education Association.
Weinstein, M. and Goodman, J. (1992) *Playfair: Everybody's Guide to Noncompetitive Play.* San Luis Obispo, California: Impact Publishers.
Wirth, J. (1994) *Interactive Acting: Acting, Improvisation and Interacting for Audience Participatory Theatre.* Fall Creek, Oregon: Fall Creek Press.
Wolf, S. (1988) A Model of Sexual Aggression/Addiction. *Journal of Social Work and Human Sexuality,* 7(1), 131-148.
Wolpe, J. (1969) *The Practice of Behavior Therapy.* New York: Pergamon.
Yablonsky, L. (1976) *Psychodrama: Resolving Emotional Problems Through Role-playing.* New York: Basic Books.
Yardley-Matwiejczuk, K. (1997) *Role play: Theory and Practice.* London: Sage.

Further recommended reading

Clifford, S. and Herrmann, A. (1999) *Making a Leap: Theatre of Empowerment—A Practical Handbook for Creative Drama Work with Young People.* London and Philadelphia: Jessica Kingsley Publishers.
Cossa, M., Fleischmann Ember, S., Grover, L. and Hazelwood, J. (1996) *Acting Out: The Workbook. A Guide to the Development and Presentation of Issue-oriented, Audience-interactive, Improvisational Theatre.* London and Washington, D.C.: Taylor and Francis.
Cox, M. (ed) (1992) *Shakespeare Comes to Broadmoor: The Performance of Tragedy in a Secure Psychiatric Hospital.* London: Jessica Kingsley Publishers.
Devlin, A. (2000) *Criminal Classes: Offenders at School.* Winchester: Waterside Press.
Fine, N. and Macbeth, F. (1992) *Fireworks: Training for the Creative Use of Conflict.* Leicester: Youth Work Press.
Home Office Standing Committee for Arts in Prisons (2001). *Including the Arts: The Creative Arts – The Route to Basic and Key Skills in Prisons.* Manchester: Bar None Books.
Jenkins, A. (1990). *Invitations to Responsibility: The Therapeutic Engagement of Men who are Violent and Abusive.* Adelaide: Dulwich Centre Pub.
Johnston, C. (1998) *House of Games: Making Theatre from Everyday Life.* London: Nick Hern Books.
Johnstone, K. (1994) *Don't be Prepared: Theatresports for Teachers—A Resource Tool for Teaching Improvisation and Theatresports.* Calgary: Loose Moose Theatre Company.
Johnstone, K. (1981) *Impro: Improvisation and the Theatre.* London: Methuen.
Novaco, R. W., Ramm, M. and Black, L. (2000). Anger Treatment with Offenders. In Hollin, C.R. (ed.) *Handbook of Offender Assessment and Treatment.* London: John Wiley and Sons Ltd.
Spolin, V. (1985) *Theatre Games for Rehearsal.* Evanston, Illinois: Northwestern University Press.
Spolin, V. (1986) *Theater Games for the Classroom.* Evanston, Illinois: Northwestern University Press.
Stordeur, R. A. and Stille, R. (1989). *Ending Men's Violence Against Their Partners: One Road to Peace.* London: Sage.
Thompson, J. (1998). *Prison Theatre: Perspectives and Practices.* London: Jessica Kingsley
Thompson, J. (1999). *Drama Workshops for Anger Management and Offending Behaviour.* London: Jessica Kingsley.
Williams, A. (1991) *Forbidden Agendas: Strategic Action in Groups.* London: Routledge.

General Index

Alphabetical Index of Exercises

\# Exercises suitable for one to one work + Exercises suitable for large groups (more than 25 people)

Index of General Games and Exercises by Aims

Note: *Interactive Observer Scenes*, *Frozen Pictures* and *Role Plays* can be used to address most of the themes listed here.

(***Italics*** indicate that the most common aim of the exercise is in this category)

Index of Offending-focused Games and Exercises by Aims

Note: *Interactive Observer Scenes*, *Frozen Pictures* and *Role Plays* can be used to address most of the themes listed here.

(***Italics*** indicate that the most common aim of the exercise is in this category)

www.ingramcontent.com/pod-product-compliance
Lightning Source LLC
LaVergne TN
LVHW081933200926
848484LV00009B/2423